IT'S ALL POLITICS

IT'S ALL POLITICS

South Alabama's Seafood Industry

E. Paul Durrenberger

University of Illinois Press
Urbana and Chicago

©1992 by the Board of Trustees of the University of Illinois
Manufactured in the United States of America
C 5 4 3 2 1

This book is printed on acid-free paper.

Library of Congress Cataloguing-in-Publication Data

Durrenberger, E. Paul, 1943–
    It's all politics : South Alabama's seafood industry /
    E. Paul Durrenberger
        p. cm.
    Includes bibliographical references and index.
    ISBN 0-252-01910-5 (cl : acid-free paper)
    1. Shellfish trade—Alabama—Gulf Region. 2. Seafood
industry—Alabama—Gulf Region. 3. Shrimp industry—Alabama—
Gulf Region. 4. Oyster industry—Alabama—Gulf Region. 5.
Ethnology—Alabama—Gulf Region. I. Title.
HD9471.U53A24   1992
338.3'727'097612—dc20   91-40916
                                                          CIP

For Dorothy

Contents

Prologue

I am drinking coffee across the table from Roland Nelson in his house in Coden, Alabama. It is the second week of October 1988. The sun has not come up yet. Mr. Nelson tells me he believes in the Bible and that there is nothing in it about plastics or industry. Farming and fishing are basic. They are in the Bible. The chemical industry and pollution are ruining the oysters. Dust from the chemical plants is in the air. There is a factory nearby that makes blue jeans. They want to stone wash the jeans and that will add to the pollution in the water. "I don't understand goofy people who want to buy old jeans. If they want worn-out clothes, they can get them at the Salvation Army and not pollute the bay. . . . The Bible says people will destroy ourselves, and we are doing it."

Roland's son-in-law comes silently into the kitchen with a baby on his shoulder. "We should save it for the kids, for the ones that are coming." There is a pause before Roland continues, "But you know it's all politics. It's all politics. . . . They can stop you from taking the oysters, but they can't stop that pollution. Or the chemical companies. It's all politics. They got nobody in Conservation [the department] that cares. . . . They don't enforce anything. How come? We need someone in there who cares."

This conversation is not unique. Roland has said the same things a thousand times or more. Other oyster catchers in south Alabama have told the same story or similar ones for years. Since the Department of Conservation was established in 1907 there has been constant discussion about who should regulate the fishing industry. Whoever has been charged with the task has been accused by others of self-interest, incompetence, neglect, maladministration, corruption, or worse.

Paul, Roland's son, comes in and we drink more coffee. We get up and go outside where Paul calls his brother, John. The sun is just coming up. Paul and John hitch a boat trailer with a skiff on it to a pickup truck and Paul drives to King Bayou in Alabama Port, where they put in at a boat ramp. Another oyster catcher, who has just put in, says, "We ought to get some federal money like they got in Florida. Oyster catching is bad lately."

By seven, the sun is up and we have motored to the west side of Dauphin Island bridge, over Cedar Reef. People of European descent have been catching oysters on this reef since early in the eighteenth century, but not always for the same reasons. French settlers caught them in desperation as starvation food when they could find nothing better to eat. Later, their descendants and other Americans caught oysters to sell locally in the burgeoning cotton port of Mobile. In the late nineteenth and early twentieth centuries, immigrants from the eastern United States and other parts of the world joined them to catch oysters for the canneries that eastern capital had established in the area. As these canneries sought more steady and reliable sources of raw material, fishermen began to catch shrimp as well as oysters, and by 1950 a shrimp boom had started. With larger boats, many fishermen specialized in shrimp for the newly constructed freezing plants. The oyster canneries went out of business but the oyster catchers continued to catch oysters whenever and wherever the pollution from the new industrial and residential developments allowed.

Paul pulls the skiff into a rank of other oyster catchers, many with women culling while the men tong for oysters. Paul places a plywood sheet across the bow of the boat and he and John begin tonging, walking along planks set just inside the coaming.

They dip the long-handled tongs into the water, shift the handles as they feel for oysters on the bottom, close the rakelike tongs, and deposit the catch they bring up on the plywood sheet. Most of the shells gape, empty, or are occupied by hermit crabs. Oysters must be three inches in some dimension across the shell to be legal.

A man-and-wife team works beside us. He tongs and she culls, deftly knocking away cemented shell from good oysters with an old file. Only one oyster in a clump of four or five shells may be good. The rest go overboard while she throws the good one into a bottomless plastic basket set inside a gunny sack. When the basket is full, she pulls up the bag, sets the basket in another bag, and starts again. He has been catching oysters since he was ten years old, and, his wife adds, he is now forty-six.

Paul explains that I am studying the seafood industry. "The conchs are a big problem," our neighbor says. "Eating the whole reef. Not enough fresh water is coming to the bay since the Tenn-Tom canal was opened. That changed everything. Now the conches are eating the oysters. Look at the number of dead ones. We need to replant the reef."

"I get tired of feeling like Bonnie and Clyde" she says, explaining that they keep undersized oysters.

Oystermen, biologists, politicians, and fisheries managers in Alabama have been talking about culling laws for about a hundred years, twice the lifetime of our neighbor. Culling regulations are still a topic of conversation.

Paul says, "You could arrest anyone out here today. That man there . . . lives on Dauphin Island. He is ninety-one years old and still tonging. Some say he would die if he quit. Here, this is a hermit conch. Some say the hermit conch eats the eye of the oyster, but I don't believe it. Different people say different things. Everyone out here has a different way of doing things and a different solution to what's wrong."

The man in the neighboring boat joins in. "It's all politics." The discussion turns to the Bentsen-Quayle vice-presidential debate and the upcoming presidential election of 1988. They say they have had enough of Reaganism and would prefer Dukakis. There seems to be a consensus that they would prefer Lloyd Bentsen as a Democratic presidential candidate.

I stand at the front of the boat and examine the oysters as they pile up, throwing the empty shells overboard. Paul hands me a rubber-covered canvas glove to protect my hand and shows me how to cull. My speed picks up a little but lacks the certain touch and speed of Paul or the woman in the boat next to us.

The boat works its way to the west at each dip of the tongs as the oyster catchers pole backward, dragging an anchor of junk metal. We come aside another boat and Paul asks if there is coffee. The oysterman says there is. Paul and John tie up to his boat and we go aboard for coffee.

Here we have the same conversation about the election, conservation, and conches. Paul suggests, "They should do like Mississippi and have people out here on the water on the reefs, not just on the highways and roads. They should test and know what is going on on the reef." Our benefactor repeats that smaller oysters are more in demand than legal-sized ones. Restaurant owners prefer small oysters to large ones. It is the same dozen oysters they sell cooked whether they are large or small, and there are more dozens of small oysters in each gallon of oysters they buy.

After coffee, we continue to work. Paul and John bring up piles of shell to deposit on the plywood sheet and I sort through them, looking for good oysters to pitch into the sack. We come alongside a couple of younger men. One is just back from sixteen days in jail. He tells about the bad food and a judge with no sense of humor. Later I ask Paul what he was in for. "Just about everything," he answers. Everyone we talk to agrees that catching is bad. They catch less and less the longer they stay at it.

Paul says, "See all these people out here? Not one of them has helped us plant shell. They all want something for nothing. They want the state to pay them to plant oysters. We, our club, wrote the proposal to get a million dollars for conservation after Hurricane Frederick. Rick Wallace [of the Sea Grant Advisory Office] helped us do that. We got the money and they [the Conservation Department] planted shells. But they were clamshells, and they form lime, and the oysters don't stick to them. With some money, I could get this reef back in shape in three years."

"How?" I ask.

"Dredge over it. Use a dredge with some chain link fence behind it, dredge it, turn it over, clean it up, so spat would catch. Plant new shell. That would do it."

This was done in the past with some success. There have been shell-planting programs for half a century or so. Some were sponsored by the federal government, some by the state, some paid for by an oyster tax.

"Have you ever dredged?" I ask.

"I have seen it in Mississippi. It makes this tonging look primitive. It takes a lot less effort. They could allow it, but there are some oyster catchers that have never seen anything else and say they would shoot anyone using a dredge. They don't like it. But they could put a limit on it like they have now. It would be easier with dredges."

This conversation echoes an old debate. The argument about the merits and dangers of dredging has also been going on for nearly a hundred years. Some oystermen swear dredges are destructive; others think they improve the reefs.

"What else do you do besides oyster catching?"

"When it plays out here, I can go to Louisiana or Mississippi or Texas and catch oysters there. Here we get twenty-five cents a pound for oysters in the shells in bags. A bag is about a hundred pounds. We can get five or six bags in a day's work. Over in Louisiana they have planted beds. I can catch them for the owner and he gives me nine dollars a bag. But you have to have two homes and buy food and pay gas and electric bills and it isn't much good."

In Mississippi and Louisiana there are privately owned or leased oyster beds. In a previous conversation I had heard Paul talking about tonging on these beds. The owner "just sits there in a beer hall while other people catch his oysters." There have been private oyster beds and leased beds in Alabama in the past as well.

I continue to cull as John and Paul tong. We stop for some lunch of coldcuts, bread, and a two-liter bottle of soft drink Paul picked up at a convenience store before we set out. After lunch, Paul endeavors to instruct me in the art of tonging. After I bring up the tongs empty or nearly empty several times, I begin to get the hang of it, though I am not consistent.

Paul explains how he and John taught their brothers-in-law to catch oysters. "They work in the boat yards, but they like oyster catching better, so when the season opens, they quit there and catch oysters. You can see why. The pay is about the same, and this is better work." He told how he and Roland built two steel shrimp boats in their yard, but sold them when the price of shrimp went down because they did not think they could get their money back after they got them all rigged out.

We make an early day of it as Paul has business in Mobile. He has to register the oyster club with the probate court to make it official. Roland and other oyster catchers organized Save Our Shells to plant shells on the reefs. V. M. Parker, director of the Alabama Seafood Advisory Commission, has advised them to register the club officially, including its constitution, bylaws, and elected officers. Paul says, "We have to get an outboard motor. I have finished reglassing the deck of the barge. We just have to keep at it. You do what you can. I have to register the club so we can get some money from Swingle [director of the Marine Resources Division, Alabama Department of Conservation and Natural Resources]. V. M. Parker is doing what he can. I told him we would hit a stump and now he knows it."

Paul mentioned that one of the oyster-planting group, Junior Wheeler, was just back from open-heart surgery, and how his own brother, John, had to have heart surgery when he was younger. Then they had a Blue Cross insurance plan for fishermen. It covered preexisting conditions, so a lot of people, some who were not fishermen, signed up, and the fund went broke. Now they are without health insurance.

We return to the boat ramp and Paul backs the trailer to the boat. He doesn't have to pay the two dollar fee for use of the ramp because he sells his oysters to the shop owner across the road. We take the bags of oysters out of the boat and put them into a truck where a kid weighs them on a platform scale and throws them into the back of the truck.

The owner's father owned the shop before. The owner has the oysters shucked in a shack down by the bayou across the road and ships them all over the United States. He picks up an eight-inch shell from the ground and says, "This is a beautiful oyster, but no one wants to buy them." He repeats the oyster catcher's observation that restaurants prefer small oysters, goes in to tend to business, and then returns behind the building.

"It's all politics. Oyster catchers and shrimpers have no money or organization so they can't get any influence. Not like chemical companies. They don't stick together. Shrimpers are different from oyster catchers. A shrimper has a hundred thousand dollar rig. When shrimping isn't good, he comes out to catch oysters with tongs, and everyone knows he has that hundred thousand dollar rig and here he is catching oysters with us with tongs. And they drag over the reefs."

It has not always been so. Earlier in the century there was a union of oystermen in Mobile. Oyster catching was not large scale yet in other areas of coastal Alabama. When the canneries were built and more and more people were catching oysters, and then shrimp, the factory workers as well as fishermen organized themselves into unions and affiliated with other fishermen and factory workers in Mississippi and Louisiana. Their organizations had considerable strength until the mid-1950s.

The kid in the truck tells a story about a shrimper who trawled with heavy chains on the trawl and got thirty sacks of oysters. Conservation caught him and made him pay $2,400 in fines. Later Paul said someone had seen the offender and had turned him in to Conservation.

The shop owner says again, "It's all politics." He went on to say that the new Navy homeport and the new industry on the west shore and Theodore outfall line would all contribute to pollution. He explained that now no oysters can be taken from Mobile Bay because of pollution, and he expected the contaminated waters would extend to the Dauphin Island bridge with the new sources of pollution.

Another truck and boat rig pulls up behind us. We get into the pickup and pull out.

I had met Paul and Roland Nelson in August, when I was accompanying V. M. Parker on his rounds of the industry. I went with V. M. to a meeting with the Save Our Shells Club. The Conservation Department collects a tax of twenty-five cents on each bag of oysters sold. V. M. was trying to arrange for the SOS Club, as it's called, to get some of the oyster-tax money. The club members have invested their own money, time, and labor to build a barge, rig it with a pump to wash shells overboard, and start their own shell-planting program. At that meeting the Nelsons and their fellow oyster catchers had invited us to come to a public meeting the Corps of Engineers was holding in Bayou la Batre to conduct a hearing on a draft feasibility report to deepen the channel into Bayou la Batre.

The present Alabama Seafood Advisory Commission has no policy-making role and can only advise the governor. It is not the first seafood commission. Such commissions have a long history, and there has been a continuing struggle between supporters of the concept of regulating the seafood industry through a commission composed of people involved in the industry and those who favor control by a bureaucratic agency of the state. When there have been industry commissions, there has been a cry that they favored themselves. When there has been regulation by biologists, there have been charges that they are incompetent and do not know the industry.

The Corps of Engineers meeting was toward the end of August in the auditorium of the Bayou la Batre community center. There were two folding tables on each side of a podium in front of the stage. Just inside the back door of the auditorium were two more tables, one on each side, with a woman at each. They asked each person who entered to fill out a card with his or her name, address, firm, and telephone number, and to indicate whether he or she wanted to speak. Some of the thirty-seven people in the folding chairs on the floor of the auditorium were in open-necked shirts and jeans or housedresses, some in neckties and suits. The ten people at the tables in front were dressed in business clothes.

A representative of the Mobile District Corps opened the meeting and outlined the history of the project to deepen the channel from twelve to twenty feet. An Alabama senator spoke of the politics of the project in Washington. There was an illustrated talk about bulkheads, disposal of spoil, and funding. The moderator then opened the meeting for comments. Six representatives of boat-building and seafood firms testified to the importance of the project. Roland Nelson had a turn and said that he had started the SOS Club and wanted to be sure the silt did not cover the shells the club members were planting on the east side of Coffee Island.

The moderator took over again and introduced the committee advocating the twenty-foot depth, thirteen businessmen who organized in

1984 to push for a deeper channel. About an hour and a half later, the meeting adjourned and I went to the lobby to chat with V. M. Parker and Paul Nelson and some other oyster catchers.

Paul says, "Lots of people have a bad attitude about this channel because some people are going to benefit lots more than others."

Junior Wheeler adds, "They are already millionaires."

I ask Paul about a controversy in the shrimping industry and he says that oyster catchers and shrimpers have conflicting interests. "We are all in the seafood industry, but they won't help others. We are all working people." He went on to discuss the effects of Hurricane Elena and the subsequent shell replanting, and the politics of getting the funds for shell planting. He discussed an allocation from the oil fund revenue for shell planting and how half of it was appropriated to make a park instead of planting shells.

Acknowledgments

My research for this book was funded by a grant from the National Science Foundation. My wife, Dorothy, accompanied me to Alabama and Mississippi and helped me with much of the archival work in the many libraries and collections we visited. She has also contributed to this study in other ways too numerous to mention, including reading earlier drafts of the manuscript. Others who read early drafts and offered useful advice include Lee Maril, David White, Jim Jones, Nicola Tannenbaum, Tony Paredes, and James Acheson. I thank them for their help. My appreciation goes to Sheriton Burr of Corpus Christi, Texas, for his hospitality while I was visiting coastal Texas and for his help with my research since. I also thank Carol Bolton Betts of the University of Illinois Press for her help in preparing the final version of the manuscript.

Many shrimpers, oyster catchers, biologists, administrators, processors, and others in the seafood industry gave generously of their time and experience. I thank them all for their contributions to this work. I am especially grateful to Roland, Paul, and John Nelson of Coden, Alabama, and to V. M. Parker of Mobile.

Portions of chapters 5 and 6 have appeared previously in the journal *Maritime Anthropological Studies* (Durrenberger 1988, 1990) and are used here with permission.

1

Introduction

Perspectives

The microscopic focus on two men in a boat, tonging for oysters, widens as we see them talking with other oyster catchers, organizing a club to plant shells, working with V. M. Parker, and attending Corps of Engineer meetings. The circle expands further as we see the Corps of Engineers organizing a project with local business elites and getting it funded from Montgomery and Washington. It enlarges in a different direction as we see the director of the Seafood Advisory Commission approaching state agencies on behalf of the industry. It widens more when we take into account the Conservation Department and the national agencies that regulate fishing. The two men tonging for oysters from a skiff become the center of these and other overlapping systems of relationships that have developed over a period of about two hundred years. Some of these relationships have remained fairly constant while others are recent innovations.

While everyone might have a different solution to every problem, as Paul Nelson said, everyone agreed that pollution was a problem that was getting worse. Everyone repeated one phrase: "It's all politics."

Since I heard it from everyone, often more than once, I thought a lot about its significance. Later, David White, an anthropologist who had worked as a shrimper and studied the shrimping industry and community in Bon Secour, on the east side of Mobile Bay, was visiting Bon Secour and showed me around the community. Over supper, I asked him what he made of the phrase. I think he was right when he explained that it is a recognition that everything is decided by power and by power relationships, and that the oyster catchers who were repeating the refrain were recognizing that they had no power, that issues were out of their hands whether they be the effects of pollution, the conservation of oysters, the planting of shells, the granting of funds, the deepening of channels, the disposal of dredge spoil, the enforcement of laws, or any of the other many issues involved in their day-to-day lives and livelihoods.

While we were unloading Paul and John's oysters behind the seafood shop, a uniformed marine enforcement officer came out to chat and have a soft drink. He represented the Conservation Department I had just been hearing about in none too kind words. The officer was Paul and John's uncle. While V. M. Parker was discussing how to get some funds to help with the SOS shell-planting program, Roland Nelson mentioned that his own brother is the mayor of Bayou la Batre and wondered why he did not or could not do more to help oyster catchers. People could not count on close kinsmen and neighbors to make common cause with them. An uncle must enforce laws on his nephews; a brother cannot direct aid to a brother.

In primitive societies people identify each other according to their genealogical connections, and the first questions one addresses to strangers are designed to place them in one's kinship system. In modern societies, kinship and community hold people together less than economic ties. The first questions one addresses to strangers are to place them in the economic system: not "How are you related to me?" but "What do you do?" People define themselves and others in terms of how they relate to economic categories and the political system that defines the rules of access to resources. Their relations with political and economic systems shape their lives more than relations with family and area. While kinship and area are still important, where people fit into the process of production as workers, managers, or regulators, and the place of the commodity in the larger economic system are more important, as these two examples suggest.

The lived experience of people, their concepts and self-concepts, is determined by the form of their political and economic system, and the form of that system is determined by historical processes. It is that process that I describe and analyze here.

The place of one commodity relative to others can change over time as seafood has changed from being a food fit only to keep the starving from death to a luxury for the well-off. The capital to produce a commodity can change as technology changes. The large double-rigged gulf-plying shrimp trawlers have replaced smaller, single-rigged bay boats that replaced seining from schooners. Capital can move out of unprofitable enterprises and into profitable ones as eastern capital moved into canneries on the gulf coast and then out again. Other aspects of the technology of production changed as freezing supplanted canning. The system of distribution changed from railroads to trucks.

Relations with the political system can change as legislatures create new regulatory agencies and laws or alter old ones. Laws may favor one group over another. Court decisions may allow a practice at one time and ban it at another. Fishermen used to negotiate with processors to set a seasonal price for shrimp and oysters but could not after the practice was found to be in violation of antitrust laws.

Except for the native American populations that left mounds of shell as testament to their use of esturine resources and the early settlers who used fish and oysters to keep themselves from starvation, few have used seafood as an important subsistence item in their household economies. True, people of coastal Alabama catch mullet for church suppers and volunteer fire department dinners as well as for family gatherings and everyday food. Everyone delights in the bounty of a jubilee when all manner of seafood literally walks out of the water and into waiting baskets and buckets. Coastal people used to catch and eat more oysters than now. The most important point is not that people ate seafood, but that they did not, by and large, depend on it as the major item of their household budgets. They were not subsistence fishermen.

While the early residents of French descent on the western side of Mobile Bay may have relied on fish and oysters along with game for their yearly subsistence, from the beginning of the American presence in Alabama the use of sea resources has been for commerce rather than subsistence. People caught fish and oysters for sale, not for their own use. They were trying to make a living in the market economy, not just provide food for their own tables. The limits on their catches were thus determined not by how much seafood they could use but by how much they could catch and sell. How much they could catch depended largely on the technology available and the size of stocks available to catch. Later it depended on regulations as well. How much they could sell depended on economic developments such as the establishment of transportation networks and processing plants. These in turn depended on the growth of the national and international economies.

Systems

Any system is composed of elements related to each other, so that if one of them changes it affects the others. Each is a variable, just as "x" is a variable in an algebraic equation and can take on different values at different times. Once we identify the elements or variables of a system, we can measure their values. If the elements are related to each other systemically, when the value of one element changes, the values of others will also change. Often some variables are more important than others, more essential to the system because their values determine the values of other variables in the system.

These central variables change through time. In this study I start with Alabama's incorporation into the United States in 1819. We can divide the history of south Alabama's fishing industry into three periods based on their most important variables: the first—from 1819, when Alabama began to be incorporated into the economy of the United States with statehood, to 1915—was the period of preservation with ice and distribution by railroad; the second, from 1915 to 1950, was the period of industrial canning; and the third, from 1950 until now, is the period of industrial shrimping and freezing. Each system was different from the others, with different variables and relationships. Each system is characterized by different dominant elements that largely determined the values of other variables. The first was dominated by the means of preservation and distribution; the second, by the means of processing; and the third, by the means of harvesting and preservation. Each system gave way to the next as people attempted to solve its problems.

I have named each of the three periods of the history of coastal Alabama's fishery for its central variables: ice preservation and distribution by railroads, industrial canning, and industrial catching and freezing of shrimp. Over time, the central variables and limitations to the industry shifted from the system of preservation and distribution to the organization of processing, and then from processing to the technology and organization of harvesting as well as processing.

We can watch the values of variables change historically and look for variables whose values depend on each other. When we find a set of variables whose values change over time together, we have identified a system. One variable might get larger as another grows. For instance, figures 1 and 2 show that the total value of shrimp caught increases as shrimp boats get larger and larger, a process that starts in 1950. On the other hand, as shrimp boats get larger, the pounds of shrimp caught for each ton of shrimp boat gets less and less (figure 3). As one variable increases (size of shrimp boats) another also increases (value of shrimp landed) while a third decreases (pounds of shrimp per ton of shrimp boat). Meanwhile another variable, the value of shrimp per ton of shrimp boat, has no relationship to the others but goes up and down over the same period (figure 4).

Figure 1 shows that shrimp boats remained about the same size

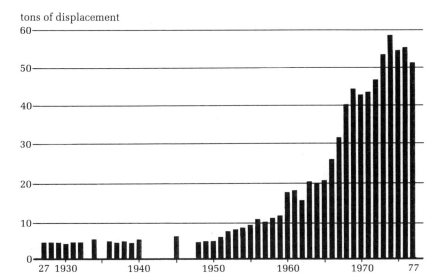

Figure 1. Size of the average shrimp boat in tons of displacement.

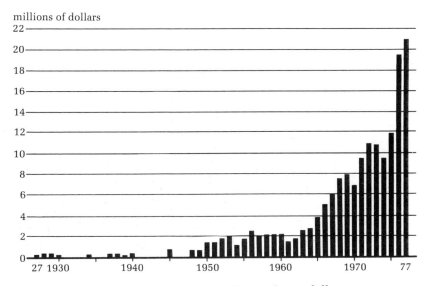

Figure 2. Value of shrimp landed in millions of 1967 dollars.

thousands of pounds

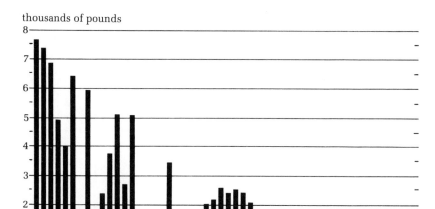

Figure 3. Pounds of shrimp catch per ton of shrimp boat.

dollars per ton

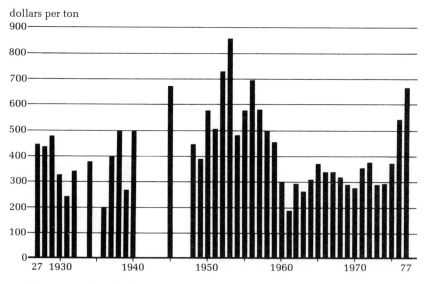

Figure 4. Value of shrimp catch per ton of shrimp boat in 1967 dollars.

until 1950 when they began to get larger. Figure 2 shows that the value of shrimp landed was variable and small until 1950 when it began to increase each year. Together, these figures illustrate the process of increasing shrimp catch and boat size that started in 1950. Since that progression was centered on the industrial-scale catching and freezing of shrimp, I call the period from 1950 to the present the period of industrial shrimping and freezing.

This designation calls attention to the most visible, central dimensions of the seafood industry of the period: the large gulf-going shrimp boats and freezing plants. As we will see, these boats and factories are among the most important variables of the system because they determine the values of other variables. People still catch oysters with tongs from skiffs and use small boats to trawl the bays and sounds for shrimp. To call shrimping industrial is not to suggest that earlier systems were pre-industrial, because all have been enmeshed in the industrial development of the United States whether via its railroads, its processing technology, or its fishing technology.

Earlier, oysters were the foundation of Alabama's seafood industry. Large industrial processing plants packed canned oysters to ship throughout the United States and abroad. Toward the end of the nineteenth century, as their local problems increased, seafood packers from Chesapeake Bay and the eastern United States began to take an interest in the gulf. They established canneries, and local people began catching oysters for them. Some local people invested capital in canneries. Since the industrial canneries were central to the industry, I call this middle period, from 1915 to 1950, the period of industrial canning.

A processing technology defines this period. While fishing and processing technology defines the most recent period, the large canning factories were not only the most visible aspects of the second system, but virtually every other dimension of the system depended on them. They were the predominant variable in the system, as central to this period as the gulf boats and freezing plants are to the present system.

Before the canneries came to Alabama and the rest of the gulf coast, preservation of seafood depended on ice. During this period fishermen caught fish and oysters to sell to dealers who iced them and sold them locally or sent them inland by riverboat or railroad. Demand was only local until the transportation system allowed wider distribution. As railroads and steamboats penetrated north into the interior to bring cotton to Mobile and ice factories were built to produce ice locally, there was a wider market for seafood products. Fish vendors began processing fish for the inland trade and then fitting out boats to seek the valued red snapper in the Gulf of Mexico. They packed oysters and sent them by rail and riverboat to consumers as far from the coast as winter weather and ice supplies would allow. The volume of seafood depended on local demand and the regional transportation system. Since seafood production from 1819 to 1915 depended on ice and railroads, I call this earliest era the period of preservation with ice and distribution by railroad.

Iced fish has a short shelf life. There are two solutions to this problem. One is to develop alternate methods of preservation. The other is to speed up transportation so that it does not matter. The transportation system was developed for the cotton trade but it allowed the expansion of the fishing industry. At the same time, processors were experimenting with canning. Some canneries were established in the nineteenth century, but they were not successful and did not dominate the seafood industry—did not become important variables—until the system of taxation and regulation was changed in 1915 to reduce taxes and eliminate double taxation for planted oysters. After conditions for cultivating and catching oysters improved with the legislation of 1915, canning became profitable in Alabama and began to develop.

The supplies of oysters were too unreliable for canneries, which began to can fruit and shrimp to even out the supplies of raw materials. When trawl nets increased the reliability of the supply of shrimp, processors turned their attention to shrimp rather than oysters. As new freezing and processing technologies, ways of rigging trawls, and boat technology developed, and new distant shrimping grounds were discovered, industrial shrimping superseded the system based on industrial canning that entailed oystering and small-scale shrimping. This system had in turn supplanted one that depended for its organization and structure mainly on short-term preservation with ice and rapid transportation by rail.

Even though I focus on coastal Alabama, it is impossible to confine the story to that stretch of the Gulf of Mexico. The impetus for oyster canning came from Chesapeake Bay. Much of the capital for the industrial facilities came from the East. Some came from local sources and some from Biloxi. Factories and unions in Biloxi and Louisiana were connected to those in Alabama.

We will see that one of the problems that have faced shrimpers since the end of World War II is imports. Imports of shrimp are part of the trade policy of the United States, and that policy is formed on the basis of considerations of foreign policy. One aspect of foreign policy is development programs for Third World countries. Some of these programs have encouraged pond raising of shrimp and increased the supply of imported shrimp to compete with domestic production. These development and trade policies are not aimed at Alabama or gulf coast or American shrimpers. The policy makers probably do not even know that there are such shrimpers or how their policies affect shrimpers. These national policies do affect shrimpers but are not local in origin. Again, to understand how the system works, we have to look outside it.

Another policy that affects shrimpers is the regulation that they equip their trawls with chutes called turtle excluder devices (TEDs) to allow turtles to escape. These are dangerous to shrimpers, reduce the catch of shrimp, and increase the consumption of fuel. Their value for preserving turtles is questionable given the lack of control of foreign shrimpers, domestic industries, and developers and water sports that decrease the turtles' shore habitat and pollute the waters. Shrimpers must endure this because of a law favored by sport fishermen in league with environmentalists, who have been trying to outlaw trawling since it was first introduced on the Gulf of Mexico around 1918. The story of this issue will take us from Alabama to Texas and Louisiana and Washington. Again, elements outside the system made significant changes in it.

This book is the story of these and other processes, the development of Alabama's fishing industry. The title of the book reflects only a single dimension of these processes, but a constant one. And, I think it points to an enduring relationship of the primary producers, the fishermen, to other aspects of the industry: their relative powerlessness. Even that has fluctuated. While politics is a constant, it is not necessarily the most important process.

If we take a broad view, we see that the dynamics of each system is determined primarily by larger processes outside the fishery itself. In the early period, the development of the cotton industry was of critical importance. In the middle period, the technological and economic incentives to establish large canneries were central. The introduction of trawl technology altered the system away from oysters and toward shrimp, and at the same time away from factory fleets and toward owner-operated fishing boats, independent fishermen, and fishermen's unions.

The new technology of gulf fishing boats and new techniques of processing, cleaning, and freezing shrimp defined the most recent period. The amount of capital involved in the larger boats undermined the independence of owners and their unions and made for some reversion toward fleet ownership.

Politics, as such, is not the decisive factor in any period, except perhaps the transition from the first to the second in which a tax crippled the oyster industry until it was lifted to begin the second period. In recent times, when fisheries management has become a profession and a concern, ironically, much of the relevant policy is a consequence of policies that do not directly concern fisheries. Foreign policy is more important than fisheries policy for setting levels of imports that determine prices for shrimp and thus the economics of the industry for both processors and shrimpers. Preservation of endangered species is the focus of the recent TEDs policy that affects fishermen. Other policies that center on industrial development, tourism, conservation, and sports fishing have similar indirect consequences.

To keep the book focused, I have discussed events outside Alabama only as they have affected what was happening in Alabama, insofar as Alabama fisheries were part of larger systems. I have mentioned a few other places for comparisons—Iceland, where fishing is the living of a whole country; Japan, where industrial development nearly destroyed chances for any fishing at all; Florida, where there is a history of shell-planting programs; and Canada, where there have been parallel studies of fishing and fishing policy. At one point I even mention the Trobriand Islands off the coast of New Guinea. However, I have kept such comparisons to a minimum. Comparisons and generalities can only be as sound as the local studies upon which they are based. With the details of local description in place, with the particulars of local history established, it is possible to compare them with other histories and other places to establish general patterns.

Themes

In spite of the great changes in the fishing industry, there have been a number of continuities. People have been saying the oyster industry has been dying since oyster catchers first started tonging. There have been repeated attempts to revive the industry with various schemes of relocating oysters from polluted areas to uncontaminated waters and by planting shells to form the foundation for oyster reefs.

The Alabama legislature has formed various bodies to regulate the seafood industry. Whoever has been unlucky enough to be put in charge has always encountered some who say everything he does is wrong, and who accuse him of incompetence, corruption, or worse. When we see the history of such attacks, we can begin to understand and sympathize with the bureaucrats in management positions at all levels, even if we don't always agree with them.

Biologists control such positions and define fisheries issues as biological, sometimes extending the definition to economics. Ironically, we know least about the most important aspect of these systems, the people in them—the fishermen, biologists, bureaucrats, legislators, factory workers, processors, and others.

Another continuous feature is the misuse of science. Ever since there have been attempts to make fisheries policy, that policy has been based on rhetoric of science. That is, every policy had to be based on some story that would pass for scientific evidence; at least, it had to be persuasive to a judge. The dredging of Mobile Bay for its oyster shells while attempts were made to reestablish an oyster industry, the policy about TEDs, decisions about dumping gas and oil drilling wastes and industrial effluent as well as domestic sewage into Mobile Bay—all depended on convincing powerful people of the scientific merits of one side of the issue.

The process has always been the same: to claim science for one side and to brand the opposition as irrational. This works well enough where there is an imbalance of power, as between unorganized shrimpers and the powerful environmentalist and sport fishing groups who can afford their own biologists and lawyers. It works less well when the environmentalists' "scientists" are pitted against industrialists' "scientists."

In this process, another constant is that money talks. Each party bends science to its own interests. As long as the Conservation Department derived a large income from shell dredging, "science" showed it to be harmless. With well-financed environmental lobbies and powerful sport fishing groups allied against shrimpers, National Marine Fisheries Service "science" shows that TEDs are the best solution to the problem of endangered sea turtles.

This emphasizes another enduring characteristic. The general pattern for any industry is for it to say it wants the government to leave it alone while lobbying as hard as it can for subsidies, tax breaks, and protection from imports and against competition. This is no less true of the fishing industry, but what becomes obvious in examining "the industry" dynamically, historically, is that it has never been unitary. There are many different interests in the industry. Fishermen do not always share interests with processors. Processors do not always share interests with biologists. What in some contexts appears to be "an industry" is, on closer examination, a complex set of relationships with conflicting interests that change over time.

It is easy to take processors as "the industry," since they are usually organized to speak for their interests. To do so is to accept only a limited view of a complex system of changing relationships. My emphasis is on the systems and how they change. This analysis illustrates the dynamics of these systems, another constant.

If anything has remained constant during the past two or three hundred years, it might be the annual cycles of the fisherman's prey, the constant spawning, growing, maturing, and spawning of the shrimp and oysters.

Biology

Shrimp spawn offshore. The young larvae enter the bay, develop in the marshes, and leave the bay as young adults to spawn in the gulf and start the cycle over. The postlarval brown shrimp immigrate into the estuaries from March to April, and juveniles leave the estuaries for deeper waters in the spring. White shrimp come into the estuaries from June to September, and leave again in the fall as juveniles (M. F. Smith 1984, 10).

The viability of shrimp populations does not appear to be affected by fishing pressure as each female produces between half a million and a million eggs. Only a small portion of the eggs survive the migration inshore to the marshes and the predators in the marshes. The catch of shrimp in any year is not affected by the number of shrimp the previous year. The major factors that control the size of shrimp populations are not fishing pressures but environmental factors such as salinity and water temperatures (Wallace and Hosking 1986).

When the temperature and salinity conditions are right (higher than seventy-two degrees, salinity above six parts per thousand), oysters spawn from April through October. Females release between seventy million and a hundred and seventy million eggs. Fertilized eggs develop into free-swimming larvae in about twenty-four hours. They form a shell that becomes too heavy for them to carry after a few weeks, and the larvae settle to the bottom. If the spat find a clean, hard bottom—for instance, one composed of oyster shells, known as cultch—they secrete a fluid that cements them permanently to the bottom. Larvae that settle into soft mud do not survive, or develop a long, narrow shape with unmarketable meat. If they come down on firm mud, they may grow into large "mud oysters." People can encourage oysters to grow by seeding areas of barren bay or sound bottom with oyster shells to provide cultch on which spat can settle.

Oysters are filter feeders and concentrate pollutants in their meat (Warner 1982). The pollutants do not harm the oysters but are harmful to people. The Department of Conservation and Natural Resources and the Department of Public Health both monitor oyster reefs and close them to harvesting when levels of disease-causing organisms are too high, usually when there is a heavy spring or winter river flow which carries contaminants into the bay.

If the annual cycle of the species fishermen catch has remained constant, the landscape has not. Marshland has been filled in, channels dredged, and roads, towns, and cities built. Forests have been cut and replanted, oyster reefs have come and gone. Clean waters have become polluted, and some polluted waters have been cleaned again.

Geography

The Mobile River forms at the confluence of the Alabama and Tombigbee rivers, flows for about five miles, and branches into the smaller Mobile, Tensaw, Apalachee, and Blakeley rivers which interlace through the delta floodplain on their way to Mobile Bay (Copeland 1982, 43), one of several bays along the northern Gulf of Mexico. Ninety-five percent of the freshwater inflow to Mobile Bay is from the Mobile River system. The bay discharges about 15 percent of its outflow west into the Mississippi Sound and about 85 percent south into the Gulf of Mexico (Loyacano and Busch 1979).

The city of Mobile and its satellites of Pritchard, Chickasaw, Eight Mile, Saraland, and Theodore spread across the northern half of the western shore of the bay. On the eastern shore are the smaller municipalities of Spanish Fort, Daphne, Montrose, Fairhope, Point Clear, Barnwell, Magnolia Springs, Bon Secour, Gulf Shores, and Pine Beach. Two causeways cross the northern end of the bay: Interstate 10 and U.S. Route 90. U.S. Route 98 connects most of the eastern shore while Alabama 163 runs down the west shore to Dauphin Island. To the east of Mobile Bay the boundary between Alabama and Florida is in the middle of Perdido Bay, into which the Perdido River empties. Perdido Bay is connected to Mobile Bay by the Intracoastal Waterway, which continues west between Dauphin Island and the mainland into the Mississippi Sound, between the barrier islands off Mississippi and its mainland, and on into the waters of Louisiana and Texas.

Bayou la Batre, the westernmost community on Alabama's coast, is industrial. Large and small fish-processing plants line Bayou la Batre's wide channel and shrimp boats float at their wharves. Boats are built and repaired at several boat yards. The drawbridge across the bayou modulates the flow of automobile and truck traffic on Alabama 188 through town. A gas refinery is to the east, on the way to Coden, a small community laid out along another bayou. Boat-building works, crab traps, and oyster boats are strung out along Bayou Coden, and a few shrimp boats cluster around several fish houses. Alabama 188 runs into highway 163 on Mon Louis Island.

At Alabama Port, an unincorporated community just north of the high bridge to Dauphin Island, oyster boats are tied up along the canal that parallels the highway, and piles of shells identify a number of oyster-shucking houses. The high bridge crosses over Pass-Aux-Herons and the Intracoastal Waterway to Dauphin Island, where there are a few shrimp and oyster boats, a couple of fish houses, but mainly a marina for pleasure boats, summer houses, restaurants, and a few condominiums. The public beach gives way to a sprawl of summer houses which ends abruptly on the western end of the island, un-developed because the owners have not been able to meet restrictions necessary to get building permits. At the eastern end of the island are old Fort Gaines, the Dauphin Island Sea Lab, a public boat ramp, and a car ferry that runs across Main Pass at the southern end of the bay to Fort Morgan, the westernmost point of Fort Morgan Peninsula on the east side of Mobile Bay. From the island one sees several gas-drilling rigs in the bay and gulf.

Turning north on Alabama 163, one drives along the west shore past Bellengrath Gardens and Fowl River to the west and a number of bayside houses to the east. The industrial city of Theodore is about fifteen miles north of Dauphin Island. Mobile and its surrounding communities harbor some industry and the port of Mobile.

From the causeway, a view of Mobile Bay opens to the south. To the north one catches only a glimpse of the complex marshlands with their quivering soils, prehistoric shell middens, and thick vegetation that obscures vision beyond more than a few feet. In the bayous and channels of the delta, sport fishermen take largemouth bass, sun-fish, channel catfish, alligator gar, and crappies. At the bottom of the bayous lie the three Confederate ironclads that were sunk to forbid Farragut's ships access to the northern reaches of the rivers, the last slaving ship in America's history, and more than a hundred years' shipping refuse including many derelict barges. Bound for paper-processing plants or coal-handling facilities, barges laden with coal and logs come down the Tennessee-Tombigbee Waterway into the bay. The boundary between Mobile and Baldwin counties meanders along the western portion of the delta.

Along the east side of Mobile Bay the houses are more opulent than on the west side. Affluence seems to peak at the Grand Hotel near Fairhope with its marina full of sailing boats and yachts. Ala-bama highway 59 continues south from Foley to Gulf Shores along the gulf and a strip of condominiums and beach houses that stretches along Perdido Key into Florida. Some of Fort Morgan Peninsula is devoted to nature preserves. The peninsula encloses Bon Secour Bay to its north. At the end of Bon Secour Bay is the community of Bon Secour, so well described by David White (1977), with its fish houses and shrimping fleet. Along the bays and bayous of Perdido Bay, Bon Secour Bay, and the other bays and inlets on the east shore and gulf coast are condominiums and housing tracts of varying affluence. Some are mobile-home settlements; others, collections of quite luxurious houses. In the bayous and bays one sees more sailboats and pleasure craft than working boats. While the ambience of the west shore is decidedly industrial, the east shore is more recreational except for parts of Bon Secour.

Wherever rivers run into the bay—the Fowl River and Dog River on the west shore, the Bon Secour River and Weeks Bay on the east shore, the Mobile Delta to the north, as well as the eastern end of Dauphin Island and the western end of Fort Morgan Peninsula to the south—there are areas of marsh where primary production of the food chain begins. They provide nursery areas and habitat for the young and juveniles of commercially important species (Stout 1979). Shrimp production is related to marsh area (Mettee and O'Neil 1982). Ninety-nine percent of the shrimp caught off coastal Alabama spend at least part of their life cycle in Alabama estuaries. Mobile Bay comprises 72 percent of the estuary system of Alabama (Heath 1979; M. F. Smith 1984, 10). By 1979, about a quarter (22 percent) of Mobile Bay's marshlands had been destroyed by dredging (Stout 1979).

The transportation of oil products through the Intracoastal Waterway, the Tennessee-Tombigbee Waterway, into the Port of Mobile, and the petrochemical industry in the bay pose additional threats to marshes as "accidents, of even minor proportions, introduce oil to the Estuary and create stress on marsh communities" (ibid., 118).

A ship channel runs between Dauphin Island and Fort Morgan Peninsula and into the Port of Mobile. The channel has been dredged since 1827, and continues to be dredged. Over more than a century the dredging spoil has altered the nature of Mobile Bay. In the past, spoil was deposited in the estuarial marshes, where it contributed to their destruction. More recently, some of the spoil has been deposited to build Gaillard Island in the western part of the bay about two miles from shore. The island has become a bird sanctuary and has been pivotal in the regeneration of the endangered brown pelicans. The Corps of Engineers, which does the dredging, plans to continue deposition on the island for the next sixty years. The corps is dredging another channel to Theodore, where the construction of a United States Navy home port is planned.

The inland waterway makes coal available for export and local consumption. Export creates a demand for a deeper ship channel and problems of spoil disposal. The generation of power for local consumption creates problems of acid rain and a potential threat to marshes and sea life.

Twelve years ago Mobile Bay was receiving 32 million gallons of treated waste water per day from 19 municipal plants, and 130 million gallons a day of industrial discharge from 38 industrial sources (Loyacano and Busch 1979; Brady 1979). In addition there were "49 semi-public and private dischargers of sanitary waste, cooling water, boiler blowdown, rain water runoff, and other nonpermitted effluents" (Brady 1979, 42). Isphording and Flowers (1987) argue that Mobile Bay has nearly reached the limits of its ecological capacity for pollution.

Approaches and Sources

Anthropology is often identified by its reliance on participant observation. An anthropologist goes to a community, learns the language, lives with the people, works with them, celebrates with them, and learns about their lives from the inside. He or she then bases analyses of the culture and society on this detailed intimate knowledge of a community and its people.

We observe particular events such as weddings, feasts, harvests, festivals, sicknesses, deaths, and funerals. Though each event is unique, it is also a representative of a type of event. After we see several events of the same type we begin to see a pattern, and we can ask people to explain elements of the pattern to us.

From our observations of such unique events and people's explanations of them we can begin to describe cultural patterns that underlie events, the categories of the culture, its assumptions and institutions that give events their form. In doing ethnographic fieldwork we also collect all manner of numbers: How many people live in each household, how many work, what work people do and how much; how much of what their work produces; how much land or labor they use for what purposes; how much they consume. These numbers reveal patterns also.

Many ethnographers find that different people understand the same events in quite different ways depending on their sex, their age, and other dimensions of their positions in the society. Sometimes the patterns people tell us about in their explanations are quite contrary to the patterns we can observe in the numbers (Durrenberger 1987). Thus, while interviews always provide data, they do not always provide analysis. I interpreted the material that fisheries bureaucrats and oceanographers told me in interviews in the same light as the things shrimpers, processors, and workers told me. I considered all of the interview material to be data to be understood, not as explanations of data or analyses of systems or historical events.

By the end of a year or two in a small community, an anthropologist may know everyone there in great detail. David White (1977) has provided this kind of view of a shrimping community in Alabama. The ethnographic approach has the strength of developing intimate familiarity with a community and its people but often at the cost of less detailed understandings of the community's regional or historical context. White's ethnography is masterful, but by virtue of the ethnographic approach, he had to limit his historical investigations largely to oral history and life histories.

The approach I take here supplements the ethnographic approach by developing an independent description of historical processes beyond the community itself. Like ethnographers, I rely on descriptions of unique events, but also like ethnographers, I take this only as a starting point for understanding the conceptual, institutional, and economic structures that shape the events. I do not appeal to people's recollection of events nor to their interpretation of events, because these are variable.

This approach widens our view but sacrifices the intimacy and detail of participant observation. It depends on documentation rather than observation. Most of the events I report are ones I have read about rather than seen. Even those events I witnessed were also witnessed and reported by newspaper reporters. There is therefore a public record of the events to rely on rather than only my personal notes. A historical approach depends on examining year after year of official statistical reports over decades to show patterns rather than collecting and analyzing numbers for a year or two. It allows us to see patterns through time.

With this approach we can widen the coverage not only in space beyond a small community but also in time beyond the narrow slice of time an ethnographic fieldworker can observe. We see that what appears to be traditional or customary in the short term may be transitory and may change as other variables change. What appears to be timeless and immutable from the point of view of ethnographic description becomes flexible and changeable in the light of historical analysis that admits of time and change.

The fine-grained detail of ethnography is irreplaceable. But it can be improved by supplementing it with a broader historical and processual approach such as I use here. My approach to the material remains essentially ethnographic rather than institutional. Rather than community members, my main "informants" have been local newspapers, official reports, and other such local sources. I have used the accounts of events and reports of statistics to construct descriptions of systems of relationships, and I trace their changes through time and the reasons for their changes.

While I emphasize systems, there are many other ways to approach the same materials and questions. One could reconstruct individual biographies or life histories, community histories, or institutional histories of agencies. One could observe that any account or story is a cultural artifact of its creator and develop a literary analysis of newspaper stories or agency reports to uncover the tacit cultural assumptions of the authors and audiences. Since the particular materials of this study involve fishing, which is now regulated by several agencies, one could conceivably develop an analysis in terms of the dynamics, assumptions, and culture of resource management. Anthropology is a many-faceted discipline and each approach offers insights and at the same time has limitations that conceal what others reveal. No single approach can do all things.

I have developed this analysis in terms of an ethnographic-historical approach, using stories from the past as ethnographic documents from which to build analyses of systems of relationships, because I think this approach complements studies such as White's and will be the most generally useful. While a cultural analyst may never read a book on fisheries policy and a fishery policy analyst is unlikely ever to read a study of culture or cultural dynamics, I hope that both could find something of value in an ethnographic-historical approach.

A tenet of ethnographic method is to make the most of the testimony of local sources, informants. A tenet of historical research is likewise to make the most of accounts of local witnesses to events. For this reason I have relied heavily, though not exclusively by any means, on local newspapers. The *Mobile Register* (abbreviated MR in the citations) started publication in 1820 and has been published continuously through the present. I have used its annual commercial report as a source of quantitative data for the value of fish and oysters from 1877 to 1908. The first report, in 1879, provides figures for 1877 and 1878. The last figures are for 1908. The 1910 report says that "some of the local firms refuse to give out the information relative to the value of their business" (MR 1 September 1910). To check on this data, I compared it with U.S. Fisheries Department data for the years where both sources overlap. The correlation is .89, which suggests that they are close.

The press is an institution and one could have approached the same materials to inform an analysis of the history of Mobile's press as an institution or its cultural assumptions as part of the complex study of journalism. As Allen (1990) points out, journalists gather immense amounts of information but, because they concentrate on the five W's of a story—who, what, when, where, why—they make little effort to show how they fit together. Piecing together stories from news accounts is typically complex. There is often a story announcing that an event is planned, or scheduled, or likely to happen. A second story may develop the description in terms of the five W's. The event may still be quite unclear until an account of another event indicates the results of the first one.

What to a journalist may be a series of daily stories, each complete in itself, may form a single event in the hindsight of historical analysis. Allen (ibid.) urges journalists to recognize that every story belongs in a context of larger stories, that ostensibly isolated events fit into larger systems. Journalists do not take the building of such perspectives to be their task. That is the task of anthropology, and it is one of the differences between journalism and ethnography.

While many of the citations in the text are to the *Mobile Register*, it was far from the sole source of information. Nor did I accept its accounts uncritically any more than an ethnographer uncritically accepts the statements of informants when he or she is doing fieldwork. I used a number of other sources of information, among them other newspapers such as the *Mobile County News*, the *Mobile News Item*, the *Mobile Daily Tribune*, the *Mobile Press*, the *Gulfport and Biloxi Mississippi Daily Herald*, *Mississippi Today*, the *Biloxi-D'Iberville Press*, and the *Biloxi Sun Herald*.

The local newspapers are one of the best sources simply because every other source has a particular stake in the fishing industry and none hesitates to pursue its own ends in the presentation of "scientific" or "historical" data and interpretation. In the many instances where I could cross-check several sources, the local newspaper reports proved to be the most valuable because they were less biased, provided social and political context, and were accurate. The editorials, on the other hand, were opinionated and, by their very nature, biased. I have used the editorial content of the papers not as evidence about the fishing industry, but as examples of rhetoric partial to one side or another in disputes and debates. This analysis approaches the cultural.

In addition, I used city directories, the U.S. census, the Congres-

sional Record, and the national press. The Federal Writers Project (FWP) produced a volume on Alabama as well as a number of unpublished descriptions of the conditions and lives of everyday working people (Brown 1982). Many of these are in the Southern Historical Collection of the University of North Carolina, Chapel Hill. The FWP also compiled a number of court documents from the files of the Mobile courthouse. Together, these sources provided much valuable information.

Because of the requirement that fisheries management should be based on scientific analyses, and the establishment of funding agencies such as the Sea Grant program (Fiske 1990), there is a growing body of agency reports, contract completion reports, planning documents, management plans, newsletters, and proceedings of agency-sponsored meetings that are reproduced quickly in limited numbers for immediate agency goals. While they are freely available to anyone who knows how to request them from their numerous and varied sources, they remain obscure and limited in distribution. They become unavailable quickly, as their purpose is to inform ongoing administrative processes rather than to be used for academic research. Thus it is little wonder that, as Paredes (1991) points out, previous work is sometimes overlooked.

Such material is referred to as "grey literature" because it is public but not reviewed or published. The subject of much of this literature is biology or ecology as the major emphasis on fisheries management has been on biology and most administrators have backgrounds in that discipline or allied ones. Some of this literature has been produced by social scientists of institutions geographically close to the management agencies, ranging from major state universities to local community-oriented teaching institutions without traditions of research. In addition, some people at community institutions have added to the grey literature by reproducing their own documents. The quality of this literature varies. Though I am aware of this literature, I rely on and cite only that material which is methodologically or ethnographically sound.

I have relied on the U.S. Fisheries statistics for most of the quantitative data on Alabama. The earliest is George Goode's 1887 report to the United States Commission of Fish and Fisheries. The second was published in 1900 for the year ending 30 June 1899 by the same agency. I compared this with U.S. census data for years that both cover, but, while they are consistent for 1930, 1940, and 1950, they diverge for 1960 and 1970. Owen (1949, 55) notes a similar divergence between U.S. census data of 1940 and Alabama Conservation Department data and attributes it to their differing techniques. The census counted oyster shops as "trade," freighters as "transportation," and canneries as "manufacturing." Such enumeration differences explain the discrepancies in their findings.

I have availed myself of the rich historical resources of Mobile and surrounding communities. They include the archives of the Historic Mobile Preservation Society; the local history and genealogy division and other holdings of the Mobile Public Library; the University of South Alabama Library; the archives of the city of Mobile; records at the Mobile County Courthouse; the University of South Alabama Photographic Archives; the library of the Dauphin Island Sea Lab; the library of the Seafood Division of the Alabama Conservation Department, also at Dauphin Island; the library of the National Marine Fisheries Service at Pascagoula, Mississippi; the archives of the *Mobile Press-Register*; the Mobile City Museum; the archives of the Bayou la Batre Historical Society; and the Mose H. Tapia Library at Bayou la Batre. The archives of the city of Mobile house a rich collection of official documents and tax records that extend back to the foundation of the municipality. The Mobile County Courthouse, like other Alabama county courthouses, contains records of all kinds of transactions and court cases from the foundation of the county.

Another source for the post–Civil War period is the records of the Bureau of Freedmen, Refugees, and Abandoned Lands. Southern states were socially, politically, and economically disorganized by the Civil War and postwar occupation. Because southern whites were not prepared to initiate an economic and political system based on free wage labor rather than forms that attempted to perpetuate slavery in various disguises, Congress established the Freedmen's Bureau in the War Department to control matters relating to the newly freed slaves.

Bureau agents wrote detailed reports of negotiations and disputes and some prepared brilliant and often prophetic analyses of the political economy, as they termed it, of the area. These records preserve a detailed portrait of some aspects of the period, but deal mainly with questions of access to land and terms of employment for newly freed blacks rather than the maritime economy that is of most interest here. These records deserve a separate detailed study as those of Oubre (1978), Peirce (1904), and Howard White (1970). Of more relevance to this study are the development of the railroads and the fortunes of the cotton and timber industries, all detailed in the local accounts.

The *Acts and Proceedings of the Alabama Legislature* provide a record of the deliberations and legislation of that body, but they do not record which interests were lobbying whom and how heavily, what public opinion was, or who in local communities supported or opposed legislation. However, they are rich sources for cultural and institutional histories. In discussions of legislation, instead of over-burdening the text with citations, I have cited the more accessible and locally relevant newspapers which provide a much richer social context than the publications of the legislature.

The *Alabama Marine Resources Bulletin*, published by the Alabama Marine Resources Laboratory on Dauphin Island, proved very useful, as did the annual reports of the Marine Resources Division of the Department of Conservation and Natural Resources. This agency has its own agenda which it pursues in its publications. For instance, the agency interpreted the 1915 legislative abolition of the Oyster Commission as political interference with scientific research and management (Swingle and Hughes 1976, 63). Everyone agreed that after six years of operation it functioned so badly that it had virtually shut down the oyster industry. The claim of interference is part of the successor agency's interest in presenting the image of scientific management and a rhetoric of neutrality, as well as trying to isolate itself from legislative "interference." Such interests interfere with an unbiased presentation of history. The United States Bureau of Fisheries claimed credit for the introduction of the trawl as well as for the discovery of offshore fishing grounds, while abundant evidence from other sources suggests that both were consequences of fishermen acting on their own. Again, local newspapers provided the best source of data.

The Mississippi-Alabama Sea Grant Program generously provided me with many of its publications. Other sources of information were the regional management plans for various species and their supporting documentation prepared by the Gulf States Marine Fisheries Commission. These materials have little sociological, cultural, or historical depth, although they are indispensable sources of economic, biological, and technical information on recent times.

From September 1987 through March 1989 I interviewed or visited with many national, regional, and state fisheries officials in coastal Alabama. I visited numerous fishermen, shrimpers, oyster catchers, processors, marina operators, and others from Pensacola, Florida, to Biloxi, Mississippi. In March 1989 I moved from Mobile to Biloxi, where I conducted a stratified random-sample survey among more than 150 Vietnamese and American bay and gulf shrimpers. I also interviewed fisheries officials as well as shrimp and oyster dealers, packers, priests, social workers, and others involved in the business between Bayou Caddy on the western border of Mississippi and Pascagoula to the east. I visited shrimping communities and attended meetings in Louisiana, and in July of 1989 I visited the area of the Texas gulf coast between Corpus Christi and Port Lavaca and was there for the shrimpers' blockade. All of these interviews and observations also enter into this work.

I do not attribute most quotations, especially from fisheries officials. I refrain from identifying sources to avoid any possible embarrassment to them. Fee and Buckmaster (1991) found that people who expressed views that diverged from those of their superiors did not want to be identified. The dynamics of these agencies deserves detailed separate treatment. Where I do identify individuals with quotations, I cite the source, always a matter of public record. I do not identify shrimpers because as part of the design of the research I quite consciously did not ask their names.

The older spelling of Bayou la Batre does not capitalize the "l" as recent usage does. I prefer the older spelling and retain it except in direct quotations.

2

1819–1915: Preservation with Ice, Transportation by Rail, and Experimentation with Canning

The modern history of Alabama's seafood industry begins in 1819 when the state was admitted to the Union. From the sixteenth century when European explorers first appeared, what is now Alabama was part of the French, English, and Spanish empires in the Americas. While fishing played a role in this history, it belongs to the history of European empires and to the analysis of imperial systems centered on foreign metropolises. As it pertains to fishing, that history is discontinuous with the history of Alabama as a part of the United States. When Alabama became a state, Mobile was importing fish to ship to plantations inland.

The seafood industry in the early days of American Alabama was mainly centered on the supply of fish and oysters to the residents of the burgeoning port of Mobile. As lands were expropriated from native peoples and incorporated into the United States, cotton production boomed in the interior of Alabama. The outlet to the American markets of the Northeast and the rest of the world was Mobile, where planters could also purchase imported tools and supplies for their plantations and the slaves who worked them.

The fish and oyster trade in southern Alabama developed against the background of this commercial history. Mobile businessmen promoted a railroad to increase the traffic through the port. As the railroad expanded and ice manufacture developed, there was an extended market for fish and oysters from Mobile Bay and the gulf coast. Alabama firms cleaned and iced fish and oysters to send to the interior, though there was still a strong local demand that took up to 20 percent of the catch. The range of rail shipping of iced seafood depended on the weather until refrigerated railcars were introduced early in the twentieth century. As the market increased, seafood firms began to cultivate oysters in and around Mobile Bay until tax provisions made the practice unprofitable. Table 1 shows the increasing number of fishermen and oystermen recorded for Alabama in each U.S. census.

Though there were earlier experiments, the first successful canneries were not established until early in the twentieth century. Early canneries leased bay bottomland from the state to cultivate oysters, but the enterprise did not flourish. The high taxes in the provisions of the oyster laws of 1911 made it unattractive to plant or harvest oysters, and canning went into abeyance until the laws were reformed in 1915. This marks the end of the early period and the beginning of industrial canning as the predominant rather than secondary feature of the seafood industry.

Table 1. Number of Fishermen in Alabama at Each U.S. Census from 1850 through 1910

	Population of			Number of
Year	City of Mobile	Mobile County	Baldwin County	Fishermen and Oystermen
1850	20,515	27,600	4,414	47
1860	29,258	41,131	7,630	210
1870	32,034	49,311	6,004	174
1880	29,132	48,653	8,603	296
1890	31,076	51,587	8,941	397
1900	38,469	62,740	13,194	612
1910	51,521	80,854	18,178	578

Source: U.S. Bureau of the Census

From Colony to State

The British and Spanish agreed to transfer Mobile to the newly independent United States in 1783, and nineteen years later the first cotton gin was built near Montgomery. With both Spanish and American claims, the status of Mobile and coastal Alabama remained ambiguous until 1813 when the United States, then at war with Britain, seized Mobile with a force from New Orleans. The next year, Andrew Jackson took his Tennessee militia into Alabama against the Creek Indians and on to New Orleans against the British. After the Creek ceded about half the lands of Alabama to the United States in 1814 and the Chickasaw Nation relinquished its claim to lands south of Tennessee in 1816, the United States Congress divided the Mississippi territory and named the eastern part Alabama in 1817. White settlers from Virginia, the Carolinas, Tennessee, Kentucky, and Georgia poured into Alabama and in 1819 Alabama was admitted to the United States.

In 1821 steamboat service up the Alabama River to Montgomery made the port of Mobile accessible to Alabama cotton planters. With slave labor and more cotton gins, the interior of Alabama produced cotton that moved through Mobile to the rest of the world. By 1833 cotton was the primary industry in Alabama. With new varieties of cotton, the newly settled lands tripled production by 1840. Until 1861 farmers and planters sold most of Alabama's cotton and purchased their supplies in Mobile (Jordan 1957; Amos 1976).

Each week the *Mobile Register* published current prices for commodities, among them beef, butter, cheese, coffee, cordage, various kinds of cloth, herring, mackerel, shad, raisins, flour, ham, lard, European iron, sugar, spirits, tea, tobacco, wax, and wine. None of the lists identifies fish as an export item. From 1840 to 1860, New England fishermen would spend their winters on the coast of Florida catching and salting seven hundred to eight hundred barrels of fish per year to sell to planters in Alabama and Georgia (Stearns 1887b). Alabama was importing fish from Europe and Florida.

Deposits from the Dog River built up a bar that prevented deep-draft vessels from entering Mobile Bay to load and unload at Mobile. The deep-water port that served Mobile was at the south end of the bay at Alabama Port, near Cedar Point (Amos 1976, 63). Goods moved between Alabama Port and Mobile by small boat (Hamilton 1911), and later by railroad. From that time to this there has been a constant effort to get support for deepening and widening ship channels and improving port facilities at Mobile (Thompson 1979).

Mobile competed with the Atlantic ports of Charleston and Savannah for the cotton trade. To expand the city's hinterland, Mobile interests sponsored the Mobile and Ohio Railroad to go to the Ohio River near Cairo, Illinois. In 1850 the United States Congress authorized a federal land grant to promote the railroad company's efforts, and the next year, Mobilians voted almost unanimously in favor of a land tax to sustain the railroad. By 1852 the railroad reached thirty-five miles to Citronelle. The same year, Congress appropriated fifty thousand dollars to dredge a channel through Mobile Bay to Mobile. In 1858 the railroad extended 260 miles to West Point, Mississippi. By 1861 it reached Columbus, Kentucky, nearly to Cairo, Illinois, and connected by ferry across the Mississippi River to the Illinois Central Railroad to join Mobile to the Midwest (Thompson 1979).

Railroads and riverboats delivered cotton from the interior to Mobile, where it was loaded onto ships for sea transportation to Europe or the northeastern United States. After the Civil War, railroads spread from east to west to connect the headwaters of the river systems directly to the East Coast. It was no longer necessary to move raw materials south to the sea to transport them north and east. Mobile was cut off from the most important trade networks and its importance as a port diminished (Isbell 1951, 50–51). In the 1870s the railroads south of the Ohio River took the cotton that would have gone to Mobile to Savannah, Norfolk, and Charleston (Alsobrook 1983, 2).

If the railroads took the cotton trade from Mobile, they facilitated a timber boom toward the end of the nineteenth century as products from the pine forests of southern Mississippi, Alabama, and the Florida panhandle gained in importance. The less than 2 million cubic feet of timber exported in 1887 had increased four and a half times to 8.1 million cubic feet by 1897. Lumber, grain, meat, coal, and iron reached Mobile for export to Europe and Latin America while vegetables, fruits, and tropical products were shipped north from Mobile by railroad.

Seafood in Mobile and an Expanding Market

Seafood was first commercially important to supply the local demand in the port town of Mobile through its local marketplace. As agriculture developed in the interior there was an expanding market. With increased transportation facilities for moving cotton to the coast, and more plentiful ice as it began to be manufactured locally, seafood was shipped to a wider area. The dynamics of the industry shifted from a local marketplace to a regional distribution network served by railroads. The seafood industry had its origins in the local marketplace and expanded from there.

Josiah Blakeley, a transplant from Connecticut, reported in 1812 that there were ninety single-story wooden houses and twenty white families in Mobile. In a letter he wrote, "This market furnishes plenty of good oysters and fish, and during the winter the greatest plenty of wild geese, ducks, etc. . ." (Hamilton 1910, 444). In 1814 Blakeley and others elected a municipal government. On Dauphin Street near the water they built a market where fresh meat, fish, and oysters were sold from daybreak to ten in the morning (ibid.).

In 1824 William Robertson petitioned the city to decide a contested claim to access to a location at the foot of Government Street. He intended to build a fish market bordering the channel to preserve live fish. A committee recommended an ordinance restricting the sale of fish, except shellfish, to the marketplace, in stalls furnished rent free to fishermen. Robertson said he had spent two thousand dollars to build the market and that it would be a public benefit to remove the fish stalls from the streets and to provide fish to the populace, especially in summer when there was a "scarcity of wholesome meats." He mentioned his risk and that "it is yet uncertain whether from the Capital necessarily employed and the expense of taking the Fish it can ever be a source of any considerable profit to the proprietor" (WPA 1939).

Four years later, because there was no sheltered place to sell fish when the market burned, a group of immigrants from Spain petitioned the mayor of Mobile and received permission to sell fish in the open without charge. In 1829 the city reaffirmed an 1824 ordinance restricting the sale of fish to the market, which William Robertson contracted to maintain (ibid.).

There were complaints of monopolistic practices and price gouging by market-stall operators because city ordinances would not allow the sale of their produce in other locales or at other than specified times. The highest bidders occupied market stalls and there could be no competition against them. They therefore set both the prices offered to producers and the prices for consumers. People complained about the system for selling meat, poultry, vegetables, and other produce as well as fish (P. Taylor 1951, 43).

In 1838 when market butchers offered a farmer seven cents a pound for his cattle instead of the ten cents he asked, he built a pen outside the town limits and contracted to supply hotels and others for half the prevailing market price of twenty-five cents. The butchers then bought his cattle for ten cents a pound (ibid., 43–44).

In November of the same year, the *Mobile Register* editorialized against high commodity prices and limited market hours:

> We know of no way of breaking into the iron-bound monopoly of the fish market, but by competition. This business is almost exclusively in the hands of the Spaniards, and they look upon the trade as a prescriptive right which it is said, requires a more than ordinary nerve to trespass upon. But the field is lawfully open. . . . Very many of the small hard-money fortunes, which have been amassed in the city, and retained while paper millionaires have been ruined, are known to have been made in the little fleet of fishing smacks huddled together in the dock of the fish market. The Spaniards greatly mistake their own interests, as the butchers do, in their systematic efforts to keep up the prices of their articles. (MR 9 November 1838)

In 1838 the Mobile city directory listed thirteen establishments that sold oysters. In 1850, before the Mobile and Ohio Railroad started, the U.S. census reports there were 34 fishermen and 2 oystermen in Mobile. Of these 36 individuals, all but one were foreign born. They accounted for less than one percent (.75 percent) of the total of the 4,815 people enumerated as members of the work force. In Mobile County, outside Mobile, there were 16 "watermen" of whom there were 5 from Alabama, 8 from other states, and 1 each from England, Scotland, and Spain. There were about twice as many fishermen in Mobile as in rural Mobile County. The category "watermen" must not be identical to the category "oystermen and fishermen" because there are only 47 of the latter in the state as opposed to a total of 52 watermen from Mobile County and fishermen and oystermen from the city of Mobile. At any rate, most of the oystermen and fishermen lived in Mobile.

Ten years later, as the railroad was about to connect with the Illinois Central, there were 71 fishermen and 37 oystermen, 1.28 percent of the work force of 8,436. Of these 108, 69 percent were foreign born, 24 percent were southern by birth, and about 6 percent were northern born. There were 45 fishermen and 57 oystermen outside of Mobile (Thompson 1979), a total of 210 in the state.

There was a strong local demand for seafood. In 1870 the Mobile city directory listed 11 oyster dealers. There was a steady increase until 1880 when there were 22. There were 21 oyster saloons in 1870, 16 in 1880, and 29 in 1895, after which the directory does not list oyster saloons as a category of business. The directory lists 70 retail oyster dealers in 1895 and 88 in 1900, 37 in 1905, and a further decrease to 26 in 1915.

The fish and oyster trade depended on ice to keep the seafood fresh. From 1827 ice was packed in sawdust and brought to Mobile from New England in sailing ships (MR 25 April 1937). In 1844 Charles P. Gage is listed as an ice dealer in the Mobile directory. As early as 1861 a company advertised fish packed in ice.

The first ice was manufactured in Mobile in 1870. The manufacturers announced that they could sell ice at rates to drive northern ice out of business (*Mobile Daily Tribune* 10, 24 February 1870). In 1872 northern ice imported by schooner was still advertised. The Louisiana Ice Manufacturing Company began producing ice in Mobile in 1879 (MR 30 March 1879). Some dealers combined the businesses of ice, fish, and oysters. By 1887 ice was being manufactured in interior towns, thus diminishing the demand for ice from ports, but in

Mobile the demand increased. People continued to build new ice-manufacturing facilities and to import ice from the North, as some preferred lake ice to manufactured ice. The *Mobile Register* (1 September 1887) reported that "as the dealers entered into an agreement as to price, the competition has been in the sale and not in the price of the article." By June of 1897 manufactured ice was so plentiful that there was a price war and the price of ice dropped from thirty-five cents to fifteen cents a hundred pounds.

In 1867 the D. J. Files Company advertised pickled and spiced oysters from their steam tugs. Two years later they advertised "fresh oysters in cans hermetically sealed packed in ice and forwarded to any part of the United States." Packers put oysters in "friction top" cans in their own liquor, fastened the tops, and placed them in ice containers for shipment. The packages had to be re-iced periodically by employees of the shipping companies. It was unlawful to place ice in the containers with oysters (MR 29 November 1914).

The *Mobile Register* was enthusiastic about the developing seafood industry and saw a bright future in oysters. It reported that "England is excited on the subject of oysters. The price charged for good ones is five times as great per bushel in 1871 as it was in 1861. The beds have been dredged to death, and cannot restock themselves" (MR 5 January 1872). The newspaper kept Mobilians informed about battles between Maryland and Virginia oyster catchers in Chesapeake Bay (10 February 1872).

The *Register* reported on the issue of riparian rights, the rights of landowners to use adjacent areas of water, from other parts of the United States (4 January 1872). In 1872 Alabama legislation granted owners of waterfront property the rights to oysters they might plant and harvest up to six hundred yards offshore as long as they did not interfere with navigation (Stearns 1887b, 571). In 1840 the *Mobile Register* started its annual commercial report. In it were published statistics and descriptions of every significant industry in Mobile. The first report on fish and oysters in 1879 proclaimed:

> These luxuries with which nature has so bountifully supplied our coast have during the past year assumed a commercial importance hitherto unknown to Mobile. A new firm with ample means and large experience in commercial pursuits has taken hold of this branch of business with the laudable design of raising it to the importance it has already attained at Baltimore, at which place the natural advantages are in no way superior to those of Mobile. We are informed that they have already obtained a foothold in the principal markets of the West, and with special freight arrangements we have no doubt that this industry, which is destined to aid in

no small measure in the commercial rehabilitation of Mobile, would soon spring into giant proportions. The quarantines [against yellow fever] which hemmed us in last fall cut down the season about one half, and the actual figures therefore do not exceed those of the previous year, but we expect our next Annual Statement to tell a far different tale. (MR 31 August 1879)

To encourage the development of a local oyster industry the *Register* published a report on the successful oyster trade of Baltimore (MR 1 October 1879). An article in the agriculture section argued that the artificial management of any animal or thing, including fish and oysters, is a branch of agriculture and described oyster cultivation practices of Chesapeake Bay (MR 23 November 1879).

Legislation was passed in 1879 to prevent nonresidents of Alabama from catching oysters (MR 1, 4 February 1879). The 1880 report says that oysters in the shell were shipped by railroad to any point between Mobile and St. Louis, Cincinnati, Louisville, and Atlanta.

In 1880 Alabama fishermen used gill nets, seines, and trammel nets. Seine fishermen went farther from Mobile than gill netters and they camped along the shores of Bon Secour Bay. Some fishermen owned small farms near the fishing grounds and combined farming and fishing. They would fish when there was sufficient ice to preserve the fish for the boat trip from their camps to Mobile. F. Kuppersmith was one of the large buyers of such "inside fish" in Mobile (Stearns 1887b, 570–71).

A distinction was made between two separate fisheries: an open-sea line fishery and an inside net fishery. The smacks that fished the gulf for the Mobile market were part of the fleet from Pensacola, Florida (ibid., 570).

Independent oystermen, who had no other occupation, tonged in pairs from flat-bottomed boats and sold their catches at a standard rate of forty cents a barrel or ten cents a box. One oysterman tonged while the other culled the oysters and placed them in boxes that held one quarter of a barrel, which they sold to carriers in sailboats. These carriers worked on contract for dealers in Mobile and sold the oysters there for seventy-five cents per barrel. The crewmen paid for provisions and received 60 percent of the proceeds, which they divided among themselves. The captain got 10 or 15 percent of the owner's 40 percent. If captains owned the boats, they hired crewmen (ibid., 572).

After the oysters had been piled in a dealer's warehouse, black and Creole shuckers, who were paid by the volume of oysters they produced, opened them with knives. The "customary" price for opening a barrel of oysters was thirty-five cents. Drained oysters were ice-cooled in vats with strainer bottoms and then either shipped or canned. For shorter distances, they were placed in cans of one to ten gallons which were in turn placed in ice. For shipment further inland, they were put in square cans of a quart to a gallon and hermetically sealed (ibid., 572–73).

There were both planted oyster beds under riparian ownership and natural oyster beds. Owners would plant about thirty vessel loads—more than 2,500 bushels—on new grounds to grow for two years before harvesting. The next plantings would be less because small oysters would grow in the meantime (Stearns 1887b).

In 1880 a Scranton, Mississippi, cannery had offices in Mobile and employed about a hundred people who lived in a company village. They traded in both fresh oysters and cooked and canned oysters as well as canned fried oysters. When Stearns visited the cannery, it had a capacity of thirty thousand one-pound cans per day but had not yet produced any significant product because of problems and delays. The company also intended to can shrimp, fruit, and vegetables (ibid., 573).

By the next year the demand was greater than the supply, but in September it was noted that "during the past few months dealers could not supply the demand from the interior on account of the extreme hot weather" (MR 1 September 1881). It was a good year for oysters "owing to the very cold weather that allowed many shipments to Cairo, St. Louis, and other distant points. The past winter, as everyone knows, was a mild one, and was not cold enough to allow many shipments to distant points, causing the principle trade of 1881–82 to be confined to a smaller space." The report complains of "certain laws in regard to fishing" that prevented fishermen from obtaining all the fish they needed (MR 1 September 1882).

In 1882 a J. J. Delchamps wrote in answer to a letter of inquiry from Mississippi about Mon Louis Island, that the reefs between the island and Dauphin Island and the oyster beds of Heron Bay and West Fowl River supplied most of the oyster trade of Mobile. He reported that the oyster beds of East Heron Bay were mostly owned by a Mr. Kuppersmith (MR 13 February 1882).

The 1883 report mentions for the first time "large shipments of crabs" to points in Alabama, Mississippi, Georgia, and Tennessee, and the 1885 report says of the fish and oyster trade that "many vessels are engaged in it, and employment is given to a large number of men in this section who depend entirely upon it for their support and spend their earnings in this port."

Cold weather in 1886 allowed shipments of fish to Milwaukee and Chicago, Kentucky and Indiana. The next year warm weather shortened the shipping season, and state laws against use of gill nets and seines in some areas reduced the supply of fish (MR 1 September 1887). The next year, the fish supply supply was not equal to the demand except for snapper. Early rains were credited for the good quality of oysters early in the season (MR 1 September 1888). Warm weather restricted the shipping radius in 1889 and again the supply for shipping was not equal to the demand.

In 1889 the Gulf Coast Oyster Company owned its own oyster beds, stocked them, and filled orders from any part of the United States. The company used its own boats for planting and delivering oysters, was erecting an oyster factory at Portersville, and had a large building at the oyster dock in Mobile (MR 1 September 1889).

Boats, Shippers, and Processors

The seafood industry started with a local market and expanded as it became possible to transport seafood while preservation with ice was still effective. This depended on a supply of ice and fast transportation. An alternative was to preserve the seafood more permanently so it could be stored for long periods and transported greater distances at leisure. There were therefore experiments with canning to increase the shelf life of seafood. While these did not change the dynamics of Alabama's seafood industry in this period, they did lay the foundations for a seafood boom in nearby Biloxi, Mississippi, and formed the basis of the next period.

In 1867 the Dunbars of New Orleans built a floating canning factory (Sheffield and Nicovich 1979, 4). After gaining experience in California and Maryland, Mr. A. Booth went to Louisiana to establish a packing plant on barges. He moved the factory from place to place in response to storms, floods, and lack of oysters. About 200 people worked in the packing plant, and 125 others caught the oysters he purchased from local dredges, but he had problems getting sufficient oysters and maintaining his factory workers (MR 17 February, 1 September 1891).

In 1890 Booth relocated to Mobile where he intended to move the processing plant ashore to enlarge and improve it (ibid.). In Biloxi, Mississippi, Booth found some people who had previously worked for him in Baltimore. They were out of work so he asked them to go to Louisiana with him. He advanced them railroad fare, and guaranteed them board and wages for the time they were on the way from Louisiana until the factory started work in Mobile, and to pay their fare back to Baltimore. They did not get the oysters as quickly as Booth had hoped and his factory was idle. The workers threatened to return to Biloxi, but Booth attached their property for repayment of the railroad fare he had advanced them.

A Mobilian, Adam Glass, came to the defense of the workers. He understood that since there were few oysters coming in, and no work for the workers, they had earned little and were hungry. To hold them would be a kind of slavery, and, in his opinion, they were not contractually liable for their railroad fares. Booth and the workers came to an agreement, and the workers stayed on. Booth did nothing to catch oysters, though he had a barge to buy oysters from catchers (*MR* 4 March 1891).

In 1881 businessmen in Biloxi had established a factory to can shrimp and oysters and to process raw oysters. A second followed in 1882. Other entrepreneurs built plants, and by 1890 Biloxi factories were importing Polish workers, known as "Bohemians," from Baltimore for seasonal labor (Sheffield and Nicovich 1979, 10–11). They were also importing Alabama oysters to process whenever they could. The impetus to build canning facilities in Alabama came largely from legislation to halt the export of canning oysters from Alabama to processing plants in Biloxi. The influence of the Biloxi seafood industry was strong and enduring.

While oysters had been planted each season before, in 1891 none were planted in Heron Bay and Bon Secour. There was some planting of shells and oysters around the Fowl River grounds. Mobile oysters were advertised in Atlanta, Nashville, Cairo, and Chicago. The "plant" oyster was said to be of the best quality, most demanded, and capable of competing successfully against eastern oysters. An 1891 newspaper article concludes:

> It is to be hoped no further time or opportunity will be permitted to escape unemployed or unimproved, and that our oyster growers will go to work and plant with the assurance that the next session of the state's general assembly will revise the oyster code and remedy all objectionable features incorporated into its terms and conditions at the last session, guided by the experience of the past and governed by the necessity for the present. (*MR* 1 September 1891)

A letter, signed only "coaster," to the *Mobile Register* of 4 January 1891 in response to the proposed oyster law of that year illustrates a sophisticated understanding of the potential prospects and problems of oyster production in Alabama from biological, political, and economic points of view. It is therefore worth quoting extensively:

> Your article a few days ago, asking comments on the proposed oyster law, affords me the opportunity to give you some dots [sic] on a subject

upon which I and a great many others have thought a good deal. We approve of the law but with one exception, that is the size, two and a half inches in width is rather a large oyster. I should think that two inches in width would be what all would call a large reefer or select, and would be considered a marketable oyster. You will no doubt hear of a great many complaints from those who are catching oysters, and that the small oysters that are taken by the three and four hundred barrels each day to the state of Mississippi for canning purposes are not fit for any other use than for canning. That is a great mistake, and any one who is acquainted with the growth of the oyster will agree with me that if they continue taking the small oyster from the shoals, that it will leave none to spawn from. It will only be a question of a short time when there will not be enough oysters on the reefs to furnish the city of Mobile.

Now, here is a great benefit the law can have; here is the line of Mississippi only twelve miles from the Grant's Pass reefs, where only a year ago capitalists invested in planting lands in Grand Bay, Mississippi, and planted thousands of barrels of oysters from our reefs in Alabama. And now suppose they would not have been allowed to take those oysters from Alabama, would not the lands have been sold in Alabama and this state been benefited by it; but Mississippi is enriched by our oysters and we are none the better off.

We have plenty of the finest planting grounds in Alabama awaiting capital to work them, and it is the duty of our legislators to look to the interest of our state. Those few who object to the proposed law have nothing at stake, only so they can make hay while the sun shines. They can pick up their little traps and put them in a pulling skiff and emigrate to any place when the oysters are no more in Alabama. Look at the large Reefs at Pass Christian and Pascagoula. No one would have thought a few years ago that all of those oysters could be taken, but, when one will enquire as to the amount of oysters those canning factories can consume, they will see that our reefs will not last long.

At present there are not less than ten to fifteen large schooners from the Mississippi canning factories loading at the Grant Pass reefs, taking anything in the way of oysters, regardless of size. Let our legislators go down to the reefs and it would convince them that I am correct. We have plenty of room in Alabama for oyster factories. Let those who want our oysters come over here. We must look out for our own state's interest or we will surely get left.

The *Register* pointed out that England had once been an oyster-producing country but that by 1891 it was not, and that the oyster industry of Maryland and Virginia had been badly managed. It urged legislation to manage Alabama's oyster resources and published a law then before the North Carolina legislature. This measure provided that no one should take oysters in the shell out of the state unless they had been in private beds for two years, and that no oysters less than two and a half inches could be exported or sold except for seed. It closed oystering from 1 May to 1 October except for gathering seed oysters (*MR* 4, 24 January 1891).

An ex-oysterman urged legislation to protect Alabama's oyster reefs since "for many years the oyster industry has been a certain means of livelihood to a great number of families living on the shores of Mobile bay" (*MR* 10 January 1891). Pointing out that boats from canning factories took everything from the reefs, including shells and small oysters which formed the foundation for future oyster reefs, he urged a law similar to the North Carolina one to forbid the export of oysters and to enforce culling. He suggested an oyster inspector should be in Mobile, where the oysters were landed, because there might be ten or twelve boats loading at the same time in Heron Bay, Cedar Point, Grant Pass, or Dauphin Island Bay (ibid.).

In February, when the Alabama legislature discussed an oyster bill, a senator replaced the provision of a two-cents-per-barrel tax with a twenty-five-cents-per-barrel tax, which he held not to be "excessive." The amendment passed (*MR* 5 February, 1891). A correspondent to the *Mobile Register* replied that he did not believe those "who have been clamoring for a law to protect the oysters know what they want," except to prevent Mississippi canning factories from buying oysters that no one in Alabama wanted or would buy, and which had not been used for the past thirty years to his "certain knowledge." "Now when our neighbor comes to buy what we consider worthless, there is a great fuss about it; when, at the same time, for over fifty years, we oystermen of the state of Alabama have had free access to the oysters of Mississippi and Louisiana, without money or price" (*MR* 18 February 1891).

He argued that Alabama's neighbors spent thousands of dollars on oysters, which helped Alabama and "the poor struggling oystermen." "Now we are in favor of the protection and propagation of oysters. But a tax of twenty-five cents would amount to a prohibition. Two cents per barrel would be a burden, but that could be borne. It has been a hard matter for our oyster dealers to compete with Mississippi in the last few years. What would they do with a cost increase of twenty-five per cent." He argued that Louisiana and Mississippi would get all the trade and Alabama none (ibid.).

In February 1891, after a spirited debate on the level of taxation, the senate passed the agriculture committee's amendment to set the tax at five cents a barrel. A conference committee later changed this to ten cents a barrel (ibid.) and the legislature passed the measure to empower the governor to appoint an oyster inspector and deputy for two-year terms (*MR* 17 February 1891). The oyster inspector was to live on Dauphin Island or Cedar Point and his deputy was to live in Mobile. They were to report to the probate judge of Mobile, and could be dismissed at the recommendation of the Mobile County grand jury if an investigation should warrant it (*MR* 26 February 1891).

The inspector and deputy were to collect a ten-cents-per-barrel tax on all oysters taken from Alabama waters for whatever reason, including canning, and explicitly including transplanting to other beds in Alabama. Sheriffs as well as constables and other peace officers were authorized to enforce this legislation. A culling law required oysters to be two and a half inches in diameter. There was a September–May oystering season on both public and private reefs, and oysters in the shells could be shipped out of state only from mid-December to mid-January. Only Alabama citizens could catch oysters. Boats were to be taxed according to their capacity at ten cents per barrel. Revenues went to the state treasury (ibid.).

The Biloxi, Mississippi, *Herald* editorialized that the legislation was absurd, impracticable, peculiar, and remarkable. The editorial continues:

> The legislative mind was wrapped in a fog as dense as ever settled down on the sound, but amidst its density one clear idea is expressed, and that is that no oysters are to be allowed to go out of the state without being shelled. . . .
>
> Now the peculiar thing about this most extraordinary provision is that the solons [legislators] of the Alabama assembly have given to a Mr. Boothe [sic], who has recently established a canning establishment in Mobile, a monopoly in the oyster canning business. The legislature says to the hard toiling fishermen of oysters, you shall not seek a market in Mississippi or Louisiana factories for the oysters you have caught in Alabama and paid ten cents a barrel for; you can only sell your oysters to Mr. Boothe's factory. Now is not that creating a monopoly for an oyster factory in Mobile . . . and limiting the toilers of the sea to . . . factories that may be in the state, and denying them an open market. No law of commerce could be more unjust. . . . (*MR* 3 March 1891)

Oyster dealers reported less trade and attributed it to the law of 1891 that taxed oysters at ten cents per barrel. They wanted it repealed as the tax gave other oyster-producing areas a great advantage over Mobile (*MR* 1 September 1892).

Influxes of fresh water in floods were credited with killing some oysters at the mouths of creeks and small rivers, but the oysters were said to be abundant and the beds in good condition. The impediment to the oyster industry was not natural but legislation that made it increasingly unrewarding for oyster catchers and processors alike.

Although there was commerce in pickled and iced canned oysters, the major trade in oysters was raw oysters. The oyster law increased the cost of oysters to shippers and decreased their profit. "Indeed, the shipping trade was so much hampered that many cargoes of oysters brought to the Mobile wharves could find no sale" (ibid.). The tax had to be paid to the oyster inspector at the reefs. Oyster boats could carry from fifty to two hundred barrels. If the oystermen could not sell their cargoes at Mobile, they lost the tax they had paid. No oysters were taken from reefs to be planted in beds. Under the law, the oyster cultivator would have to pay tax on the seed oysters when they were first collected and pay tax on them again when they were finally harvested (ibid.).

The oyster fishermen wanted the law amended to reduce the tax and to provide for the preservation of reefs. They supported a tax, but not more than 20 percent of the sale price. There should be no double taxation on planted oysters. There should be no license fee "inasmuch as these craft already pay tax . . . are owned by poor men as a general thing, and the effect of the license of ten cents per barrel laid on the oyster boat's carrying capacity is an additional and unjust levy upon the industry" (ibid.). They also wanted a rebate on tax paid on oysters they could not later sell, as "this impost falls very heavily upon a class that has already lost its labor in taking the oysters from the water, and carrying them twenty-five or thirty miles to market" (ibid.).

Biloxi canning companies, which got some of their supply from Mobile Bay, took the matter to court. Judge Oliver J. Semmes held the law unconstitutional but was reversed by Alabama's supreme court. A newspaper account recorded, "It is believed that the result of this litigation will be the establishment in this county of other oyster packing companies, increasing the labor demand in the lower end of the county and building up a very healthy and as yet sparsely settled section" (ibid.).

The Booth Company had already moved its packing plant on barges south to Bayou Coden to be closer to the oyster beds. The *Register* reported, "The labor demand of this company will add materially to the resources of the oystermen, as women and children are given light and remunerative work in the canning business" (ibid.). A storm destroyed the factory in 1893 (MR 11 December 1904).

P. B. Dorlon opened a plant in 1896 to can vegetables and oysters, but insufficient supply of raw materials was one of the reasons he abandoned the business (MR 1 September 1922). In 1896 Mobilians established a new factory in Bayou la Batre to can oysters and crabs and to pack fish (Bureau of Fisheries *Report* 1900). They also established a terrapin farm. In 1896, 1897, and 1898 the *Mobile Register's* annual commercial reports said that the supply of cultivated oysters had not been increased by planting and that the main limit in the trade was the supply of oysters. Each report urged planting the oyster beds of Mobile and Baldwin counties. The 1898 report mentioned a fear of the oyster drill or conch.

Even so, oyster catching was the most important branch of the fishery in 1897. Oysters were taken from planted grounds in Bon Secour Bay, Heron Bay, and the Mississippi Sound as well as from natural reefs in the sound and Mobile Bay. Most of the catch was sold to Mobile dealers. Vessels had purchased oysters from tongers to transport to Mobile, but the returns to this enterprise declined until it was abandoned and in 1897 each boat took its own catch to market. The Biloxi canneries and the one at Bayou la Batre paid 25 to 30 cents a barrel for canning oysters. Vessels of over 5 tons displacement predominated slightly over smaller boats in the quantity and value of oysters they caught (Bureau of Fisheries *Report* 1900). Baldwin County supplied 331,940 pounds of oyster meats valued at $18,890 compared to Mobile County's 562,957 pounds valued at $21,991. More of the Baldwin County catch were the highly valued large cultivated oysters (ibid.). The 894,897 pounds for both counties was about 22 percent more than the 1880 production of 731,500 pounds, and its total value of $40,881 was about 10 percent lower than the value of $44,950 produced seventeen years earlier (Stearns 1887b, 569).

In 1897, 9 Mobile firms processed oysters and produced ice (MR 1 September 1897). There were 53 fishing vessels of more than 5 tons of displacement (19 in Baldwin County and 34 in Mobile County), more than double the 24 of 1880 (Stearns 1887b, 568) employing 150 people. There were 254 boats of less than 5 tons of displacement (85 Baldwin, 169 Mobile), about double the 119 of 1880 (ibid.) with 443 fishermen involved in boat or shore fishing, fewer than the 545 of 1880 (ibid.). That same year, 196 people were employed in packing and fish houses of all kinds. There were 789 people involved in the fishing industry. The apparatus on the vessels were 3 seines, 10 trammel nets, and 110 tongs. In the shore fishery there were 10 seines, 116 lines, 25 spears, and 170 tongs (40 in Baldwin, 130 in Mobile). Seines were used mainly from small boats for taking fin fish. Using only hand lines, 5 vessels engaged in the red-snapper fishery which had recently been established at Mobile (Bureau of Fisheries *Report* 1900). Apparently at least some of these vessels from Mobile worked out of Pensacola (Stearns 1887a, 585).

These figures are divergent from those of the U.S. Census, which reports 296 fishermen for 1880 as opposed to Stearns's 545, and 612 for 1900 versus 443 given by the 1887 fishery report. The census used local enumerators who were familiar with the area. While outside observers may have had a keener eye for some kinds of detail, they may not have enumerated as well as local observers. The enumerators may have used different categories.

Mobile was the principal market for all fishery products. There were no railroads to Bayou la Batre or Coden. The most important aspect of the shore industry was the wholesale trade in fresh fish and oysters. There were four fish wholesalers in Mobile to pack and ice fish. Eight wholesalers dealt in oysters, and two of these were also fish processors. There was one wholesaler at Coden and one at Bayou la Batre, a total of ten wholesale establishments in the state (Bureau of Fisheries Report 1900).

In 1899 and 1900 more railroad lines were constructed in Baldwin and Mobile counties and there was increased employment not only in railroad construction but also in timber production. These alternatives attracted oyster catchers away from the bay and caused a decrease in the supply of oysters (*MR* 1 September 1900).

The Mobile and Ohio Railroad had built a branch line to the factory in Bayou la Batre by 1899 so it could ship iced oysters to Chicago and Oklahoma, then known as Indian Territory. The factory could shuck and ice fifteen hundred barrels of raw oysters per day, most of which came from Mobile Bay (*MR* 1 September 1899).

By 1900 the Mobile Fish and Oyster Company (established in 1864) maintained its own fishing fleet of schooners and unloaded fish, oysters, crabs, turtles, and shrimp at its wholesale depot. It started the red-snapper industry and shipped them in carload lots to northern cities (*MR* 1 September 1900, 1 September 1911). In 1898 the Spanish immigrants S. Gonzales, Victor A. Perez, and Charles E. Perez, Jr., had founded the Gonzales Fish and Oyster Company.

Because the 1901 market had been overstocked and none of the packers could control the market price to insure the margin of profit they wanted, in 1902 oyster canners of Louisiana, Mississippi, and Alabama discussed joining together in a combine (*MR* 7 August 1902). Rumors spread along the west shore of Mobile Bay that the oyster combine was sponsoring legislation to revoke riparian rights and to lease bottoms until then held in riparian ownership. The rumors said the combine would create such conditions that only industrial concerns could use the oyster beds. Riparian-rights owners protested until legislators assured them that no such legislation was being contemplated (*MR* 31 October 1902).

The 1902 annual report said that "Expansion certainly characterizes the facilities offered to shippers and the regularity, frequency and certainty of daily express trains and steamboats give guarantee of assurance to consignee and shipper." It added that more people and boats were active and the oyster beds of Mobile and Baldwin Counties were planted:

> A good force of "catchers" got to the work after their summer's rest and a supply of well "culled" stock was by them uninterruptedly furnished to the "fleet" skippers, all of whom were soon engaged in making steady, regular runs.
>
> During the season the number of boats was the largest in the history of the trade. Several boats made regular runs with the oysters to the westward shipping points, shippers there quickly realizing the desirability of the Mobile bay stock and offering to skippers advantageous terms and facilities for quick unloading.
>
> It is gratifying to observe the constantly increasing local consumption. (*MR* 1 September 1903)

In the same year in Biloxi, Mississippi, there was dissent between union and nonunion fishermen, and the factories weathered a short and ineffective strike of fishermen (Sheffield and Nicovich 1979, 23). In Mobile there was an Alabama Oystermen's Protective Union (*MR* 6 September 1904).

In 1903, 104,000 barrels of oysters were received in Mobile. Of these, a fifth, 20,800, were for local consumption and the rest were shipped as far as Denver and Seattle, but the biggest markets for both fish and oysters were Chicago and St. Louis. The Mobile Fish and Oyster Company, then the largest processor, handled about 60 percent of the oysters.

Local consumption of oysters in Mobile resulted in a problem of disposal of their shells from downtown establishments (*MR* 30 August 1903). The street department had constructed receptacles across the gutters in front of oyster bars, where the shells accumulated during the day. The city removed the shells each morning to use for paving. As the streets were paved and asphalted, the shells were put in barrels at the edge of the sidewalks, where they were obstructive and sometimes became rank before they were removed. One establishment had to dispose of between five and twenty-five barrels of shells a day during the oyster season (ibid.).

In 1903 about thirty-five or forty fifteen-ton schooners brought about 500 barrels of oysters a day from the first of September until the end of April. Of these, about 150 barrels were for the local market. The Mobile Fish and Oyster Company, Alabama Fish and Oyster Company, Gonzales Fish and Oyster Company, and F. Kuppersmith banded together to form the United Oyster Company, which controlled the oyster trade. This "oyster trust" owned the most extensive oyster beds in the South. Mobile Fish and Oyster Company owned oyster beds at Coden, then the largest cultivated beds on the Gulf of Mexico (MR 15 July 1909). There were only two "independent" firms: Star Oyster Company and the Southern Oyster Company.

The next year the John Bayles Company of Baltimore announced it would build a cannery at Alabama Port to can oysters, fruits, and vegetables (MR 13 January 1904). It imported two hundred "Bohemian" workers for the winter season of 1904 (MR 9 October 1904). There was a fresh-fish packer in Bayou la Batre and two firms intended to establish raw-oyster processing houses in Coden and Bayou la Batre, but most oysters were going to Mobile (MR 9, 30 October 1904). By the end of November the canning factory had started operations at Coden and had twenty boats working for it (MR 27 November 1904). The cannery at Alabama Port was doing a lively business and Baltimore interests investigated sites at Bayou la Batre for more canneries (MR 4 December, 18 December 1904). At Coden

> there were two gentlemen . . . from Baltimore, Md., . . . looking over the field here for a location for a canning factory to be ready for business next season. They told the writer they could buy better oysters here for one dollar a barrel than they could buy in Baltimore for two dollars and fifty cents a barrel. I've been told this before. It is most wonderful to me how Baltimore can compete at all with oysters canned in Alabama, Louisiana, and Mississippi. It is only a matter of time when Baltimore will close her canning factories and they will come South. There is room here for two more canning factories. In time our people will plant tomatoes, corn, beans, and other vegetables in such quantities that one factory can run the year round. It is done in many places South and why not here. (MR 4 December 1904)

In 1903, 5,811,000 pounds of fish went through Mobile. The Mobile Fish and Oyster Company packed fish in barrels of ice for shipment in refrigerated railroad cars. The red snapper, fished off the coast of Mexico on the Campeche Banks, was the major fish because it kept fresh longer than others and withstood icing well (MR 1 September 1910).

There was some snapper-fishing from Mobile and New Orleans as early as 1845 by sloops that spent most of their time seining for shore fish. In 1874 Pensacola interests chartered Connecticut schooners to fish for snapper off Pensacola, but because of poor shore and transportation facilities, it was not very successful until 1880 when the fleet was enlarged and larger crews of deep-water fishermen from northern countries were employed. Ice storage facilities were added to the schooners to replace the storage of live fish in wells. Fishing skippers were instructed in navigation techniques so they could find fishing locations. Some experimented with trawling, but hand lines were found to be the best gear. Larger vessels previously used in the northern cod and mackerel fisheries were brought to Pensacola (Stearns 1887a).

Between Pensacola and Cape San Blas there were numerous small fishing spots. Different fishermen gave such locations different names, such as "Roger's Hill Bank," "First Yellow Bluff," and "Second Yellow Bluff." Some were named for conspicuous landmarks fishermen used to navigate to the spots (ibid.).

Fishermen located fishing grounds by sounding and testing with a hand line. The schooner would then drift through a small bank or anchor over a large one while the crew fished using weighted lines with codfish hooks on the ends. Because of the fast change of pressure as they were brought to the surface, fish from depths of thirty-five or forty fathoms had distended swimming bladders which the fishermen pricked before storing the fish. Fishermen got bait by seining close to shore, or used salted bait (ibid.). Snapper fishing technology did not change much in the following years.

Unloading catches directly into its warehouse from its eight fifty-ton schooners, the Mobile Fish and Oyster Company handled and shipped fish, turtles, crab, and shrimp from its depot and warehouse in Mobile. The company contracted with another thirteen schooners, which averaged about nine thousand pounds of fish per month each, for beach fishing. The Star Oyster Company owned a fishing boat and contracted with several schooners (MR 1 September 1909).

There were fourteen other smaller schooners that fished closer to Mobile and sold their catches to various wholesale houses. There were also about twenty lone fishermen, known as the "mosquito fleet," who worked in the rivers and an equal number in the bay to produce about two hundred pounds of fish per week. Though snapper was the major fish, other species caught with seines in shallow waters included pompano, Spanish mackerel, fresh and saltwater trout, flounders, croakers, perch, spade, sheepshead, blue fish, and mullet (ibid.).

Shippers were compelled to improve their methods of shipping and handling fish to compete with Atlantic shippers (MR 1 September

1910). Improved refrigerator cars and rapid transportation allowed the interior market for fish and oysters to expand (*MR* 1 September 1906).

On the western shore of Mobile Bay, the Bayou la Batre Canning Company, which started operations in 1896, processed oysters from Mobile Bay, but because of "a change in the holding of the stock of the company the plant was shut down" for two years in 1900 (*MR* 1 September 1903). In 1903 Charles Torsch, of the Torsch Packing Company and Aughinbaugh Canning Company of Baltimore Maryland, bought (ibid.) or leased (*MR* 1 September 1905) the plant. He also established a large oyster and shrimp cannery at Bay St. Louis, Mississippi, and was president of the Peerless Oyster Company of Mississippi (*MR* 16 August 1915).

In 1904 a second cannery was built in the south of Mobile County, at Alabama Port. By 1905 the oyster industry had expanded due to the enlargement of the oyster beds. Two canneries in the southeastern part of Mobile County were canning six hundred barrels of oysters a day. The *Mobile Register* reported that at Coden, "the canning factory here is running full blast" (*MR* 5 February 1905).

The fourteenth of August 1904 is recorded as the first catch of shrimp for canning (*MR* 1 September 1905), but there must have been shrimp canning earlier, as the *Mobile Register* for 1 September 1903 reports a meeting of the Oystermen's Protective Association to reach an agreement with canners about the measure for shrimp before they would go to work.

Taxation and Regulation

Canneries had more processing capacity than they had seafood to process. This fact is central to the understanding of the subsequent history and politics of the seafood industry to the present day. Processors needed a constant and steady supply of oysters, so they tried to cultivate their own supply by planting oysters. The canning industry did not develop more quickly in Alabama because of legislation that taxed planted oysters twice, once when they were caught for seed and again when they were caught for canning. The tax was so high that it was unprofitable to plant oysters for canning. The problem of an unsteady supply of oysters continued to plague canneries. To solve it they began to explore shrimp canning and thus inadvertently pointed the way to the modern system, which relies on shrimp. While the technology and institutional structures for industrial canning had developed in Alabama, the law had not kept pace. The legislature managed the marine resources of the state by direct legislation. This is quite a different system from the more modern one of technical regulation by means of an administrative agency. The politics of the two systems are quite different as well, as events showed.

The *Mobile Register* suggested in 1906 that the cultivation of oysters was "quite a business" but that "the natural oyster beds could be made to yield a more abundant supply by a little legislation tending to the preservation of the small oysters. Thousands of the baby oysters, not large enough to be salable, are caught along with the fully developed oysters, instead of being 'culled' and thrown back into the water to grow until they become of a suitable size for the market" (*MR* 1 September 1906). In 1907 and 1908 the *Mobile Register* called again for a culling law.

In July 1909, Alabama's first game and fish commissioner, John H. Wallace, visited Coden and Dauphin Island and the oyster reefs of Portersville Bay in the company of friends interested in the development of the oyster industry. He heard complaints about legislation governing the industry and said that he had been studying the question with the advice of competent authorities in Alabama and elsewhere and had concluded that "Alabama has been sleeping on her opportunities" (*MR* 7 July 1909). He suggested there was no proper culling on the reefs, and pointed out that Mississippi had expanded its public reefs by planting shells to produce good surfaces on which oyster spat could settle and grow (ibid.). The newspaper reported:

> Mr. Wallace concluded with a description of the Alabama coast as in his opinion it will appear when the canneries and raw oyster shops are kept running all of the cooler months with oysters from public reefs and private beds and when the canneries will be operated in the warmer months putting up figs and other fruits and vegetables. He painted a picture of prosperity, growth and development which was pleasing to his hearers. (ibid.)

J. A. Joullian of Coden negotiated between different interests and helped to frame a bill satisfactory to all concerned, on the east and west shores alike (*MR* 7, 15 July 1909). There was conflict between oystermen in Baldwin and Mobile counties because most of the oyster beds of Baldwin County were privately owned under riparian ownership or leased, while most of the oyster catchers who depended on the public reefs for their livelihoods lived in Mobile County. These oystermen resisted anything that seemed to threaten their access to public reefs. They perceived dredging for seed oysters to be taking from public reefs for the disproportionate benefit of private interests. They disagreed with the concept that ownership rights should extend seaward from adjacent land—riparian ownership—and resisted the practice of leasing areas of the Mississippi Sound or Mobile Bay to private interests for oyster cultivation. To them, this was private control of a public resource that should be available to everyone equally.

Oystermen met in Bon Secour to oppose the 1909 legislation which they saw as operating in the interest of the "oyster trust." Wallace denied this and pointed out that the combine owned factories in Louisiana and Mississippi and used the threat of buying oysters in Alabama to keep prices down in those states. He also argued that the trust would not want to encourage further competition in either buying or selling oysters and that Alabama's antitrust laws prohibited its operating a factory in Alabama (MR 15 July 1909). In a letter to Representative Sam C. Jenkins of Baldwin County, Wallace said:

> There is nothing in the bill that affects or conspires against the oystermen of Baldwin county. They are planters, they are given free use of the oyster reefs and are not even required to cull oysters they take for planting purposes. The best experts contend that the leasing of water bottoms is the best plan for the development of the oyster industry; this places the oyster business at once upon a fixed and stable basis and will be a source of great encouragement to the oyster industry. Any natural assets so valuable as that comprised in our oysters should not be longer neglected but should be regulated by the state, not only for the benefit of the present generation but in order that a vestige of our shell-fish may be transmitted to people yet to be. (ibid.)

The bill would prohibit the exportation of oysters from Alabama for canning. Wallace contended that no oyster factory would be able to survive in Alabama as long as Mississippi factories could buy oysters in Alabama at higher prices than an Alabama factory could afford to pay. He suggested that when the Mississippi factories drove up the price of oysters, Alabama factories would close, Mississippi packers would no longer come to Alabama, and the oyster industry would perish (ibid.).

Wallace continued in his letter:

> I have endeavored to aggregate the best ideas embraced in the best oyster laws on the continent and this I confidently believe I have done. It is the history of all oyster legislation that the oyster catchers, who at first resist civilized legislation for the protection of oysters, have come to be the greatest benefactors of such statutes, completely changing front and developing into the strongest and most enthusiastic supporters of such laws. (ibid.)

Steam dredges were prohibited, but sailboats with dredges were allowed in some areas where the water was over ten feet deep and oysters could not be caught with tongs. The oyster grounds were to be patrolled and the laws strictly enforced (ibid.). Steam dredges were first used in Mississippi in 1893 and were banned on public reefs there in 1902. In Mississippi, dredging by sail was still allowed until further controversy led to a 1904 law that allowed steam dredging in deep waters but reserved shallow waters for tongs and sail dredges (Sheffield and Nicovich 1979, 15–19).

Alabama's oyster laws were not at the top of the list of the legislation Governor B. B. Comer asked for in his proclamation of a special legislative session, but they were on the list (*MR* 26 July 1909). By August, Mobile and Baldwin county interests had agreed on the provisions of the bill, and the main features of the "Mobile" bill were retained (*MR* 5 August 1909). There was no organized opposition to the bill (*MR* 16 August 1909) and it passed without a dissenting vote. The *Mobile Register* applauded the law because it established an Oyster Commission and allowed for the leasing of bay bottoms that were not covered by natural oyster reefs (*MR* 20 August 1909).

By 1910 a thousand acres had been leased and the *Mobile Register* lamented Alabama's slowness to develop its oyster resources. The article pointed out that 90 percent of the oysters consumed in Alabama were imported from other states and only 10 percent were from Alabama.

> Nature has been so lavish in bestowing that there has scarcely been any incentive in this state to assist by artificial cultivation. The growth is spontaneous and so heavy that this feature has actually damaged the industry.
>
> Adjoining states have provided improved methods of oyster culture which have yielded better grades to the detriment of the Alabama natural growth. The time has gone by when the Alabama natural growth oyster can find a market. These oysters commonly called reefers, small and impoverished in quality though they be, furnish the finest seed in the world for transplanting to artificial beds where they grow larger. (*MR* 1 September 1910)

In 1910 the son of Rhode Island's shellfish commissioner came to Mobile to engage in oyster cultivation. The *Mobile Register* took this as an indication that even "those high in the councils of oyster men in the prosperous East" were taking note of the importance of Alabama's resources (*MR* 1 September 1911).

The 1909 law included a provision concerning oyster culling and prohibited "the taking of oysters from our reefs by boats from other places, a system of piracy largely practiced by the canneries at Biloxi and other places" (*MR* 1 September 1909). The Oyster Commission was credited with inducing canners from Biloxi, other places in Mississippi, and Louisiana to form the Alabama Canning Company and build a cannery between Bayou la Batre and Coden on Portersville Bay in southern Mobile County (*MR* 1 September 1910). It had a capacity of twenty-five hundred barrels of oysters per day and its own ice plant. It was set up like others in coastal Mississippi and Louisiana to pack oysters and shrimp in the winter and fruit and vegetables in the summer (ibid.).

John Craft, president of the Oyster Commission, reported that the commission had many applications for oyster leases and suggested that leasing would improve the industry. He said: "A few years ago absolute want prevailed among many of the oystermen, who to-day are placed in a position to easily earn a good living and accumulate money from the fruits of their toil" (*MR* 3 September 1911).

In addition to leasing areas for oyster cultivation and inducing a new seafood-processing plant to locate in Alabama, the Oyster Commission had sixteen miles of natural oyster reefs worked to break them up and scatter them to provide more area of natural reef (*MR* 1 September 1910).

A United States–sponsored oyster reef survey published in 1913 (H. Moore 1913) suggested that about six hundred thousand bushels of oysters, twice the quantity taken during 1911, could be harvested without fear of depletion. It counseled transplanting oysters from beds that did not produce good-quality oysters to depleted natural beds or private bottoms (ibid., 59). The report predicted that canneries and raw-oyster trade would provide greater and greater demand for oysters. The canneries could be satisfied by the natural reefs, but the raw-oyster trade would demand better, cultivated oysters. It concluded that increased demand for quantity and quality of oysters could "not be fully satisfied excepting by a resort to oyster culture under private ownership, with its consequent demand of personal interest and attention. Until recently the laws of Alabama have restricted the rights to engage in oyster culture to riparian owners and their lessees, but the present law permits the lease of any barren bottoms belonging to the State."

The surveyor located about twenty-five thousand acres of suitable bottomland in the Mississippi Sound, which he suggested would be ideal because of the yearly set of spat and rapid growth. He established survey reference points and recommended strict surveys to determine boundaries of lease holds to prevent disputes (ibid.). He observed that:

The sparse population on the shores near the oyster bottoms renders the oysters little subject to injurious pollution from drainage and sewage discharges. This consideration is an important asset at a time when the spread of infection through oysters is a matter of such widespread public concern, and for business reasons, if for no others, the cleanliness of the beds and the treatment of the oysters should be jealously safeguarded. (ibid., 60)

In 1912 an oyster cannery planted twenty thousand barrels of oyster shells on unoccupied areas, mostly on the western edge of Grant's Pass Reef. They were well covered with young oysters and considered promising. The Rhode Island oysterman planted ten thousand barrels of oysters from White House Reef in upper Mobile Bay to the Mississippi Sound, where, he hoped, they would not be subjected to the killing freshwater floods of the bay. In 1912 oyster planters were optimistic and thinking of expanding their areas. They could rent areas for one-third cash and pay the balance after marketing the oysters. The maximum charge was a dollar per acre per year. The oysters on Grant's Pass Reef were large and abundant, so the Oyster Commission forbade the use of the reef for collecting seed oysters. It was afraid that the reef would be depleted, that the large oysters would all be in private beds, and the price would be then increase "to a point where consumption would be prohibitive." This would also deprive oyster catchers of their livelihood on the reefs (*MR* 1 September 1912).

Two years later the Mississippi Oyster Commission, financed by a five-cents-per-barrel tax on oysters, planted 53,292 barrels of seed oysters it had removed from congested reefs (*MR* 8 September 1914). Workers planted 180,000 barrels of shells (*MR* 30 December 1915) and continued transplanting oysters and planted 175,000 barrels of oyster shells in 1915 (*MR* 7 July 1915, 30 December 1915).

In the six years between 1909 and 1915 the Alabama Oyster Commission planted 35,000 barrels of oyster shell at a cost of $1,559.56 ($.045 per barrel). This is an average of 5,833 barrels a year. In spite of the fact that oyster planters in Baldwin County and elsewhere had provided ample proof of the plausibility of planting oysters, the commission transported an "unreported number of seed oysters" to an experimental plot in Portersville Bay at a cost of $1,147.50 "to demonstrate oyster management" (Swingle and Hughes 1976, 62–63). In the 1887 review of the American fisheries, Ernest Ingersoll had outlined the history of legislation concerning oysters from colonial times and had discussed oyster conservation, cultivation, and depletion, so plentiful data were available by the turn of the century.

Factory Workers and Oyster Catchers

Antebellum industries drew on an abundant supply of unskilled labor from small, infertile farms. In 1850, twelve cotton factories employed 7,636 people, and in 1860, fourteen mills employed 1,312 workers. Other people found employment in sawmills, small mines, and furnaces. Illiterate whites were not much better off than slaves, and often worse off than 2,690 free blacks who, in 1860, worked at skilled jobs of brickmaking, masonry, carpentry, and tinsmithing. There was little industry in Alabama through the period of reconstruction. Eastern capital revived coal and iron industries, and lumbering and turpentine operations began in south Alabama.

Industry adopted the pattern of plantation paternalism. Illiterate farmers were accustomed to living in houses owned by employers, buying supplies from their commissaries, and getting medical attention on their orders. Company towns were established for factories, mines, and mills under similar arrangements. Employers deducted charges, percentages, and service fees from wages and there were many opportunities for exploitation (Federal Writers Project 1941, 70). Forcing people to work against their will was an offense called "peonage," and early in this century such charges were brought against employers in several southern states (MR 12 January 1904, 8 January 1905).

There were similar charges in the seafood industry of coastal Alabama. Two boys from Bayou la Batre were arrested for vagrancy in 1903. With some others, they had left the cannery at Bayou la Batre. All had been advanced railroad fares from Baltimore with the assurance they could make seventy-five cents a day opening oysters. They said they made only a little because the oysters were small, and that while they were advanced food, they said it was meager. The sheriff's deputy said the story was false and that shuckers were generally contented (MR 21 November 1903).

A United States grand jury in Mobile investigated a charge of peonage against the cannery. It was alleged that it held people against their will for debt. Witnesses said they left the cannery because insufficient work made it impossible to make a living, they had been returned to the factory after they left, and they had been guarded by an armed deputy sheriff.

One man testified that all of the five members of his family worked for a week to earn forty cents among them. He went to a logging camp to work, but a deputy sheriff came and forced him back to the cannery. In Baltimore he had been a clerk. He said that the stories of peonage were not exaggerated and that the cannery had treated people better since the first stories had gone out. Not able to afford train fare, the witnesses walked from Bayou la Batre to Mobile to testify against the cannery (*MR* 2 December 1903).

The president of the Bayou la Batre cannery, Mr. Torsch, met a delegation of Mobilians, including John Craft, who went to Bayou la Batre to investigate the charges against the cannery. After visiting houses of all cannery employees, they found the company furnished each family a house, a mattress, a stove, and free wood to burn. The complaints, they discovered, were made by inexperienced workers who did not know how to process oysters. Many of the people came with families. Those who were inexperienced, all apparently Americans, found it difficult to make any money on the piece-rate system that paid five cents per five-pound can.

The "Bohemian" workers, also from Baltimore, were reported to be satisfied with their conditions and earnings. The committee concluded that the complaints were from persons unaccustomed to the work who had deceived labor agents by saying they were expert oyster processors; that accommodations were superior to those of the past six years (to 1897) when the cannery had operated; that fuel, house rent, and other accommodations were free; that medical attention was accessible and paid for by the company; that there was sufficient work for all at prevailing scales, and payments were made weekly; that the location was healthy, and no force had been used to keep workers at work (*MR* 8 December 1903).

An article from the *Mobile Register* of 1 September 1912 entitled "Wild Life, that of Oystermen" gives a picture of the life of the oyster catchers of 1912. It carried three sub-headlines:

"Ours Is a Poorly Business,"
Says Those Who Bring Their Boats

OFTEN HAVE TO FIGHT

Men and Their Families Arise at 3 A.M. for Bare Subsistence.

Did you ever visit the oyster docks and see those rough, unkempt looking men lounging about on the decks of small schooners? And did you ever engage one of these men in conversation?

If you are familiar with the scene it's unlikely that you ever addressed one of the men, for their appearance is not prepossessing, and if you did it's almost a surety that the first remark about their work that greeted you was:

"It's a poorly business."

That short sentence conjures up more before the oysterman's mind than a page of description. After those or similar words, the old oyster runner will sadly shake his head. It will be nearly a minute before he answers another question.

Your first inquiry has reminded him of his wild, hard, hazardous life, of the raging, freezing, bleak, wintery nights he has spent on the oyster reefs; perhaps with his wife and daughters beside him. It is often the case, especially within the last year.

Times Have Been Hard.

"It's getting worse," he'll tell you, and, perhaps unjustly, the Alabama Oyster Commission is blamed for the state of affairs. Every oyster runner—the exceptions are very scarce, if they exist—will tell the same story—a tale of their almost perfect contentment in their half wild homes along the coast, rudely shattered by laws regulating the industry.

2,500 Make a Living at It.

There are some 2,500 souls—workmen, all of them—who eke out their existence from the oyster reefs in Alabama waters. The most prosperous of these men, women and half-grown children own boats. One boat each, some of them have only sailing skiffs, just large enough to carry them to the oyster reefs. More than a thousand of the others just have a "bite of bread," they call it.

Most of the people engaged in the business of catching oysters for a livelihood have been at it all their lives, and in most cases their families for several generations have been oystermen. They are raised up to the life and know it from their childhood.

During the oyster season the father, his sons and, if the year has been bad, mother and daughters, awake at 2:30 o'clock, dress in the cold winter air, perhaps get a bite of fish and bread, and by 3 o'clock the sailing skiff is under way heading for the oyster reefs.

As the boat approaches the reef, to which the oysterman is on his way, he is not alone. About him as far as his eye can reach, he will see through the half daylight white sails flung to the breeze and when the morning breaks about him, in all directions, will be anchored his neighbors' boats.

Every hand holds a pair of oyster tongs and the scene is one of great activity. No one is loafing. The life is too hard for that. Every oyster counts and the sooner the holds in each boat are filled, the sooner will money be realized. Competition is keen.

Down goes a pair of tongs into the water. You see it moved about, the handles opened, closed, and then pressed together tightly. Up, up, the tonger pulls. Someone calls "good." He seems to have had good luck. And when he had finished culling the catch there are fifteen good oysters left. The tonger is happy.

May Catch Barrel a Day.

Three times has the man beside him lifted his tongs and one out of those three times he has caught two oysters larger than the culling size.

The tonger is not discouraged, for next time he may get twenty-five. And maybe he won't catch a barrel in a day, but that seldom happens.

The work of tonging the oysters will continue until late in the afternoon when a motor boat appears on the horizon. She is sent out from the canning factory to buy a load of oysters from the tongers. She had scarcely appeared in sight when suddenly everyone quickly, and quietly, begins hauling up anchors and hoisting sail.

The day's fun begins. A race for the freight boat is on. The man who reaches her first sells his load first and the others getting theirs afterwards discharge their oysters into the motor boat in the order in which they arrived. The last boats in the line oftentimes are forced to wait all night before their turn comes.

So the race is for blood, for no oysterman wants to stay out on a reef all night if he can avoid it. With every inch of sail set and tongers standing on deck to add to the speed of their respective crafts by catching as much wind as their bodies will stop. Everything possible to increase the speed of the boat is done.

It is dangerous to be in one of those boats as they approach the freight vessel. Sails remain set until within a few feet of the big boat and the oystermen manoeuvre for position. In the grand rush at the close of the race it is not an unusual thing for a boat to be smashed and go to the bottom.

Oystermen will tell you this happens several times a week during the winter season. It is then that the true man shows in the oysterman. No matter how much in the wrong the man who sailed the sunken boat was he does not lose his all.

It's an unwritten law among the oyster tongers that everyone must give two or three barrels each to the man whose boat was lost to help pay the cost of raising and repairing. The canning factory boat usually donates three barrels.

But if the man believes the sinking of his boat was intentional, and sometimes they do, the result is a general fight, pulled off in the plain American way. For maybe an hour two factions will fight each other, fists being the only weapons used. If it gets too rough the man in charge of the factory boat will get a crowd together and stop the row.

After the blood is washed off everybody gets together and laughs about how hard the other fellow can hit, showing to corroborate the statement, a hickey on the head, a place where a tooth was a short time before, or pointing to a black and swollen eye. There is no enmity. It's done up in American fashion as only men of the open know how.

The small boats return home when they have unloaded, while the larger schooners, catching oysters for Mobile markets, remain at the reefs all night, or until they get a load. In winter, when the sleet freezes the hands of the tongers, it's just the same as the fall of the year to the oysterman. He must do his work or starve. Finally loaded, he points his vessel toward Mobile and he remains at the oyster dock here until he has sold his load.

Summary

As the transportation network expanded and ice production increased, the market for fish widened. The small-scale fishermen who had operated from market stalls enlarged their operations and purchased more boats. Eastern industrialists noticed Alabama's oysters and began to invest in canneries. These early experiments were only sporadically successful for the following reasons: There was no sure and steady supply of raw materials. Policies might make the industry unprofitable. Oyster catchers might seek alternative sources of income if prices for oysters were too low or taxes too high. Finally there were natural hazards such as hurricanes.

The Lyons Bill of 1909 established an oyster commission to manage oysters. The oyster tax was to support the commission and its activities on behalf of the industry as a whole. Like their successors, they could not fail to be political. The commission started a rhetoric of scientific management that continues to this day. Like fisheries managers today, they used science as a way to justify the policies they developed.

Canners and oyster planters were in business to make money. They could not absorb the increased costs of the new tax. The oyster planters were taxed twice, when they took seed oysters and when they harvested the oysters, and they went out of business. The tax on oysters had the effect of shutting down the industry because it was not worthwhile to harvest oysters or to can them.

Not until a hurricane crippled seafood production in Biloxi and conditions got worse in the East would Alabama oysters look good to processors. Then they would usher in the next phase of industrial canning, bringing in capital and reviving the factories.

The period of preservation with ice and transportation by railroad thus came to an end, but it laid the foundations for the period of industrial canning that was to follow. The experiments to overcome earlier problems resulted in a distinctive new system of production. It involved the formation of fishermen's unions and cannery organizations to negotiate prices with each other for the whole gulf region; the development of new technologies for harvesting shrimp, making the supply of raw material more reliable; and changes of policy.

3

1915–50: Industrial Canning

The technology of canning was developed in the nineteenth century. G. W. Dunbar Sons of New Orleans first attempted to can shrimp in 1867 but did not develop a satisfactory process until 1875. By 1880 the company was producing canned shrimp in one-and-a-half-pound cans. A second cannery was started in Galveston, Texas, in 1879, and a third in Biloxi, Mississippi, in 1880 (Johnson and Linder 1934, 25). The oyster-producing areas of coastal Alabama were well known and there were people who made their livings by catching oysters. The supply of oysters was readily accessible. The technology of canning was available. Everything was favorable for the development of a canning industry in the communities of coastal Alabama, but the system of laws then in place inhibited it.

With the development of more and larger canneries, there was even more processing capacity demanding more seafood. The supply of oysters was too erratic and too small to meet the demand. The canneries therefore outfitted schooners to seine for shrimp and later were glad of the opportunity to purchase shrimp from independent trawlers. They encouraged greater and greater supplies of shrimp and thus set the stage for the next system of industrial shrimping and freezing.

In the early part of the twentieth century, taxation had discouraged oyster planting to the extent that it had ceased. The oyster canneries were closed. Oyster catchers and processors alike petitioned their legislators for relief from what they found to be unworkable laws.

A state representative named Sorrell reported to the legislature that during his visit to Mobile he had learned that "many" Mobile businessmen said "the oyster commission is the greatest fraud ever perpetuated upon the people of Alabama" (*MR.* 17 February 1915). He read from a state auditor's report that six thousand of ten thousand dollars collected by the commission was paid for salaries to commissioners and their employees. A bill was introduced in the legislature to abolish the Oyster Commission.

As early as 1904 there was an Alabama Oysterman's Protective Union in Mobile (*MR* 6 September 1904). In 1915 the Alabama Oystermen's Protective Association protested the taxing and licensing provisions of the 1909 oyster law (*MR* 24 January 1915). Some asserted that the revenues of the commission went to pay exorbitant salaries to its members and that a few monopolists were trying to gain control of the oyster industry (*MR* 26 January 1915).

Biloxi interests owned a factory in Bayou la Batre that had been closed until a hurricane destroyed their Biloxi plants, when they reopened the factory with Frank E. Smee as its manager. He telegraphed Representative Grayson that thousands of dollars would be invested in oyster planting that year if a new bill regulating seafood were passed. Another telegram signed by thirty Baldwin County citizens urged passage of the bill. It passed by a vote of eighty-four to four (*MR* 17 February 1915).

The 1915 bill abolished the Oyster Commission and mandated the appointment of a warden and assistants. The revenue they collected was to be placed in the state treasury instead of the Oyster Commission treasury (ibid.). This change of law set the stage for the development of the next phase of Alabama's seafood industry. Oysters were the attraction for canneries, but the supply of oysters was not dependable. The canneries therefore began to process shrimp in addition to vegetables.

At first, canneries purchased schooners and hired captains and crews to seine for shrimp in Louisiana. Shrimp gained prominence with the introduction of trawling technology a few years later. As more fishermen owned their own boats, they were more independent of processors, and they began to band together into unions to negotiate the prices of shrimp and oysters with processors. Processors had no other source of raw materials, so they were dependent on the fishermen. With the encouragement of New Deal legislation, the unions became an important component of the system, negotiating every year for prices.

With abundant shrimp to make the supply of raw material more reliable, processors needed more labor to work in their factories. The demand for labor put the processing workers in a more favorable position to organize into unions with fishermen. Because factories depended on local products, they had to rely on local fishermen and workers, and a system of negotiation between them developed.

Fishermen and Factories

Alabama's only seafood-canning factory at Portersville Bay, Bayou la
Batre, which had been closed since 1912, was unharmed by a hurricane that damaged a number of Biloxi's factories and ships. The
Biloxi interests that controlled it brought some machinery and material by boat from Biloxi and opened the cannery in November to
pack oysters (*MR* 10 October; 13, 14 November 1915). They arranged
to bring 276 "Bohemian" men, women, and children from Baltimore
to work in the factory, and recruited local labor for shuckers (*MR*
11 November 1915).

All of the schooners and power boats (two sloops, eight schooners,
and six power boats were named) of Frank E. Smee, the factory manager, as well as a number of other boats from Mobile County and Dauphin Island were fitted out to catch oysters. The thousand-barrels-a-
day quota would require "nearly every available boat now in Alabama
waters suitable for that purpose" (*MR* 14 November 1915). Gasoline-
powered boats were used to tow sailing boats and reduced the danger
of losing cargoes by becalming.

An enthusiastic report in the *Mobile Register* said:

> The prospect of having nearly $1,000 per day turned loose in that com-
> munity, chiefly for labor, has caused a small boom at Coden and Bayou
> la Batre, and the latter place has other and further cause to rejoice. The
> county authorities have agreed to build a drawbridge across the bayou at
> the town. This will open three miles of the bayou now closed to naviga-
> tion, and will permit schooners and power boats to reach two sawmills
> and numerous charcoal kilns above the town. (ibid.)

The canning factories became the center of south Alabama's seafood industry after 1915. The number of canneries fluctuated between
one and four. There were four in the late twenties, only three in the
thirties, two or three in the forties, and only one in the sixties. After
1965 there were no canneries. They had been replaced by freezing
plants.

In 1917, World War I was blamed for a shortage of labor in the canning industry in Biloxi. Furthermore, only about half of the usual two
hundred to three hundred boats that fished for shrimp had set out by
the end of August (*MR* 29 August 1917). The plants were idle for some
days because there were no oysters to buy. Arguing that increased
costs of living made a pay increase necessary, oyster openers in Biloxi
struck for a raise in pay from sixty-five cents to a dollar per thousand
oysters opened. With no organization and unassociated with boat-

men or laborers, the workers saw their action come to nothing (MR 13 September 1917).

By 1918 oyster producers were renting about five thousand acres of propagating grounds in the Mississippi Sound from the state of Alabama. Each acre could produce as much as three hundred barrels of oysters valued at a dollar a barrel while the costs of planting, rent, and interest were about twenty-five cents a barrel. In 1918 the Bayou la Batre Cannery had been packing shrimp and vegetables for two seasons, the Alabama Canning Company had been canning shrimp and oysters, and two additional canneries financed by Boston interests were under construction on the west side of Mobile Bay. Two of the canneries had refrigerating plants for cold storage and ice making. Much of the labor was still brought in from the Chesapeake. Biloxi firms were considering opening plants on the west side of Mobile Bay (MR 1 September 1918).

In 1912 the first experiment with a power boat and otter trawl in Biloxi produced forty barrels of shrimp (Sheffield and Nicovich 1979, 35–37; Walker 1975, 169). In 1912 and 1914 the Bureau of Fisheries used small otter trawls at its laboratory in Beaufort, North Carolina, to collect marine fauna. When fishermen saw the quantities of shrimp these experimental hauls yielded, they began to devise larger trawls for shrimping. About the same time, shrimpers began trawling near Fernandia, Florida (Johnson and Linder 1934, 9). In 1917 the U.S. Bureau of Fisheries introduced a new kind of trawling net from North Carolina in Florida and Louisiana (Rushton 1979, 107). The new technology of trawls and power boats would open new fishing grounds and transform the shrimping industry. The newspaper reported:

> A new process of taking these shrimp has completely revolutionized the industry. Formerly, with the equipment then in use, it was possible to take shrimp only at certain seasons and in comparatively shallow water. Now they may be taken in much deeper water and much larger specimens are secured. The process consists in taking the large shrimp from their winter bed by a system of trawling.
>
> The mechanical device employed is merely a net attached to two horizontal boards which are kept edgewise down on the bottom by means of iron shoes. These boards assume the shape of an open V, with the larger opening towards the boat which pulls them through the water. This at once keeps the net open and guides the shrimp into the mouth of the net.
>
> Men operating these trawls can earn, as a rule, from $25 to $50 a day, and the process is very simple. It is this feature that is attracting shrimp fishermen to the Alabama coast. Those who have knowledge of the fisheries resources claim that at no distant day the trawl will be introduced into

the business of taking salt water fish of all kinds in countless thousands of tons from the salt waters of Alabama. (*MR* 1 September 1918)

A 1938 account from Bayou la Batre describes trawling from L. W. Rabbie's thirty-six-foot *Bernie Geneva* with a cabin aft, hatch forward, two gasoline drums lashed in the bow, and a twenty-horsepower Bridgeport Marine engine. There was a trawling platform about four feet over the stern to protect the nets from catching on the exhaust pipe. The trawl was thirty or forty feet long with two trawl boards. The nets lay on the rack until they were taken down and laid on the trawl boards. Ropes from the trawl led through a single tree about six feet up the mast in the bow and then to a wooden hand-powered winch over the cabin. The captain had two helpers. He headed for Mobile Bay, where word had it shrimp had been sighted, anchored off Cedar Point for the night, and began to test the waters with the try net, a small hand-held net, early the next morning. When he found shrimp, he stepped on the rear platform and threw the trawl overboard, the trawl boards following, and let out the lines slowly so as not to foul the boards on the bottom. After dragging an hour, the boat slowed, Rabbie stopped the motor, and the crew winched up the ropes until the trawl boards reached the platform. With the brake on the winch, they lifted the boards onto the deck, then caught the tail of the trawl with a float on it, and tied it to the center of the boat. The crew then bailed out the shrimp with long-handled scoop nets (Hartley 1938). Johnson and Linder (1934, 12) reported the same process but indicated that the net was emptied on deck for sorting. They said that hand winches were almost universal in the gulf while there were power winches on the larger boats of the south Atlantic.

When the trawl was empty, the crew began another drag and sorted the catch on the deck. In a one-hour drag, they had caught fifteen barrels of shrimp. Shrimpers all carried binoculars to watch each other, and when one boat would turn for a round trip, indicating it had located shrimp, everyone else would race toward it and the whole fleet would trawl together. The crew stowed the shrimp in the ton and a half of ice the boat carried. After spending another night in the bay, the captain took the boat to Bayou la Batre to unload. Shrimpers did not drag at night (Hartley 1938).

Gulf fishermen almost invariably fished from single ports, and often for only one factory throughout the season. The fishing grounds were therefore those areas that the small boats could reach in a reasonable time. Shrimping was confined to inside waters. In Alabama, shrimpers fished the southern half of Mobile Bay, the Mississippi Sound, and the coastal waters up to four miles offshore. Where there was some distance between factories and fishing grounds, either the area remained unexploited or factories sent freight boats to buy shrimp from the trawlers. These boats were supplied with ice, and the shrimpers who sold to them used none (Johnson and Linder 1934, 6–7, 21).

This new fishing technology relied on the new power boats (*MR* 1 September 1923), though diesel power was not introduced in the south Atlantic until the thirties, and later in the gulf. Seining, however, remained the primary technology for some time. In 1923 a new packing company in Pascagoula, Mississippi, had 8 shrimp trawlers (*MR* 2 September 1923). In Alabama in the twenties there were 3 or 4 motor vessels of more than five tons seining and between 18 and 23 trawling. There were between 8 and 16 boats of less than five tons displacement seining and between 120 and 155 boats trawling. From then until the fifties there was a steady increase in the number of trawlers, and seining for shrimp was insignificant in Alabama after 1930. No sailing vessels are recorded as seining in Alabama in the twenties or thirties, though there may have been some before 1927 when systematic data on gear began to be recorded in the U.S. Fisheries reports.

As soon as trawling was introduced, sport fishermen began their opposition to it, which continues to this day. In 1925 a spokesman from the Izaak Walton League addressed the Rotary Club of Pass Christian, Mississippi, to tell them that trawling would destroy gulf fishing. He argued that Mississippi, Louisiana, and Alabama should regulate commercial fishing as a unit, if the United States government would not, and promote sport fishing opportunities because a year-round fishing season would bring ten thousand sportsmen to the gulf to spend a million dollars a year (*MR* 15 August 1925).

The number of canning plants in the south Atlantic and the gulf peaked in 1924 and shrimp increased in importance all over those areas (Johnson and Linder 1934, 2, 25). In 1922, five canning factories in Bayou la Batre canned 2,235 tons of shrimp and 55,935 tons of oysters and shipped 150 tons of raw fish and 325 tons of raw oysters (*MR* 1 September 1922, 1 September 1923). There were five canneries and about twenty seafood dealers in Bayou la Batre in 1923. Three or four boatloads of Alabama and Florida red snapper had been landed there, but the channel was too shallow for larger boats (*MR* 1 September 1925).

All of the products moved by the bayou, and in 1922 the merchants of the city began to sponsor the idea of deepening and widening the bayou. They argued that since the channel over the bars leading to the bayou was only four feet deep at average tide, tons of shrimp and fish were lost because the vessels carrying them could not enter the bayou until the tide was up, and larger vessels could not enter at all. They sponsored a movement to get federal funds to provide a ten-foot channel over the bars to promote the canning industry (MR 1 September 1922, 1 September 1923). By 1926 work on the $20,000 project was under way (MR 1 September 1926).

Coden was shipping raw oysters and crab. Most of Dauphin Island was owned by nonresidents, but most of the residents worked as shrimp and oyster catchers, shuckers, or in other aspects of the seafood industry on the mainland. At Bon Secour there was large-scale oyster cultivation under riparian ownership. Mobile was the center for the distribution of raw oysters and shrimp and had one large cannery. The oyster and shrimp industries were intertwined since the same canneries processed both and the same boats caught them at different times. Though foreign workers had been brought in in the past, and some stayed, by the early twenties most workers and fishermen were residents.

Collecting workers in cannery-operated trucks or buses in the mornings and returning them when the work was finished, shrimp and oyster factories drew labor from an eight-to-ten-mile radius and provided supplementary income to truck farmers and satsuma growers of the area (MR 1 September 1925). The season for shrimp for canning was 1 August to 1 June; for oysters, from 1 September to 1 June; but for factories and workers alike, seafood processing was a matter of "feast or famine," as the supply of shrimp or oysters depended on weather and other unpredictable conditions (MR 1 September 1923). Canneries had to renovate their machinery every season and were out of use when there was little or no shrimp or oysters to process (MR 16 September 1923).

"A considerable part" of the product of Bayou la Batre packing houses went to Biloxi by schooner for labeling and reshipment. The balance went by rail across the country as far as Portland, San Francisco, Los Angeles, and San Diego (MR 1 September 1923).

About a hundred boats were licensed for oysters in 1923. Each shrimp trawl also had to have a license. Many boats were licensed for both (ibid.). In 1925, 160 boats from one to thirty-five tons were licensed to take oysters and about the same number to catch shrimp. In addition to the six canneries of Bayou la Batre and Mobile, two new ones were slated to open: one on the west side of Mobile Bay on the west Fowl River and one on Weeks Bay in Baldwin County on the east side of the bay.

While "congested population" in the northeast Atlantic polluted the waters, contaminating the oysters and reducing the harvest, in 1925 the Bureau of Fisheries of the Department of Agriculture determined that oysters from Mobile and Portersville bays were not contaminated (*MR* 1 September 1925, 1 September 1927). Representatives of state and county boards of health, the Department of Agriculture, the Conservation Commission, and representatives of the canning industry agreed in the same year that processors could steam and open oysters and shellfish only from areas the state board of health had approved. They also adopted cleaning regulations for canning apparatus (*MR* 1 September 1926). A U.S. Department of Agriculture chemist held meetings to advise canners on proper procedures (*MR* 13 August 1925). By 1928 at least one Mobile firm, the Star Fish and Oyster Company, had a freezing facility and a refrigerated storage facility (*MR* 1 September 1928).

In 1929 floods brought an accumulation of mud and silt to Mobile and Bon Secour bays and thirty miles into the gulf of Mexico to kill thousands of acres of oysters. The oyster harvest declined from 89,200 barrels to 1,811 barrels. Production also dropped in Biloxi and Apalachicola Bay due to predators. The situation of Alabama oystermen was dire until 1933, when there were more floods. The Federal Civil Works Administration was established that year and the oystermen went on relief. The oystermen included descendants of original French settlers, Cajuns who came from Canada, as well as newer immigrants such as Czechoslovakian and "Bohemian" families who had first come to Alabama for seasonal work.

The oyster industry of southern Alabama was shut down, and Mississippi's was not far behind. The reduction of the oysters and the Depression together left the oystermen without any means of livelihood. They could catch shrimp or fish, but this had always been a supplement to their main income from oyster production. Shrimping could provide summer income, but was insufficient for annual income (*MR* 6 November 1936).

In the thirties about 250 boats, most individually owned, caught shrimp and oysters to sell to local markets for fresh local consumption and shipment to the interior. They also sold directly to canneries to supply the raw material for a large industry, dominated in south Alabama by the Dorgan-McPhillips Packing Company with headquarters in Mobile and factories in Bayou la Batre and other locations (*MR* 26 November 1933).

Shrimp seines were up to twelve hundred feet long and eighteen feet deep. Handling them required at least six and up to twenty men and several skiffs. Schooner fishermen tested for shrimp with try nets, sailed until they located a school, and anchored. Fishermen on skiffs lay out a circle of net about a quarter of a mile long. Throwing out the unwanted fish, the crews then hauled in the net (Johnson and Linder 1934; Federal Writers Project 1939).

A Biloxi shrimper recalled:

> . . . I went on the boats right away. I happened to get a place on the boat but it wasn't trawling then. It was just seining. They used to have seines then. We used to have about nine or ten men to a crew. Because you had to have muscle to pull on that seine. . . . The seine was only about eight or nine feet deep so whenever the shrimp would work out in deep water, well, we would go drudging oysters then. . . .
>
> . . . you had the seine in one skiff and we'd keep throwing the net. . . . we'd change if we'd get tired, there was about eight or nine persons there and they'd throw the net. If we'd find shrimp we caught them and round them up and put the seine overboard . . . then we'd have to pull it in and we'd have to scoop the shrimp out and the fish or whatever we had, then ice them down. We used to have maybe ten or twelve ton of ice. All them big blocks. We'd have to shave it and ice our shrimp.
>
> . . . The seine, you just round the shrimp up and you gotta haul it in, but when you trawling you put your trawl overboard and in the back you got some big wooden boards and you just drag . . . and you pull it up once in a while and if you catching a few shrimp you don't trawl too long. . . . Then I found it much easier trawling all you done was you pick up and you had the wench and hoist it up and dump it on deck and then you pick the fish out and wash the shrimp and put them in the boat. I found that much easier I guarantee you, that's much easier than seining, I tell you. (Powell 1976)

The seines were twelve to fourteen feet deep at the center and tapered to five to seven feet at the ends. About half the crew would hold one end of the net while the boat laid out the rest in a circle. One to three men were placed at intervals to walk on the bottom line while the seine was being pulled in. When the net was drawn into a small circle, the crew bailed the shrimp from it into the boat (Johnson and Linder 1943, 12–13; Becnel 1962, 6).

Two men could handle a trawl. The schooners, with their large crews, were sizable investments, but individual fishermen could afford power skiffs. With trawling technology, shrimp-boat ownership shifted from factories to fishermen. By the end of the 1930s the schooners were out of use and, because they worked on their own rather than factory owned boats, fishermen were much more autonomous (Sheffield and Nicovich 1979, 35–37; Federal Writers Project 1975, 169).

From 1 August until 1 December, crews of two to five men trawled Mobile Bay and the gulf just outside it for shrimp. They used a small test net to locate schools of shrimp, then dragged a trawl for about an hour to catch up to twenty-two barrels of shrimp. Frequently as many as a hundred boats would work a single school of shrimp (*MR* 26 November 1933).

The same fishermen would catch oysters from 1 December to 1 March. Sometimes, when shrimping was going well, they continued to shrimp after oyster season opened and oysters were late reaching the market (*MR* 1 September 1942). Oystermen used tongs, and from time to time, with strict supervision and regulation, dredges (*MR* 26 November 1933).

The period from 1915 to 1950 was dominated by the industrial canning of oysters and shrimp. While fish and oysters could provide a steady supply of raw material for fresh-seafood processors and shippers in local and regional markets, oysters alone did not provide a reliable resource for canneries. They therefore experimented with other products such as fruits and vegetables. They also began to can shrimp, when it was available. The canneries in Biloxi processed shrimp from Louisiana. Shrimp canning meant a wider range of possibilities for fishermen as they could provide both shrimp and oysters.

After the repeal of the 1909 law regulating seafood in Alabama, there were continuing debates, competition, strife, and conflict over the regulation and management of the fisheries of the state. As the canneries grew and grouped together to form powerful blocks, fishermen, empowered by the new laws of the New Deal, began to organize themselves into effective bargaining units.

Taxation, Regulation, and Management

Until 1918, fishermen seined for shrimp in shallow marshes, especially in Louisiana. In 1919, Mississippi fishermen were seining for shrimp and catching oysters in Alabama. Acting at the request of a delegation of oystermen from Mobile and Baldwin counties, Alabama legislators Holmes of Baldwin County and Craft of Mobile County introduced legislation to prohibit the water transportation of shrimp and oysters in the shell. The bill specified license fees on shrimp and oyster boats to be paid to the oyster inspector and forbade shrimping between 15 December and 15 January and from 1 June to 1 July except for in-state use at local markets and domestic consumption (*MR* 7 February 1919).

No one could take shrimp and oysters out of Alabama by water unless their states allowed Alabamans to remove shrimp and oysters from their states. Shrimp could be taken out by water only if Alabama factories and dealers were unable to purchase them. Oysters were to be inspected for size on the reefs, and factories and dealers were to check to be sure that the oysters were properly culled (ibid.).

The 1919 legislative assembly placed the oyster and shrimp fisheries under the Department of Conservation, which began a study of them (*MR* 1 September 1920). This department had been established in 1907 largely through the efforts of John Wallace, Jr., who was named its first commissioner. When he died in 1921, I. T. Quinn took the office (A. Moore 1927, 983). A tax on reef oysters was to defray the expense of enforcing oyster law and planting additional bottom areas (*MR* 1 September 1920).

There was a chief oyster inspector in the Department of Conservation. George Sprinkle held the office in the early twenties. There was a two-cent tax on every barrel of oysters and twelve cents for every barrel of shrimp landed in Alabama ports. The money went into a Conservation Department account at the Alabama treasury. Part of it was used for enforcement of shrimp and oyster laws.

Conservation Commissioner I. T. Quinn favored legislation to allow dredging for oysters to increase production. He argued that oysters that could not be dredged in deep waters of Mobile Bay were wasted (*MR* 29 May 1923). He suggested that while oystermen opposed dredging because they thought it would ruin oyster beds, Alabama's seafood laws were obsolete (*MR* 6 June 1923). The *Mobile Register* pointed out that something had retarded the development of Alabama's seafood industry since 90 percent of Alabama's seafood was imported (ibid.). Quinn suggested dredging could be confined to deep waters and regulated to prevent destruction of oyster reefs (*MR* 8, 9, 10 June 1923). The legislature's conservation committee heard Quinn's arguments in Mobile and went to Mississippi to investigate the policies there. The committee also scheduled public hearings and tours of Bayou la Batre (*MR* 8, 9, 11 June 1923).

At the hearings, oyster packers favored dredging while some oyster catchers opposed it. Those who favored dredging argued that Alabama had the most prolific oyster beds in America but the least oyster production and that other states allowed dredging with good results. All factions supported the idea of the state's planting public oyster beds for public use (*MR* 12 June 1923).

During the early twenties there was a debate about ownership of oyster reefs. Some claimed that at least part of the leased beds had always been natural reef, never planted (*MR* 1 September 1923). This is the same debate that developed in the Chesapeake region and gradually removed most private leases to public reefs (Hedeen 1986). The Mississippi Oyster Commission claimed that it extended the area of public reefs by enforcing culling laws and by returning shell to the reefs for cultch material to which spat could attach. The commission required canners to return a portion of their empty shells for replanting. While the reefs of Mississippi were said to be depleted around the turn of the century, their rehabilitation was attributed to such measures (*MR* 1 September 1923).

The Alabama legislature's conservation committee recommended that all oyster bottom leases should be abolished, that the state should plant seed oysters and oyster shells in depleted and barren areas, that the oyster tax should be increased from two to five cents per barrel, that 15 percent of all shells from public reefs should be replanted, that dredges should be allowed in deep open waters where hand tongs could not be used, and that riparian rights should be curtailed. Some members opposed the dredging provision because oyster catchers opposed it (*MR* 19 August, 3 September 1923).

Under the influence of Mississippi, the Holcombe bill was passed in 1923 to allow the state Conservation Department to use some of its revenues to dredge oysters in May and June from areas too deep for tonging to replant in shallower and more protected areas (*MR* 1 September 1925, 16 September 1923).

The chief oyster inspector and his assistant patrolled the reefs in a power boat to keep out-of-state boats from taking oysters and shrimp and to enforce culling laws which required that oysters measure two and a half by two inches. While packers had to file monthly reports, the Conservation Department required daily reports of shrimp and oyster catches (*MR* 1 September 1923). It also required that canneries and shippers set aside 10 percent of their shells for replanting. Alternatively, the Oyster Commission could take the value of the shells, ten cents per barrel. Since a cost of ten cents a barrel was imputed for replanting the shells, and fifteen cents per barrel for transplanting live oysters, it was deemed better to dredge and transplant oysters. To create a fund to be used to hire oystermen to seed public oyster beds, processors and canneries were to be taxed according to the volume of their production (*MR* 16 September 1923). When the legislature did not provide a $25,000 fund for seafood development (*MR* 21, 23 September 1923), proponents of the bill said the tax of the oyster bill would allow the same results (*MR* 26 September 1923).

The attorney general of Alabama held that the oyster fund did not have to be given to the state treasury, but that it must be used by the commission to conserve and develop additional reefs. In 1924 the Alabama Conservation Department contracted for the planting of thirty-five thousand barrels of oysters at a cost of $5,250 (fourteen cents per barrel). There was a revenue of $4,985.45 from the oyster tax, then five cents per barrel. The oysters were planted in 120 acres of Portersville Bay and 120 acres of Heron Bay. Using two dredges and a gasoline-powered hoist, a schooner could load four hundred barrels of oysters in three hours. Oystermen had objected to the tax and license, but other residents of the coast said "that this is real conservation," and did not object (MR 1 September 1925).

In 1925 the Conservation Department planted 25,000 barrels of seed oysters on about 1,000 acres of new ground (MR 1 September 1926). In 1928 I. T. Quinn reported that there were 6,000 acres of commercial oyster reefs, to which the state had added 2,000 acres during the past two years. He estimated that there were another 8,000 acres of reefs in water too deep for tonging, and 200,000 acres of bottoms suitable for oyster culture. He emphasized that there was a balance of 186,000 acres of unused oyster land.

He contrasted this vast resource with the fact that the seafood canneries of Alabama had operated only about a third of the time during the 1927 season because they could not get sufficient oysters or other seafood to keep them occupied. He concluded that "the greatest drawback and handicap to even a reasonable development of Alabama's oyster industry, was due to the state's wholly inadequate and antiquated laws, which not only retard, but actually prohibit constructive development of this great potential industry" (MR 1 September 1928).

Quinn went on to point out that oysters could only be taken by hand tongs and that an expert tonger could get twelve to fifteen barrels of culled oysters in a day. Deep waters could not be harvested by tongs. With the 1923 legislation to allow dredging of deep-water oysters, he began contracting for the dredging of White House Reef and relocating the oysters to shallower waters accessible to tongers. After three years of dredging, he found White House Reef oysters better and more plentiful than when he started. He attributed opposition to dredging to poorly supervised and unregulated dredging in the past (between 1909 and 1915), which left oyster beds in poor condition. Proper dredging, Quinn said, had demonstrated that it broke up clusters of oysters and allowed better and more rapid development of oysters and extended the beds.

He urged a "system of sea farming with modern and up to date machinery and on a more intelligent and scientific basis," and said that "so long as we cling to the antiquated method of hand tongs, to the exclusion of other devices for harvesting oysters, just that long will we be unable to develop the raw trade, and just that long will we be unable to increase the oyster pack and just that long will we be unable to furnish labor to hundreds of men, and support to thousands of men, women and children, who depend on the sea food industry" (ibid.).

Quinn cited a 1923 survey that showed that raw oysters were shipped to Birmingham from every Atlantic coast and gulf state except Alabama, and that 97 percent of the oysters of Montgomery and 90 percent of the oysters of Mobile came from outside of Alabama.

He concluded the shrimp pack was good and nothing could be done to improve laws relating to shrimping. Pointing out that there was no regulation of taking fish, that any gear could be used at any time of year and that mullet, speckled trout, and other food fish were becoming depleted and had declined in commercial importance, he urged laws to protect fish during their reproductive periods.

Quinn congratulated the Mobile Chamber of Commerce for its co-operation during the legislative session and reported that he had taken some legislators to the coast to study the oyster and other industries in Baldwin and Mobile counties. He concluded that the seafood division of his department should have a direct appropriation since funds provided from taxes and licenses of the seafood industry were inadequate to the development of the industry (ibid.).

In 1930 the Mobile Chamber of Commerce named a committee to investigate the "rehabilitation and enlargement of the oyster industry" along the coast "with the view of making it one of the major businesses of this section. . ." (MR 1 August 1930). The committee was to work out legislation to help develop the industry (ibid.). It favored a report by Paul Golstoff of the Bureau of Fisheries in Washington, who surveyed the oyster bottoms of Alabama in 1929 and recommended changes in laws (MR 2 August 1930).

A 1930 Alabama law was passed to restore the oyster beds, but no money was allocated. In 1931 Senator John Craft of Mobile, who had been on the first Oyster Commission, which had been dissolved in 1915, proposed a bill to dredge deep-water oysters and replant them in shallow waters under the supervision of the Department of Game and Fisheries. The bill was styled an unemployment relief bill (*Mobile News Item* 23 January 1931). He also proposed a new licensing and taxing scheme for oystermen and dredging of oysters in certain areas while setting aside other areas for tongers (ibid., 25 February 1931).

In 1932 I. T. Quinn declared that "oysters are fast recovering from the disastrous season of 1929 and the canning factories around Mobile are shipping as many oysters as they can secure. . . . The protection

that the oyster beds are receiving from the state has helped them recover rapidly from the chaotic condition of 1929" (*MR* 22 April 1932).
There continued to be controversy over funding for seeding oyster
beds and the extent of seeding needed (*MR* 23 April 1932). In May of
1932 a number of cases were brought against oyster catchers for in-
fringing on private beds around Cat Island and Heron Bay. The court
upheld claims to riparian ownership when it found the defendants
guilty of removing oysters without written consent of the owner. The
defendants claimed the beds were natural reefs from which they had
taken oysters for a living for years (*MR* 4 May 1932).

Quinn allowed the designation of certain areas for oyster dredging.
In 1933 the Conservation Department allowed supervised dredging of
Cedar Point Reef, Kings Bayou Reef, Buoy Reef, White House Reef,
and Fowl River Reef (*MR* 12, 13 September 1933). Quinn appealed to
the state relief administration in 1934 for a project, finally approved in
Washington, to employ out-of-work oystermen to replant the oysters
and restore the industry.

In 1935 the United States was in the throes of the Depression, and
the Bayou la Batre Chamber of Commerce and other coastal groups
and individuals were organizing to try to get federal money to combat the depredations of the oyster drill or conch (*MR* 26 January
1935). President Roosevelt vetoed a half-million-dollar appropriation
to study methods to control shellfish predators in the Atlantic and
gulf states. Mobile interests had intended to request funds from the
appropriation to dredge a canal between West and East Fowl rivers to
let more fresh water into Portersville Bay to destroy the conchs (*MR*
26 February 1935). I. T. Quinn took a delegation of twenty legislators
to visit Bayou la Batre and Baldwin counties to study the seafood
industry (*MR* 16 March 1935).

In March, state legislators met with oyster packers and growers at
Bayou la Batre and Baldwin County to discuss plans for obtaining
federal aid to rehabilitate the oyster beds depleted by the oyster drills
(*MR* 19 April 1935). Committees from each county were formed, and
there was more discussion of the plan to open a canal from the Fowl
River to the Mississippi Sound to decrease the salinity of the sound
(*MR* 20 April 1935).

In May, Bibb Graves, the governor of Alabama; Baldwin County representative A. B. McPhaul; I. T. Quinn; and Senator Swift of Escambia
County decided to apply for a $500,000 loan from the federal govern-
ment. They proposed an oyster-planting program and other means to
improve conditions for the oyster industry to be handled by a five-
member Oyster Commission or authority, which would include Com-

missioner Quinn. The loan would be repaid through a tax on each barrel of oysters, and all other laws governing the oyster industry in Alabama would be repealed (*MR* 3 May 1935).

McPhaul's bill to establish a commission to try to get a half-million-dollar federal loan passed the House in June. The governor would appoint to the commission the state game and fish commissioner, an oysterman from Mobile and Baldwin counties, and two others. The bill passed the Senate in July without dissent (*MR* 11 July 1935). The governor appointed a legislator from Baldwin County and McPhaul from Mobile County to the commission. Three members of the commission, including Nelo Gonzales from the Star Fish and Oyster Company of Mobile, Wakeford of Baldwin County, and Staples, the legislator from Baldwin County, were involved in the oyster business. The board was empowered to collect taxes on oysters and to seek a federal loan (*MR* 13 July 1935). The commission met on 31 July and agreed on a three-cents-per-barrel tax on oysters and a twelve-cents-per-barrel tax on shrimp to pay off a $250,000 loan they would request from the federal government through the Works Progress Administration (*MR* 1, 2 August 1935).

In November, $92,000 in federal WPA funds matched with $18,000 of state funds and equipment were allocated for an oyster rehabilitation project. Paul Golstoff of the U.S. Fisheries Department, who had previously surveyed the oyster reefs in Mobile Bay in 1929, made a two-day survey of the oyster reefs of Mobile and Perdido bays to determine where to plant 100,000 barrels of seed oysters and 150,000 barrels of shells during 1936 (*MR* 15 November, 1 December 1935). Mississippi received a $204,000 WPA grant for an oyster-planting project (*MR* 26 March 1936). There was a similar project at Pascagoula (*MR* 18 May 1936). Between January 1935 and February 1937 the WPA project in Alabama had expended a $92,365 federal loan and an $18,255 state grant to plant 180,248 barrels of oyster shells taken from Indian mounds and 25,846 barrels of seed oysters from shallow beds and deep reefs. The Alabama Oyster Commission deemed the project successful enough to continue when Swepson Earle, a former conservation commissioner of Maryland, inspected Alabama's reefs (*MR* 21 February 1937).

The Oyster Commission banned all oyster dredging in January 1936 and declared itself satisfied with the progress of the WPA project to rehabilitate the reefs (*MR* 16 January 1936). Marco Skremetta of the Deer Island Fish and Oyster Company at Bayou la Batre got an injunction preventing the commission from criminally prosecuting him for dredging oysters in violation of its ban. He attacked the constitutionality of the act that created the commission and claimed he would suffer great financial loss if he were prohibited from dredging and required to use tongs. Defending the constitutionality of the act and denying that Skremetta would suffer losses (*MR* 14, 28 January 1936), the commission said it adopted the regulation against dredging at the suggestion of the U.S. Department of Fisheries. The Alabama Supreme Court upheld the constitutionality of the 1935 act that created the state oyster commission and upheld its powers to regulate dredging of oysters. The court held that the state had the power and duty to protect the paramount interest of the public by prescribing the manner of taking oysters and prohibiting dredging (*MR* 15 May 1936).

In March, McPhaul introduced a bill to place the control of all aspects of the seafood industry in the hands of the Oyster Commission so that it could regulate the harvest of all fish and shellfish from all state waters, privately or otherwise owned. The commission would make all rules and regulations, open and close areas, and determine gear (*MR* 27 March 1936). The bill was opposed by the Deer Island Fish and Oyster Company, whose lawyer argued that, though he had no objection to present members of the commission, those commission members who had interests in the seafood industry might act in their own rather than public interest (*MR* 1 April 1936). Both sides lobbied the legislature heavily. A newspaper reporter wrote:

> Certain oystermen around Mobile and Bayou la Batre object to passage of the bill because Staples, Gonzales and Wakeford are engaged in the oyster industry. They do not question sincerity of these gentlemen but say the bill, if the commissioners so desired, would make it possible for the companies of the three to have unfair advantages. The commissioners deny this, saying any rules they make must apply to all alike.
>
> Oyster suppers are becoming quite the thing, with the McPhaul bill pending. The Legislature is becoming well acquainted with Mobile and Baldwin oysters. (*MR* 10 April 1936)

The McPhaul bill got lost in a legislative session devoted to taxes and debates about repeal of prohibition, a session that passed only one act and was called a "trail of failure" (*MR* 18, 19 April 1936). It was removed from the House roster with a number of other bills that had no chance of passage because there was no time to debate them (*MR* 15 April 1936). The Senate approved the bill seventeen to fourteen, which fell short of the required two-thirds majority, and the bill failed (*MR* 18, 19 April 1936).

The present Alabama Conservation Advisory Board was established in March of 1939 in a reorganization that abolished the Oyster

Commission. The Division of Game, Fish, and Seafoods was given a seafood branch with a chief enforcement officer and five assistants to enforce seafood laws and collect taxes and license fees (Swingle and Hughes 1976, 64).

In 1940 Walter Jones, Conservation Commissioner, and his chief oyster inspector examined the oyster beds and announced a dredging ban because the beds were depleted. The chief of the Seafood Division, Ben Morgan, said that there were, however, sufficient laws and regulations for the protection of Alabama's seafood. The division planted sixty-five thousand barrels of oyster shells in Mobile Bay during the summer. A Mobile oyster dealer observed that the price for oysters had been constant for several years in spite of the decline in local production and the increased demand on American food brought on by the war in Europe (*MR* 25 September 1940).

Five years later the United States Fish and Wildlife Service issued the first comprehensive report on American fisheries in fifty years and argued that regulations were piecemeal, localized, and "often based on lay opinion, superstition or snap judgment, rarely on knowledge." The report recommended that expenditures for fisheries be raised to a level comparable with those of other food industries, as well as more fisheries research, and federal legislation to control water pollution (*MR* 1 June 1945).

In November of 1945, Fred Kuppersmith, whose father, also named Fred Kuppersmith, was an early oysterman, said that dredging for "dead" and "buried" shell was damaging live oyster reefs by covering them with silt (*MR* 25 November 1945). Southern Industries Corporation began dredging shell in Mobile Bay in 1946 (*MR* 25 April 1965). The Conservation Department received a royalty of twelve cents per cubic yard of shell dredged with a guarantee of fifty thousand dollars per year. Shell royalty funds went to the Division of Seafoods (*MR* 1 August 1965). Southern Industries used about 400,000 tons of shell per year to manufacture masonry products, poultry feed supplements, and other products at its Mobile plant (*MR* 25 April 1965).

The Ideal Cement Company had approval from the Conservation Department to dredge dead shells in Mobile Bay (*MR* 17 August 1946). Joseph Collier, president of Bayou la Batre's Mobile Bay Seafood Union, and Frank Nelson of Bon Secour's seafood union lead a delegation of oyster catchers that called on the governor to halt the dredging. Director of Conservation Morgan said geologists held the reefs to have been dead for decades or millennia and covered with several feet of mud, so they could never be made into living oyster beds. The oystermen petitioned against "the sale of vital food resources, belonging to all the people of the state" (*MR* 5 September 1946). The petition argued that the reefs were neither dead nor covered with mud and had been sold to Radcliff Sand and Gravel Company, which was dredging the living oysters of Cedar Point. Although the Conservation Department had not planted the reefs for the past several years, the reefs were in fact not dead. The petition continued: "In this respect they may be compared with a fertile farm that has been sparsely planted for one or two seasons. The sale of the oyster beds from these reefs at 5 cents per cubic yard is like the sale of top soil from a rich and fertile farm that grows a special crop beloved by the people of the entire state" (ibid.).

At the request of the governor, Morgan halted dredging around Cedar Point and scheduled a public hearing in Mobile. He reiterated that the dredged reefs were dead and covered with mud and argued that dredging could help restore oyster culture by removing the mud and dead shell (*MR* 6, 7 September 1946). The Congress of Industrial Organizations (CIO) supported the dredging ban (*MR* 8 September 1946). At the hearing, oystermen and the Radcliff Sand and Gravel Company reached an agreement. Witnesses testified that mud from the dredging operations was damaging the oysters of Cedar Point. McPhillips, president of a packing company, testified in favor of the gravel company and said he had found no damage from the dredging (*MR* 12 September 1946).

In 1948 Allan Archer of the Alabama Museum of Natural History directed the planting of forty thousand barrels of seed oysters and twenty-five thousand barrels of shells (*MR* August 19 1948). The Conservation Department's shell-and-oyster-planting program of the late 1940s was given credit for a bumper crop of oysters in 1950. The director said that research to find the best planting areas and good water conditions as well as enforcement of seafood laws were "bringing back to Alabama the sea food industry that wavered in past years on the brink of despair" (27 January 1950). Others, however, contended that "mother nature was responsible for this season's big oyster production on Cedar Point reef," and that the state had not planted oysters there.

A. J. Bride of Mexican Gulf Fisheries spoke for a group of seafood packers on Bayou Coden to urge the deepening of the bayou. They argued that their boats were damaged when they ran aground in the shallow channel and that Coden had more seafood processors than Bayou la Batre. They had to unload boats on Bayou la Batre and truck the fish to their plants. Bride foresaw new seafood industries, including a shipyard and quick-freeze storage plant in Coden if the channel were deepened (*MR* 1 August 1948). Numerous people of the area telegraphed U.S. Senator Boykin in Washington, who appealed to the U.S. Army Corps of Engineers, which agreed to dredge the bayou (*MR* 4 August 1948).

At a meeting with candidates for the legislature, the Bayou la Batre–Coden Chamber of Commerce argued that the Seafood Division of the Conservation Department was an underfunded "stepchild" whose director had too much power. Chamber members said the seafood industry was drying up, that oyster production could not compete with Maryland's. To correct the "poor economic condition" of Bayou la Batre, they advocated a return to the 1935–39 system of a five-person seafood commission to regulate the industry (*MR* 27 April 1950). The candidates said they would seek legislation in line with Bride's recommendations (*MR* 21 May 1950).

Bert E. Thomas, director of the Department of Conservation, replied: "If the sea food industry is drying up in Alabama . . . it is not because of lack of interest nor because of lack of scientifically prepared and administered programs on the part of the department. . ." (ibid.).

He accused the Bayou la Batre–Coden Chamber of Commerce of selfishly inspired criticism and cited catch figures to indicate that the oyster harvest fell from 73,626.3 barrels in 1935–36 to 71,326.3 barrels the next year and "took a headlong plunge" to 55,254.25 barrels in 1937–38 when Bride was chief enforcement officer and secretary of the Alabama Oyster Commission. Thomas argued that under his departmental management in 1948 production was 98,408.75 barrels and in 1949–50 it was 117,719 barrels. He concluded that oyster production for the two years of his management was the same as the production for the four years under the management of the Oyster Commission. He continued: "We were criticized when the shell dredge worked in that area, but do you not think it significant that the Cedar Point reef has been more productive in the last two years, since the dredge's work in that area, than has been the case in years? From a layman's viewpoint it would seem the trenches that the dredge dug above the reef helped trap some of the silt that normally washed over them" (ibid.).

Thomas resigned his position in May to take another appointment and Phillip J. Hamm was appointed to succeed him, but the debate continued. Bride replied that the Bayou la Batre–Coden Chamber of Commerce was determined "to press for legislation to set up a commission to administer the affairs of the sea food division, to be composed of men who are acquainted and have a monetary interest in same" (*MR* 28 May 1950).

Bride argued that the commission had planted 115,652 more barrels of shell than the department with $310,051.64 less revenue. Bride cited the seafood dealers' request of several years earlier to close inside waters to shrimping and allow shrimping in the gulf. They had to get an injunction against the Conservation Department, which finally resulted in an amendment to allow gulf shrimping. Bride held that this procedure was expensive, and that the director of conservation had too much power. Rather, a body of people involved in the industry should make such decisions. He also pointed out that the Oyster Commission called on scientists of the U.S. Fish and Wildlife Service for scientific advice.

By that time, oyster canning had ceased in Bayou la Batre because the processors would not comply with the new United States minimum wage legislation that required seventy-five cents per hour. They argued that oyster shuckers had always been paid for piecework. In 1935 the National Recovery Administration approved a petition by the Biloxi Oyster Exchange to allow processors to pay shrimp pickers and oyster shuckers by the pound instead of by time. The ruling covered both coastal Alabama counties as well as Harrison, Hancock, and Jackson counties in Mississippi (*MR* 26 January 1935).

Many inexperienced shuckers had started working in 1950 in response to the large supply of oysters. The slower shuckers could not work fast enough to make the seventy-five cents an hour mandated by the 1950 legislation, though faster ones could. The first response of packers was to petition for an exemption from the regulation (*MR* 8 February 1950). When this was denied (*MR* 14 February 1950), the processors began laying off those who could not produce the 4.17 pounds of oyster meat per hour at eighteen cents per pound the processors were paying. Packers said because they had to pay the fishermen's price for oysters and compete with other seafoods, they could not raise the price for shucking. Both the McPhillips and Graham Sea Food Company, the two packing companies of Bayou la Batre, stopped oyster production. They cited 15 to 20 percent increases in plant operation costs and said that "competitors who are not living up to the law have been able to undersell us" (*MR* 25 March 1950). L. W. Graham said his plant closed because of "bad market conditions and because of conditions imposed by the 75-cent wage minimum" (ibid.).

One of McPhillips Packing Company's activities was dredging for shell for cement production. The South Baldwin Chamber of Commerce and union representatives toured the reefs and concluded that the dredge was destroying live oysters. They said they would attempt to have the dredging halted (*MR* 17 February 1950). F. Sprinkle, president of the Mobile Bay Sea Food Union, which was affiliated with the

American Federation of Labor (AFL), suggested that the McPhillips company "shut down because they heard the union was instrumental in efforts now being made to halt oyster shell dredging by the dredge Pelican in Mobile Bay." The McPhillips company denied the allegation (ibid.).

The season had been the best in ten years with prices of $1.50 a barrel at the reef and $1.90 at the plants. Fishermen's union president Sprinkle said the only hope for employment for the fourteen hundred to fifteen hundred oyster catchers out of work because of the plant closings was to plant oysters for the state (MR 25 March, 1 April 1950). The two packing companies and the union bid on the contract to plant forty thousand barrels of seed oysters in Mobile and Baldwin counties, and the union won on the basis of price (MR 1 April 1950).

The dredging of oyster shell from Mobile Bay continued to be controversial until it was stopped in 1982. Environmentalists claimed the dredging harmed the bay. Oyster catchers said it destroyed the oyster reefs. Studies provided only ambiguous conclusions. Opponents charged that the Seafoods Division would never stop it as long as most of its budget continued to come from dredging. The courts refused to intervene.

Various coalitions of seafood interests clashed in their endeavors to control the rules governing the industry. In 1937 the Federal Trade Commission charged the Biloxi Oyster Exchange and its twenty-four member companies, including fourteen in Mississippi and two in Alabama, with "fixing uniform seasonal sales [sic] prices, brokerage fees, discounts, label allowances, and terms governing oyster trade; regulating oyster canning and processing, and 'arbitrary' limiting packing periods" (MR 9 April 1937).

A spokeswoman for the exchange responded:

> We have never fixed the price of raw materials. We have had to adhere to what the unions demanded as to what we paid per barrel for steamed oysters, as well as for packing room labor.
>
> As far as brokerage and label allowances are concerned, those are prices, or rather discounts, which were allowed for many years prior to the existence of the Biloxi Oyster Exchange.
>
> Through the medium of the association we have raised the price to fishermen approximately 65 per cent and to the factory employees have gone wage increases of approximately 25 per cent.
>
> Our activities, our aims and our purposes have not only been welcomed, but sanctioned by the unions. (ibid.)

There were other struggles for control of the seafood industry in south Alabama. The same canning and packing firms owned factories in Biloxi and Bayou la Batre. Prices fixed in Biloxi, for instance, were used in Bayou la Batre. The processors organized into "trusts" as they had in the past. With their increasing independence from factory-owned boats, and the support of New Deal legislation, fishermen began to organize.

Labor

Labor organization was strongly opposed in Alabama. While the Knights of Labor had attempted to organize labor in Alabama as early as 1882, by 1886 only a small number of coal miners in Birmingham had established a local union affiliated with the American Federation of Labor. Other craft unions could not organize majorities in their workplaces. In 1901 an Alabama Federation of Labor was formed, but it remained insignificant because of competition with company unions. The "rural-born workers, individualistic in temperament, often joined their employers in opposition" to unions (Federal Writers Project 1941, 72).

In the wake of National Guard action to break a 1908 strike organized by the United Mine Workers in Birmingham, union organizers fled Alabama. Miners remained unorganized in Alabama and when there was a national strike in 1922, Alabama's coal production increased greatly. In 1933 the National Recovery Act gave Alabama workers the privilege of union membership without fear of company reprisals. Organizations were formed for almost every craft. Workers in mines, steel mills, and textile factories organized quickly and there were strikes in these industries for wage increases and better working conditions (ibid.).

In 1915 the International Longshoremen's Association organized a fisherman's union in Biloxi to negotiate better shrimp prices from packers and processors. Packers, claiming a poor market, engaged nonunion men for their schooners to seine for shrimp in Louisiana marshes. Seventeen hundred longshoremen were "on lockout" and refused to collect shrimp. The packers refused to recognize the union or negotiate (*MR* 14 September 1915; Biloxi and Gulfport *Daily Herald* [DH] 2, 7 August 1915). At the plant where boats were taking on ice for their voyage, union fishermen protested against the use of non-union labor. The police and hastily appointed deputies dispersed the union men. On 14 August one of the schooners arrived with eighty barrels of shrimp and the Biloxi branch of the ILA again demonstrated (*DH* 14 August 1915; *MR* 15 August 1915). There were several fights (*MR* and *DH* 16 August 1915). The shrimpers continued their strike into September, but the packers said they did not "care whether the men go back to work or not" (*MR* 10 September 1915).

Biloxi merchants, who depended on cannery workers for their business, called for a settlement (Sheffield and Nicovich 1979, 38; *DH* 19 August 1915). The mayor of Biloxi appointed two aldermen to try to bring about a resolution. The processors stated they were willing to take the men back independently but would not recognize the union. The packers did not have much shrimp; a number of people were talking of going after shrimp as independent fishermen and some shrimp was unloaded (*DH* 8 September 1915). On 16 September the canneries were kept busy processing some five hundred barrels of shrimp. Packers rapidly fitted out twenty boats and sent them to Louisiana to fill their demand for shrimp. On 17 September the members of the union voted unanimously to return to work as independent fishermen. Forty fishing boats, the largest fleet ever, left Biloxi for Louisiana the next weekend (*DH* 16, 23 September 1915; *MR* 13 November 1915). The packers did not recognize the union (*DH* 16 September 1915; Sheffield and Nicovich 1979, 39).

There was a hurricane at the end of September that damaged a number of the canning factories as well as ships. The strike and the storm damage foretold a bad shrimp season, but processors hoped for a good oyster season. In mid-November twenty-five boats returned to Biloxi from Louisiana with a record thousand barrels of shrimp and a large catch of oysters that kept the canneries operating full time (*MR* 13 November 1915)

While early attempts to organize fishermen had met with little success, the National Recovery Act and other New Deal legislation provided a new context for labor organization. Canneries could operate best with a dependable and uninterrupted supply of oysters. They relied on local fishermen for their raw material and had no alternative sources. By the mid-1930s most fishermen owned their own boats and gear and were independent of processor control. They were therefore free to organize and, to the extent they could organize, they were in a position to bargain with the processors. Fishermen all along the gulf coast were organizing.

In 1932 Biloxi shrimpers struck until the Mississippi Coast Packing Company increased the price of shrimp (*MR* 23 August 1932). The fishermen, who were asking $4.50 a barrel on the fishing grounds, the price being paid in Louisiana, met and declined to accept the offer of a single factory and decided to continue the strike until all factories met the requested prices (*MR* 21, 23 August 1932).

Two days later the Dorgan-McPhillips packing plant in Bayou la

Batre closed when it did not meet fishermen's demands for increased prices (*MR* 23 August 1932). Organized in 1922 by Mobile businessmen, this company had main offices in Mobile and four factories in Alabama, Mississippi, and Louisiana to can shrimp, oysters, and vegetables (*MR* 22 October 1936). With two shrimp- and oyster-canning plants there, it was Bayou la Batre's major packer and one of the largest on the gulf (*MR* 26 November 1933). The price for good medium shrimp delivered at the company's wharf at the end of the 1931 season had been $4 per barrel, which the packers had increased to $4.50 at the start of the 1932 season. The shrimpers asked for more and the plant closed. Julian McPhillips said his company, like others in Louisiana, was paying $4.50 per barrel in Louisiana, and that the cannery in Biloxi was closed due to demands for higher prices. Oystermen also began to organize to negotiate for higher oyster prices (*MR* 23 August 1932). To end a nine-day strike McPhillips agreed to pay $5.50 for delivered shrimp. While he had stated earlier that there was no incentive to pack shrimp at that price, he now said: "Only by having this advanced scale of price adopted throughout Louisiana and Mississippi can we hope to maintain it here in Alabama. With the reopening of our Bayou la Batre plant and the operation of our Louisiana plant, we will be producing at 75 per cent of our capacity. We are hopeful of increasing this to 100 per cent capacity in the near future, in which event, we will open our Biloxi plant" (*MR* 29 August 1932).

In the meantime, the sheriff had placed thirteen armed deputies in Bayou la Batre to prevent trouble. Two boats were scuttled during disagreements about settling the strike. The deputies were withdrawn when the thirty-five shrimp boats returned to work, and the Gulf Fishermen's and Oystermen's Association, the union that represented two hundred boat owners, agreed to deliver shrimp at the price of $5.50 until September (*MR* 1 October 1932). Then, if processors in Louisiana and Mississippi were not paying the same price, the Bayou la Batre canner would reduce its price to the Louisiana price. George Sprinkle; C. J. Cain; Allen Everett, Jr.; and J. E. Dobbis represented the fishermen (*MR* 30 August 1932). In Mississippi, Biloxi oystermen formed an organization to maintain oyster prices and agreed to organize oystermen in Alabama and Louisiana (ibid.).

Striking shrimpers patrolled the streets to prevent Biloxi packers from trucking Louisiana shrimp to the factories. A Louisiana truck driver with a cargo of shrimp took a wrong turn and fell into the hands of Biloxi police, who arrested him for violating Mississippi laws against importing shrimp; they released him on $100 bond and sent him back with his truck and cargo (*MR* 1 September 1932).

A thousand fishermen and sixteen factories remained out of work for the fourth week as the Mississippi oyster season opened early in September. A representative of the canners said they could not meet the demands of striking fishermen. Some factories announced they would move to Louisiana or Alabama (*MR* 6 September 1932). The canners' representative was quoted as saying: "With such unfortunate economic conditions and a large stock of seafood left from last year, and the fact that Louisiana already has packed such a large volume of shrimp this season, makes it impossible for us to operate at the price asked" (ibid.).

The factories announced they would not pay the $.40 a barrel price Biloxi oyster catchers requested to replace the 1931 price of $.25 (ibid.). The fifteen hundred union-organized shrimpers of Biloxi rejected an offer of $3.50 for un-iced shrimp and $5.00 for iced shrimp and held to their demand for $4.00 and $5.00. They decided to shut down all packing, even at those facilities willing to pay the prices, until all packers agreed. Fishermen called on city officials to help bring about a resolution and set up a fund to feed their families (*MR* 8 September 1932). The fishermen continued to fish for food and sold their catches in the streets of Biloxi to finance a strike support fund (*MR* 10 September 1932).

A group of Biloxi businessmen offered to arbitrate the controversy (ibid.) and met with owners and fishermen, but they failed to bring about an agreement. When four of their fishing schooners were sunk, factory owners requested more police protection, and guards were placed at the factories (*MR* 15 September 1932).

While it was unlawful to land Alabama shrimp in Mississippi, the Dorgan-McPhillips company trucked 75 percent of its Alabama purchases to canneries in Biloxi. Biloxi fishermen intercepted a truckload of Alabama shrimp and distributed them among the strikers. When the Biloxi packers stopped importing shrimp by truck, the Bayou la Batre purchases declined markedly and seventy-five Bayou la Batre shrimp boats were idled (ibid.). Biloxi shrimpers agreed to accept five dollars per barrel if packers would supply the ice. Packers refused and the strike continued for a sixth week (ibid.). Louisiana canners said the price of ice was the decisive issue since shrimpers trawled in Louisiana waters. It cost more to ice shrimp and transport them to Mississippi than to buy them in Louisiana. In Louisiana, shrimpers trawled for shrimp and sold them to freight boats, which iced and delivered them to canneries (*MR* 18 September 1932).

Some Biloxi canneries prepared to catch shrimp with their own boats. Five canneries requested injunctions against the fishermen to prevent them from interfering with cannery operations (ibid.). After the factories had been idle for seven weeks, some of their owners discussed plans to move to Pascagoula, where better police protection had been promised, or Bayou la Batre, or Louisiana (*MR* 22 September 1932).

Saying there had been less violence in Biloxi during the strike than usual, the Biloxi chief of police responded to the suggestion that he had not provided police protection to all parties: "The striking fishermen have not only promised the city officials to abstain from any violence or unlawful act, but since making this promise have kept it. The departure and return of shrimp boats has resulted in no violence, but some other reason is keeping the workmen of Biloxi from continuing in their regular occupation" (*MR* 1 October 1932).

By the end of September, some small packers acceded to the fishermen's price demands and some fifty of Biloxi's seven hundred boats returned to work. A federal conciliator got factory owners, who had refused to recognize the unions, to agree to recognize them verbally and to agree on price, but they refused to sign any contract with a union (*MR* 5 September 1933). The fishermen continued their strike and prevented others from unloading at the factories. C. L. Richardson, commissioner of conciliation of the U.S. Labor Department, tried to reach a compromise (*MR* 7 October 1932).

Factory owners issued statements that nearby towns had offered them new inducements to move their factories from Biloxi and they were seriously considering doing so. Some factories signed a compromise agreement, but most did not (ibid.). The federal negotiator worked out an agreement whereby the packers would recognize the union and set the price for shrimp at $4.50 (*MR* 8 October 1932). Out of work for nine weeks, fifteen hundred shrimpers agreed and marched through the streets of Biloxi to celebrate (ibid.). The next week two hundred shrimp boats were bringing shrimp into the factories at a rate of three hundred to four hundred barrels per day (*MR* 13 October 1932).

In 1933 Biloxi shrimp pickers were paid ten cents for twelve pounds of picked shrimp. Bayou la Batre pickers were paid ten cents for fourteen to sixteen pounds. Representatives of the AFL-affiliated picker's union of the Central Trades Council conferred with officials of the Dorgan-McPhillips Packing Company to ask for the same remuneration as was paid in Biloxi. The negotiators assured the factory representatives that they did not want to call a strike, and if one were called, they would process shrimp on hand so it would not spoil. McPhillips asked shrimp-boat operators not to go out for shrimp until the matter was resolved.

A group of four men claiming to represent businessmen and boatmen of Bayou la Batre came to the organizer's house and warned him to have his family at the shrimp factory by 3:00 A.M. the next morning ready to go to work and to retract his statements about increasing wages for workmen. The organizer, with AFL support, had the threatening men arrested (*MR* 24 August 1933). A strike was averted and the packing company's boats went shrimping again (*MR* 25 August 1933).

In Mississippi, Biloxi shrimp-processing workers struck but returned to work pending a settlement (*MR* 24 August 1933). By September they were on strike again and a federal conciliator was sent to help reach a settlement. "Several thousand" striking fishermen and women factory workers marched in Biloxi's Labor Day parade (*MR* 5 September 1933). By the end of September, they had been out of work for two months and physicians were pointing out cases of malnutrition in workers' families. Shrimpers refused a settlement proposed by the mayor, which met the demands of fishermen except for one that freight boats take shrimp from independent boats without restriction (*MR* 29 September 1933). A federal conciliator helped attain an agreement.

The fishermen of Pascagoula met and 116 joined a new branch of the Gulf Coast Shrimpers' and Oystermen's Association. Rev. Edward G. Maxted of St. John's Episcopal church explained the advantages of unions and cooperative action with employers. Union leaders explained bylaws and purposes and stressed that the principal purpose of the association was to put the organized strength of fishermen and oystermen behind the National Recovery Act (*MR* 3 September 1933).

Two hundred and fifty boatmen from Bayou la Batre were trawling in Mobile Bay in what observers considered to be a good year. Captain W. E. Akridge, the state oyster inspector, reported that while trawling was risky:

> The fascinating part of shrimping is the gambling element. When the trawl is placed overboard one never knows whether the quantity caught will be one pound or 4,000 pounds.
>
> Oftentime the trawl will be caught on an obstruction or lost entirely, or maybe a shark will rip it to pieces trying to get the fish gilled in the net.
>
> This means patient hours of repair work for the shrimper, but he knows there is a good living awaiting him in the long run. It takes an hour to make

a drag and frequently there may be 22 barrels of shrimp in a drag, worth $6 per barrel at the factories. (*MR* 28 September 1933)

I. T. Quinn observed that better prices were being paid for shrimp and oysters and more people were engaged in the shrimp industry than in the past two years (*MR* 5 September 1933).

A year and a half later, at the end of March 1935, Pascagoula packing houses shut down because they could not reach an agreement with shrimpers on the price of shrimp. One firm said it would send its own boats to Louisiana to get shrimp (*MR* 31 March 1935). In August the Biloxi fishermen's union cited increases in living expenses as a reason for asking for higher prices (*MR* 4 August 1935). Union shrimpers in New Orleans had requested an increase in their prices, but processors said the market could bear no increases. Three boatloads of between 100 and 150 men raided two shrimp processors and threw their shrimp into the water (*MR* 11 August 1935).

Alabama shrimp were found to be too small for packing, so the state Oyster Commission deferred the opening of shrimping season from the first to the tenth of August (*MR* 2 August 1935). The order was appealed to the attorney general, who ordered the commission to revert to the prior opening date of 1 August (*MR* 8 August 1935). During the first week of the season, fishermen delivered two thousand barrels of shrimp to Bayou la Batre, and three canning factories were operating at full capacity. The Bayou Packing Company, Independent, and the Deer Island Company had not set prices as they were waiting for Mississippi and Louisiana packers to settle their differences with fishermen there and set their prices.

All available boats were shrimping, most close to Fairhope on the eastern side of Mobile Bay. Freighters picked up shrimp from the boats and delivered them to the canneries in Bayou la Batre.

Biloxi shrimpers came to Bayou la Batre and tried to persuade the shrimpers to strike until they received increased prices. Sheriff's deputies were sent to investigate. The Bayou la Batre shrimpers said the Bayou Packing Company had refused their shrimp because it was not sufficiently fresh. Shrimp inspection and quality also became an issue (*MR* 13 August 1935).

Members of the Gulf Coast Shrimpers' and Oystermen's Association at Bayou la Batre struck for better prices. They held a meeting to try to persuade the nonunion workers of the Deer Island Fish and Oyster Company to join the union as the two other plants were at a standstill until they could negotiate a satisfactory price for shrimp.

Workers of the other two plants were represented by the picker's union of the Gulf Coast Shrimpers' and Oystermen's Association. The factories bought their shrimp from members of the boatmen's union of the same organization, which represented two hundred boatmen from one hundred boats. When the boatmen struck, the union factory workers struck in sympathy (*MR* 15 August 1935).

The processors said they had already accepted orders for some shrimp and could not increase their prices. The boatmen's union refused the offer. The shrimpers said the price should be increased because the two union packing firms had government inspectors who turned down some of their shrimp, which could cause large losses.

In Bayou la Batre a crowd of nonunion people passed a gathering of union people and shot and wounded three union men with birdshot. Four union men were alleged to have attacked a nonunion boat engineer on his way to work. He brandished a gun and was charged for carrying a concealed weapon. A woman union worker fought with a nonunion woman in an attempt to stop her from going to work. Both were arrested (*MR* 16 August 1935). Deputy sheriffs were sent to Bayou la Batre to break up such altercations. Fifteen people were arrested (*MR* 15 August 1935). Meanwhile, in Biloxi, shrimping was at a standstill (ibid.).

When seven boats landed six hundred barrels of shrimp at Bayou la Batre, there was a temporary settlement and strikers returned to work to process the shrimp. The threat of violence abated when the employees of the Deer Island Packing Company agreed to join a company union affiliated with the Gulf Coast Fisherman's Association and the company agreed to buy shrimp for the prevailing price.

Striking fishermen of the Gulf Coast Fishermen's and Trappers' Association in New Orleans suspended their strike in Louisiana when they agreed on a price. The Bayou la Batre unions and processors followed suit and settled on the same price (*MR* 22 August 1935). By the twenty-first of August, 125 shrimp boats representing all three Bayou la Batre packing plants had resumed operations (ibid.).

In mid-October the Gulf Coast Shrimpers' and Oystermen's Association shut down most of the packing plants in Alabama and Mississippi including two in Bayou la Batre, ten in Biloxi, one in Ocean Springs, two in Pass Christian, and two in Bay St. Louis. In Biloxi two thousand boatmen refused to operate their five hundred boats, and another thousand boatmen in Mississippi walked out. The Deer Island Fish and Oyster Company at Bayou la Batre, with its company organization, continued to operate. Another plant at Gulfport agreed to pay the additional fifty cents per barrel the shrimpers requested. The *Mobile Register* reported:

> The Register correspondent at Biloxi Thursday night said there was no possibility of any labor trouble, as the shrimpers' union—the Gulf Coast Shrimpers' and Oystermen's Association—has 100 per cent control over the workers. It was explained there is no strike—it is just a shut-down.
>
> The Bayou la Batre branch of the association also expects no trouble, despite the fact the union does not have full control in that Mobile County town. The association representative there said the Bayou boatmen were leaving negotiations to the heads of the organization at Biloxi. (*MR* 18 October 1935)

The union sent an organizer to Louisiana to organize shrimpers there because most Mississippi shrimp came from Louisiana (ibid.). All of the processing companies were members of the Biloxi Oyster Exchange. They agreed to refuse the price increase as the season was nearly over and some had a backlog of unsold canned goods after a year of large catches and a busy season of packing.

Toward the end of the month both sides were standing on their initial positions and the same two packers continued to operate— one with its own union and the other because it had met the price increase request (*MR* 30 October 1935). After a two-week shut down, the members of the Biloxi Oyster Exchange agreed to meet the price increase the shrimpers' union had proposed (*MR* 4 November 1935).

The sometimes tumultuous efforts to organize fishermen on the gulf were not isolated events. Many attempts at organizing labor in other parts of Alabama and the United States were met with official and unofficial ferocity. There were violent disputes up and down the gulf coast over whether local "company" unions or local branches of international unions should represent longshoremen and other workers. When companies recognized and negotiated with local "benevolent" associations, the international workers would block access to the workplaces. While they were not above using violence and threats of violence to keep their opponents out, law enforcement officials along the gulf arbitrarily arrested union leaders, branded them Communists, aliens, and undesirable. In Florida, out-of-uniform law enforcement officials beat and killed some labor organizers.

There was shooting and violence in the International Longshoremen's Association struggle against nonunion longshoremen all along the gulf. It was not just the gulf coast that was involved in a violent struggle over the organization of labor and other matters. There was murder in connection with a massive mining strike in Birmingham, Alabama (*MR* 2 November 1935). There had been armed uprisings in Louisiana during the past years under Huey Long, and the National Guard had been called out on many occasions in many states. Labor, government, and industry all used violence to achieve their goals.

In August of 1937 violence was again threatened in Bayou la Batre when crewmen tried to unload ten thousand pounds of fish from John Clark's two boats, manned by fishermen who had quit the Gulf Coast Shrimpers' and Oystermen's Association. The crews of the vessels were armed and three sheriff's deputies were dispatched to patrol the wharfs. In Pascagoula some fifty fishermen withdrew from the same union and attempted to fish as independents. The Coast Guard escorted a boat of nonunion fishermen into Pascagoula where it unloaded at the Coast Guard docks. Bayou la Batre fishermen were active in Pascagoula (*MR* 4 August 1937). The *Mobile Register* called the situation a "fish war" (*MR* 4, 5 August 1937).

The next day a boat came to Bayou la Batre from Pascagoula with a Coast Guard escort. The boat had tried to unload in Mississippi but the governor had declined to protect the boat because, though it was a Mississippi boat, it was selling its fish to two Alabama companies. The fish were unloaded at Bayou la Batre and the Shriner and J. W. Clark seafood companies each took one truckload to deliver in Montgomery. The Highway Patrol escorted the trucks to protect them from fishermen lying in wait for them.

A group of men gathered at the wharf of the J. W. Clark Company. Shots were exchanged and J. W. Clark himself wounded three men with a shotgun, none seriously. Sheriff Holcomb arranged a truce and set up a meeting between I. T. Quinn, the union secretary, and Mobile and Bayou la Batre businessmen. All sides were heavily armed and the sheriff's deputies continued their patrols (ibid.). By mid-month the situation was still tense as a fishing schooner with a cargo of fish from Louisiana requested a Coast Guard escort to Bayou la Batre (*MR* 17 August 1937).

There was labor strife in Louisiana in 1938 as members of the Gulf Coast Fishermen's and Trappers' Association, in conjunction with the Biloxi union, demanded $8.50 per barrel for shrimp. Jules Fisher, a Louisiana state senator and a canner, said he would not open his cannery until fishermen accepted $7.50. Union men patrolled the bayous to dump any shrimp they could find, including large cargoes from forty trawlers on Lake Salvador and many truckloads of shrimp. Sheriff's deputies had to protect people who landed shrimp, and they arrested twenty men (Becnel 1962; *MR* 13 August 1938).

In eastern Louisiana 236 shrimpers formed the East Louisiana Trappers' and Fishermen's Association, and vowed to deliver their shrimp. Their spokesman argued that the dumping and raids on independents since the season opened were for the benefit of certain canneries that wanted to dispose of their carryover surplus from the past season. These men trapped and trawled for shrimp and had a reputation for violence, having killed several lawmen in the past (Becnel 1962; *MR* 18 August 1938).

Three hundred union shrimpers in Pascagoula attempted to close a cannery. Armed posses rode shrimp trucks through union ranks and a Coast Guard patrol boat protected boats while they unloaded. The shrimpers were in the same union as the Louisiana shrimpers and were demanding $8.50 a barrel for shrimp. The canner agreed to negotiate during a three-day truce. He said, though, that he could not pay higher prices for shrimp than Louisiana and Alabama canneries (*MR* 21 August 1938).

Thirty boats of shrimpers in Louisiana said they would rather take whatever price they could get than continue the strike, and they sold their shrimp in New Orleans under a heavy sheriff's escort. The canneries remained closed (*MR* 23 August 1938). The next day one hundred union shrimpers on three trawlers patrolled the bayous of Louisiana to board and destroy the catch of nonunion boats (*MR* 24 August 1938; Becnel 1962). Unarmed union men intercepted and destroyed truckloads of shrimp on the way to New Orleans. They were arrested (*MR* 25 August 1938).

The canneries of Bayou la Batre did not operate for twenty-six days in 1940 during a dispute over the price of shrimp. Early in September the six hundred members of the local branch of the Gulf Coast Shrimpers' and Oystermen's Association withdrew from the Mississippi-based organization to form their own Mobile Bay Seafood Association. Women were active in the labor movement ashore, probably because, as in later times, the men were occupied much of the time fishing (Smith 1988). The seafood association's president (Mrs. Emma Curren) and secretary-treasurer (Mrs. Leonora Landry) were women and one of the four trustees (Mrs. Anna Nelson) was a woman (*MR* 12 September 1940). The factory workers also withdrew and formed a new union called the Seafood Workers' Union of Bayou la Batre (*MR* 14 September 1940). The president of the Gulf Coast union was a woman, Miss Deannie Duvall (ibid.).

Only one factory was packing seafood in Biloxi. Pass Christian members of the Gulf Coast Shrimpers' and Oystermen's Association formed the local Pass Christian Seafood Association in December of 1939 and negotiated an agreement to sell shrimp for the price in Louisiana or the rest of Mississippi, whichever was higher (*MR* 12 September 1940).

In 1943 all fishermen of the west coast of Florida were organized in the Gulf District Fishermen's Union. A strike that year idled the fishermen when wholesalers refused to negotiate yearly prices of mullet, mackerel, and grouper. Three hundred and fifty boats stopped production of 150,000 pounds of fish per day while a Department of Labor conciliator negotiated a settlement (*MR* 21, 24 August 1943). A similar strike followed in 1946 (*MR* 3 September 1946).

Wholesalers were organized into the Florida Fish Exchange of Jacksonville. As a result of the arbitration, the Seafarers' International Union, headquartered in New Orleans, requested a federal investigation of the exchange (*MR* 26 August 1943). M. D. Biggs, president of the international union, said: "Our findings convince us that the exchange is guilty of monopolistic practices. We are satisfied that the exchange has deliberately forced down the wholesale price of grouper and mullet paid to commercial fishermen and at the same time has held fish off the market to push up the price to dealers in other Southern states" (ibid.).

Price disputes abated during World War II because of good prices, wartime price controls, and fewer fishermen as many joined the armed forces.

Another effect of the war was to reduce the supply of tin for cans. The canneries developed fiber containers and continued to process seafood. Another consequence was the loss of factory and fishing labor as young men joined the armed forces (*MR* 2 August, 1 September 1942). A third was a shortage of ice. In August of 1943, the ice companies of Mobile jointly published an advertisement to explain that they were doing all they could do to import ice and to increase ice production.

After the lack of ice had idled Louisiana shrimp boats for a week, the shrimpers of the Fishermens' Supply Association picketed the Westwego ice plant to prevent the sale of ice to domestic dealers until ten boats were supplied with ice for shrimp trawlers in Jefferson and Plaquemines parishes. Louisiana Representative Herbert appealed to Washington's Food Distribution Administration that "the ice famine in New Orleans has tied up more than 1,000 fishing boats, caused destruction of thousands of pounds of seafood and threatens the health of the population" (*MR* 13 August 1943). He urged wage adjustments for the ice industry and additional transportation facilities to restore production. The United States Employment Service said the scarcity was due to labor shortages (ibid.).

In 1946 shrimpers in Alabama and Biloxi stayed in port when the nineteen members of the Biloxi Seafood Shippers' Association refused the price request of the Gulf Coast Shrimpers' and Oystermen's Association. A representative of the Biloxi packers said they could not negotiate with the union as they had to compete in the same market with Louisiana packers who paid lower prices (*MR* 15 August 1946). Members of the Mobile Bay Seafood Union, whose president was Walter Bosarge, voted 151-8 at Bayou la Batre to reject the packers' offer for shrimp. The union represented about a thousand fishermen of Bayou la Batre, Coden, Herron's Bay, Alabama Port, Dog River, Fowl River, Dauphin Island, Mobile, and Bon Secour (*MR* 16, 17 August 1946). The strike ended after six days when processors agreed to the union's terms (*MR* 17 August 1946). Biloxi packers extended the strike for sixteen days until the end of August when they agreed to shrimpers' initial price demands. Shrimpers and packers agreed that they had lost no money as shrimp had been small and scarce (*MR* 28 August 1946).

When the oyster season opened on the first of October in 1946, it was also delayed for two weeks by a price dispute as processors of the Alabama Wholesale Sea Food Dealers did not pay what the Mobile Bay Sea Food Union requested (*MR* 2, 16 October 1946). Shrimping was off and some fishermen moved to Mississippi and Louisiana to avoid their out-of-state taxes (*MR* 3 October 1946).

The next year, Alabama shrimpers and packers agreed on prices at the beginning of the season, though there was less agreement in Mississippi (*MR* 17, 20, 22, 24 August 1947).

In 1944 oyster dredging had been allowed in Alabama because there was a shortage of meat (*MR* 9 January 1944). The same year the Biloxi unions and packers were able to cooperate in a request to the War Labor Board for higher wages. The Gulf Coast Shrimpers' and Oystermen's Association, Biloxi Seafood Shippers' Association, Sea Coast Packing Company, and Antioch Canning Company applied for adjustments and were granted them for about twelve thousand workers (*MR* 16 April 1944). The state oyster-planting program was continued in Alabama as 100,000 to 120,000 barrels of shells were to be planted in Alabama waters (*MR* 30 April 1944).

There were good catches, but in some areas there were shortages of cannery labor. In Biloxi only five hundred of fifteen hundred necessary processing workers were available for work (*MR* 31 August 1945). The booming business of the seafood industry was attributed to the wartime meat shortage (*MR* 19 September 1945).

The principal shrimping grounds in Alabama remained the Mississippi Sound south of Bayou la Batre between Petit Bois and Dauphin islands and Mobile Bay (*MR* 4 August 1946), though Alabama shrimpers also worked off the coasts of Louisiana and Mississippi. The "traditional" boat was sixty feet long with a crew of two, though some fishermen used skiffs. Large ships picked up shrimp from other boats. The boats rarely stayed out longer than three days on a trip and most returned every night. When a run of shrimp was found, the whole fleet would assemble to drag their trawls through it. By the late forties, shrimp boats were outfitted with mechanical hoists and ship-to-shore telephones (*MR* 8 August 1948).

In 1939 Lawrence F. Evans, writing for the Federal Writers Project, interviewed a skipper of the thirty-eight-foot shrimp boat *Grover Cleveland*, which he had owned for eighteen of his thirty-five years in shrimping in Bayou la Batre. The three factories had some boats, but shrimpers preferred to work on their own vessels because "working a factory boat is like being a share cropper" and did not pay unless one owned his own boat, according to the skipper. The factories would indicate when they needed shrimp, and shrimpers, regulated by the union, would take turns going out (Brown 1982).

The skipper and his wife had eight children. The older sons and one son-in-law were also shrimpers. The wife and three daughters worked in a factory picking shrimp when there was work, about two or three days a week at the busiest (Brown 1982). The same boat was still shrimping in the 1950s (Rayford 1956, 155, 161).

Next to a cannery a half block from the shrimper's house were seven shotgun houses whose front doors opened onto the street and whose back doors opened onto the factory. Evans's impressions were vivid:

> But houses is not the name for these hovels. They are all of a pattern, long, ugly, unpainted, dilapidated, with a half porch caving in and pasteboard patches here and there for window panes. One does not need to enter to feel the hopelessness and desolation of the occupants. Ill kept, with scrawny, stooped women sitting on the doorsteps, tousel-haired and dirty-faced children; nondescript garments hanging on a wash-line between the buildings, all make a picture of despair.
>
> These are the homes of shrimpers who work for the shrimp factories on "shares." Here live the wives and daughters of the men who go to sea and fight for an existence; here live the women who strip their fingers to the bone, beheading and picking the shrimp, so that they may earn a few dollars to eke out the meager earnings of husbands and fathers. (Brown 1982, 235)

The other factories were similar in appearance. Evans estimated that about three hundred families worked for the shrimp factories (ibid.).

A similar contemporary account (Prine 1938) describes the Dorgan-

McPhillips Packing Company's camp for its workers as several small houses and two long houses, each with a long porch along the front. Ten families lived in each building and used part of the porch. The structures were built off the ground so water from the nearby bayou would not flood them. Prine described the place as "bleak and bare." Six hog pens faced the houses, and people made gardens nearby (ibid.).

Prine interviewed a seventy-seven-year-old worker, Joe Vaughn, and his sixty-seven-year-old wife, Ezora, in the camp where they lived with their daughters and grandchildren. Vaughn had left Canada for New Iberia, Louisiana, where he married a French-speaking Louisiana woman. When news of work in Biloxi spread, he worked there for a while. Then when he and others heard work was better in Bayou la Batre, they went there in 1923 or 1924 (ibid.).

Vaughn lamented that during the past year there had been only a month's work at the factory because of a strike, but before there had been as much as nine months of work in a year. Husband and wife worked in the factory when there was work, and they made between four and six dollars a week. The workers did not pay rent but had to be available to work for the packing company when they were needed (ibid.).

In addition to the big factories there were some small oyster processors. A seventy-year-old Bayou la Batre oyster catcher and his sixty-four-year-old wife, both born on Dauphin Island, caught oysters together and, with their daughter and daughter-in-law, shucked them in a tin shack near their house before selling them to the National Sea Food Company in Mobile. In addition to shrimping and oystering the man had split rails, rafted logs, and burned and hauled charcoal. Ownership of the shop made the family ineligible for relief programs (Prine 1939).

Lawrence Nelson started catching oysters in Bon Secour when he was thirteen years old. His father was a Dane who had come to Bon Secour when he was young, and began oystering. The main oyster reef was at the mouth of Bon Secour Bay where it merges with Mobile Bay, close to an island known as Oyster Reef. In 1938 Nelson told Lawrence Evans that about fifty families in the area made their livings from oysters, and that while prices may have been bad, oyster catchers did better than farmers. He had a new boat that cost him twelve hundred dollars; it was thirty-two feet long with six bunks, a cabin, a place to cook, and a Cadillac motor. He tonged for oysters but was familiar with dredges, which were outlawed. He said that no one did that because no one could afford to be arrested. He had also bought a new car and built a new house, though there had not been enough money to furnish it (Evans 1938).

Nearly fifty years later, when Cathy Donelson of the *Montgomery Advertiser* interviewed Lawrence Nelson at the age of eighty-two, he recalled playing his trumpet while resting from tonging. He reported that he continued working until the oysters disappeared in the early 1970s. He told his story of running away at the age of seventeen to go to sea, returning to meet his wife, and fishing from Bon Secour. He said he was shucking oysters from other areas for six dollars per gallon (*Montgomery Advertiser* 8 November 1987).

In November of 1945, several fishing boats owned by the Clark Seafood Company and the McPhillips Packing Company of Bayou la Batre and the C. C. Company of Biloxi were impounded in Louisiana because they had not cleared the exit port at Grand Pass, Louisiana, and did not have proper licenses to fish in the state. The captains were charged with exporting seafood but were released with their cargoes after their companies posted bond with the Department of Wildlife and Fisheries (*MR* 16 November 1945). Because the out-of-state taxes were high, some shrimpers moved from Bayou la Batre to Mississippi and Louisiana in the mid-forties. About the same time, those who had been in the armed forces were returning (*MR* 4 August 1946).

In 1946 Louisiana imposed a license fee of $2,500 on out-of-state fishing boats and $200 on each crewman. Because Mississippi had sent a delegation of fifteen to Louisiana's legislative assembly, its fishermen were exempted from the provisions of the law. Mobile's senator in the Alabama legislature, Vincent Kilborn, wrote to Alabama's conservation director, Ben Morgan, that Louisiana's tax law would "in a large measure close up South Alabama's fishing industry." Morgan requested that the attorney general consider a test of the constitutionality of such tax laws in the U.S. Supreme Court (*MR* 14 August 1946). While the governor of Alabama, Chauncey Sparks, wrote to Louisiana's governor and Morgan tried to get a reciprocal agreement like Mississippi's, seafood company officials in Bayou la Batre accused both of negligence toward the seafood industry as it dried up in Alabama (*MR* 4 September 1946).

When the attorney general declined to sue Louisiana, a fishing industry spokesman said he confirmed "the opinion of many that the Governor and the State Department of Conservation have no interest in the fishing industry" (*MR* 12 September 1946).

In 1947, 69,288 barrels of oysters and 13,334 barrels of shrimp were caught in Alabama waters. Oysters were about five times the volume of shrimp. The million dollar value of oysters was about twice that of shrimp (*MR* 19 August 1948). By 1948 Coffee Island Company's Bayou la Batre freezing plant was shipping frozen shrimp as well as fresh oysters from its own beds (*MR* 12 September 1948).

If dredging and pollution made oyster catching more and more precarious, trawling provided a more secure and dependable supply of raw material for processors, and shrimping became well established. With the processors' insatiable demand for shrimp, shrimpers began exploring the gulf for new fishing grounds and a new system developed, one that centered on industrial shrimping and freezing.

Red Snapper and Finfish

In the earliest period, when oysters and fish were predominant, red snapper was the major fish. In the second period, the period of industrial canning, snapper was still important, but the canneries gave oysters and shrimp increasing prominence.

During the second period, red-snapper fishing in the Gulf of Mexico was the most risky branch of the fishery. The technology and techniques had not changed much from the late nineteenth century. The Star Fish and Oyster Company of Mobile operated a fleet of seventy-five-foot two-masted schooners modeled on the Nantucket cod-fishing boats. Their nine- or ten-man crews and captains sailed them to the Campeche banks off the coast of Mexico to fish for red snapper in waters thirty to sixty fathoms deep (*MR* 1 September 1920, 26 November 1933). Once the boats anchored over the snapper banks, it became an endurance contest between the fisherman and the fish (*MR* 1 September 1920).

> When a smack sets out on a red snapper expedition in the gulf it carries a crew of not more than ten men and is gone some times two weeks, some times three, according as schools of snapper are located. Hook and line is the tackle used.
>
> After a few days of scouting along the coast of Mexico a snapper school is generally found after which it is but a matter of pulling them in, weighing from three to sixteen pounds each. It is an interesting sight to watch these fishermen lined along the edge of a smack, smoking their pipes and pulling in the bright red fish day in and day out, until they have twenty to thirty thousand pounds of them stored away in the hold.
>
> From sun up until after night the fisherman stays at his post and seems never to tire of his work. In spite of the fact they have but to bait a hook and drop it into the water in order to make a catch they find sport in fishing and never fail to call a neighbor's attention when they pull an extraordinary large one. (*MR* 1 September 1923)

Jarvis (1935) provides a similar account and adds that most of the fishermen were foreigners, many of them, Scandinavians.

The schooners brought their iced catches to Mobile where they were prepared for market locally or shipped to cities of the interior (*MR* 1 September 1920, 26 November 1933).

By 1918 the Star Fish and Oyster Company was the largest in Mobile with its own wharf, ice plant, and five gasoline-powered ocean-going vessels to fish the Gulf of Mexico, each with a capacity of twenty thousand pounds. They went on trips of three to five weeks. Sometimes they would land their fish at other ports such as Galveston and ship the fish by rail to Mobile (*MR* 1 September 1918).

Summary

With between one and four plants, Alabama never had as many canneries as Mississippi. There were four factories in Alabama in the last three years of the 1920s but only two in 1930 as the Depression deepened. The number fluctuated between two and three for the rest of the thirties, but by 1945 there was but one left and none was operating after 1965. Table 2 illustrates this decline.

Table 2. Canneries in Alabama

Year	Canning Oysters	Canning Shrimp
1930	2	4
1935	2	2
1940	2	2
1945	1	1
1950	2	2
1955	3	2
1960	2	1
1965	0	0

Source: U.S. Bureau of Fisheries *Reports*

Canneries continued to operate longer in Mississippi and other gulf states, and one still operates in Biloxi, but freezing has replaced canning as the major preservation technology. This process started to gain in importance after World War II. As shrimpers began to explore more distant fishing grounds in larger boats and to increase the amount of shrimp landed, the technology of freezing became an integral part of the system with industrial shrimping.

4

Since 1950: Industrial Shrimping and Freezing

Communities all along the coast of the Gulf of Mexico are famous for their seafood. Menus of restaurants that overlook a bay or sound feature oysters, shrimp, and crab. Wherever there are municipally owned docks and local law allows it, people come from inland towns to purchase fresh seafood from shrimpers as they come in. "Recreational" shrimpers with their sixteen-foot nets contract with friends and friends of friends to bring in enough shrimp to fill a freezer or an ice chest. Local festivals feature seafood suppers.

As in the early days, local consumption of seafood is still important, though Mobile no longer paves its streets with shells from oyster saloons. Likewise, transportation of seafood along the coast is still important. Semi-trailer trucks from as far south as Brownsville, Texas, back up to processing plants where workers shovel shrimp layered with ice into wheelbarrows to move them to the machines that clean, devein, and sort the shrimp so other workers can pack them in boxes for freezing. A Louisiana packing firm has a fish house in Biloxi, Mississippi, where it collects shrimp in season to ship west for processing. A Mississippi processing firm has a collection outpost in Texas. A fleet of boats owned by a Mississippi firm has operated from facilities of a processor in Bayou la Batre, Alabama. A processor in Bon Secour, Alabama, gets oysters from Louisiana to sell to restaurants.

A cannery is still in operation in Biloxi, but the balance has shifted away from local consumption and canning. Today most shrimp is frozen for sale in other areas. Although the canneries were established to process oysters and developed shrimp as a sideline, now shrimp is the predominant product. There is still an oyster industry, though it is beset with the old problems of floods and predators as well as more recent ones of industrial and residential pollution.

The shrimping industry has expanded greatly. This expansion and new technology for fishing and processing set the stage for the development of a different system with different relationships and different dynamics. Whereas negotiations between processors and fishermen's and workers' unions had been a regular feature of the previous system, they declined and disappeared within a few years in the new system. The fishermen's customary round of work changed from daily shrimping and oystering in season to specialization in one or another and in gulf or bay shrimping. The work conditions and daily life of gulf shrimpers are radically different from anything known to fishermen of the previous period.

New shrimping grounds have been discovered far out in the Gulf of Mexico. Shrimpers have invested in larger, gulf-going boats to reach these shrimp and have developed changes in the trawl nets to make them more efficient. At the same time processors have invested in machinery to clean, process, and freeze shrimp. The combination of the new fishing grounds, larger boats, and new processing technology that developed explosively about 1950 started the modern system of industrial shrimping and freezing, forming the foundation of a new system.

Unions were losing influence as more shrimpers were heavily in debt for their new boats and dared not miss any opportunity to sell shrimp for fear of losing their means of livelihood. At the same time, freezing technology made the importation of foreign shrimp possible. As more and more shrimp was imported from foreign producers and as the aquaculture of shrimp developed to provide even more shrimp for importation, processors depended less and less on local producers for their raw materials. Shrimpers depended more on processors to buy their shrimp than processors relied on them to provide it.

American trade policy has not limited or taxed these imports. This is a matter of policy that is directed at foreign policy rather than the fisheries, but it has a great consequence for them. The open importation of shrimp has swamped the market so that domestic production no longer affects prices. The legal and political situation of unions has changed as well. A judge found fishermen's unions to be in violation of antitrust legislation and outlawed them. Rather than thinking of each fisherman as a worker for a packer or factory, the judge held that each owner-operator was a corporation and the banding together of corporations to fix prices was against antitrust laws.

As trawling became more efficient and more boats were doing it, it met increased resistance from sport fishermen. When a connection was made between the mortality of certain species of endangered sea turtles and shrimp trawling, a new law requiring changes in gear was implemented. I will discuss this in detail in the next chapter, but I should note here that the expansion of the shrimping industry is the reason it became an issue.

During this period, shrimp became the most important species. Shrimpers in small boats still catch them in bays, but even more shrimp come from large boats that can drag continuously in the gulf, which is an industrial process. The shrimp are processed largely by machines in another industrial process. While fishermen still fish for finfish and continue to tong oysters, these other dimensions of the fishery have declined in their relative importance. The seafood industry in this period is dominated by industrial shrimping and freezing.

Shrimp

The Expansion of the Shrimp Industry

As early as 1944 a Biloxi shrimper, Bozo Delchambre, had explored fishing grounds about twenty miles off the Alabama coast. In 1946 two Bayou la Batre captains followed and in 1947 eight other captains joined to make an offshore fleet of ten. About 150 trawlers from Bayou la Batre and Biloxi shrimped in ten-to-twenty-fathom waters in the next two years (MR 6 August 1950). In 1950 large shrimp boats converged on newly discovered distant shrimp grounds (MR 6 August 1950, 27 July 1950; van Dresser 1950; Burman 1954; Idyll and Sisson 1957). There was a rush throughout the gulf to trawl the deeper waters at night for the newly discovered shrimp (Sass 1950) and to build new boats for the rougher outside waters and longer voyages.

Shrimping in Alabama was never the same after 1950 when forty of the Texas Fishermen's Cooperative Association's sixty-five-foot diesel-powered trawlers equipped with radios and fathometers joined in to "dwarf" the boats of the Alabama fleet (MR 27 July 1950). An additional 150 to 300 boats from other parts of the United States coalesced. They went on three-night trips and returned with about twenty 210-pound barrels of heads-on shrimp which they could sell for fifty dollars per barrel. John W. Nelson, president of the Texas Co-Operative, praised the cooperation of the Alabama Conservation Department and said the co-op would continue to land its hauls in Alabama (ibid.).

A local account of a trip to the new shrimping grounds reports:

About dusk, we pulled up behind Petit Bois Island. . . . Off to our right, a small shrimp boat attempted the rough pass between Petit Bois and Horn Islands. It pitched and tossed, then finally turned back. The incident was

somewhat symbolic of the experience of many an Alabama shrimp boat
operator, whose vessel and equipment were built for inland water shrimping operations. Many of them just can't take it out in the deep and rough
Gulf. (*MR* 6 August 1950)

A few years later, a Florida shrimper described the contrast this
way:

> Shrimping ain't what it used to be. All these fancy boats with radios
> and going off to Mexico and then China next maybe. You make a pile of
> money now, but it ain't good living.
> Old days you'd go in a boat a couple of miles and catch your shrimp
> and be back home for supper. You'd shrimp that way six months and oys-
> ter three months, and the other three months you'd go bootlegging. Them
> was what I call good times. (Burman 1954, 98)

There had long been a distinction between bay and gulf fishing.
In previous times only the large schooners sailed to the gulf to fish,
while shrimp and oyster boats remained in inside waters. The line
was just south of Dauphin Island, where even the Conservation Department did not patrol because the waters were too rough for its boat
(*MR* 11 August 1951).

The anthropologist Bronislaw Malinowski reported (1948, 13–14)
that people of the Trobriand Islands, off the coast of New Guinea,
used no ceremonies when fishing in the lagoon where they could
rely on their knowledge and skill, but used "extensive . . . ritual to
secure safety and good results" when they fished in the dangerous
and uncertain open sea.

We see the same contrast in inside and gulf shrimping, first in
Biloxi and then in Bayou la Batre. The first fleet blessing on the gulf
was in Biloxi in 1929 when priests started blessing those vessels and
fishermen bound for outside waters (*MR* 11 August 1930).

In 1949 Carl Carmer commented on Biloxi's "Latin religious fer-
vor" and suggested it was saturated with the "spirit of fiesta." He was
struck by the Catholicness of Biloxi as opposed to Pascagoula. The
fleet was blessed on the Sunday before 15 August. Newly painted
boats decorated with flags lined up in front of a white cross on Biloxi
Bay, and at midnight, priests began to pray for safety and prosperity,
moving from boat to boat to bless the fishermen and sprinkle the boats
with holy water (Carmer 1949, 105).

The ceremony moved to the front beach in 1950, and in the next
year over 250 boats were blessed. When the gulf-going boats came to
Bayou la Batre in 1950, the people of the port adopted the practice
(*MR* 30 July, 7 August 1950). Riding in a state conservation depart-

ment boat, a Catholic priest blessed each boat in turn (ibid.). The next year, a Baptist clergyman blessed the forty to fifty boats of Bon Secour in what he styled a solemn religious service rather than a gala civic celebration (*MR* 9 August 1951). Whatever their ritual purposes, such festivities later became important as ways to draw attention to the problems of the fishing industry and as tourist attractions to generate income for coastal communities.

Table 3 documents the expansion of the shrimping fleet and the increasing place of the large gulf-going trawlers in Alabama. These figures are from the U.S. Fisheries reports. While they do not always agree precisely with data from other sources, they are very close.

The 1950 U.S. Fisheries report recognized a trend of fleet expansion, discovery of new fishing grounds, and larger shrimp boats in the gulf. In the gulf states, there were three hundred new vessels of greater

Table 3. Numbers and Percentages of Vessels and Boats Trawling for Shrimp in Alabama

Year	Vessels over Five Tons (Number)	(%)	Boats under Five Tons (Number)	(%)	Total Number
1930	15	11	123	89	138
1936	26	17	131	83	157
1940	29	17	146	83	175
1945	45	21	167	79	212
1948	39	10	342	90	381
1949	57	14	344	86	401
1950	72	18	336	82	408
1951	117	25	358	75	475
1952	116	37	193	63	309
1953	122	40	178	60	300
1954	115	40	170	60	285
1955	130	46	151	54	281
1956	148	40	224	60	372
1957	166	44	209	56	375
1958	194	48	210	52	404
1959	222	52	201	48	423
1960	222	52	206	48	428
1965	295	59	206	41	501
1970	448	75	149	25	597
1975	455	77	133	23	588
1977	469	77	139	23	608

Source: U.S. Bureau of Fisheries *Reports*

than five tons displacement, and the boats were larger, more powerful, and better equipped, with longer cruising ranges than before. They could remain at sea longer and fish in deeper waters than older boats. New shrimping grounds were discovered off Florida, Pascagoula, and Campeche off Yucatan (Bureau of Fisheries *Report* 1950, 250).

The vastly increased catches taxed local processing facilities all along the gulf in the United States as well as Mexico. In Florida, ice had to be trucked into the shrimping ports of the keys, and the shrimp was trucked to New York, Philadelphia, Baltimore, Washington, and Chicago. Loads had to be re-iced four or five times en route and were only steamed, frozen, or packaged for sale fresh after they arrived at their northern destinations (van Dresser 1950). Some of the shrimp caught offshore in 1950 moved through Mobile where the quick-freeze plant at the State Docks cold-storage facility processed them. Some went through Bayou la Batre and Pensacola and some through Foley, where Gulf Frosted Foods established quick-freeze facilities (*MR* 27 July, 18 August 1950).

By the time the 1950 inland-water shrimping season opened, Alabama canning factories had already canned hundreds of barrels of shrimp. The Texas and Louisiana boats increased Bayou la Batre's business and Conservation Department revenues through its shrimp-landing license fee and twelve-cent-per-barrel tax on shrimp (*MR* 6 August 1950).

In 1950, 57 licenses were issued to freight boats to collect newly discovered Brazilian shrimp from shrimpers and to bring them in from the gulf. In addition 341 licenses were issued to trawl inshore shrimp beginning in mid-August. The inshore shrimp, along with the unprecedented haul of gulf shrimp, provided raw material for full capacity processing at Bayou la Batre. Texas interests leased some of the places to process deep-water shrimp (*MR* 18 August 1950). Shrimp production increased 60 percent in Alabama, 65 percent in Mississippi, 17 percent in Louisiana, and 100 percent in Texas (*MR* 10 November 1950). Shrimping was so good that most fishermen delayed harvesting oysters (*MR* 14 September 1950). Normally idle canneries canned small shrimp and froze larger ones (Bureau of Fisheries *Report* 1950, 250).

This process continued the next year and there was more mechanization of landing and processing facilities (Bureau of Fisheries *Report* 1951, 183). Only thirty or forty boats were shrimping in Alabama's inside waters at the August opening of the 1951 season. Gulf shrimp had kept the market supplied with large shrimp all summer (*MR* 15 August 1951).

Shrimp landings reached an all-time high in 1952. Conversion and construction of large vessels continued and 161 received new licenses in gulf states. Beginning in 1952 some vessels had mechanical refrigeration (Bureau of Fisheries *Report* 1952, 187).

In response to record shrimp landings, the emphasis in 1952 was on marketing. There were improvements in handling and treatment as processors began to install grading machines and deveiners (Bureau of Fisheries *Report* 1952, 187). In 1949 J. M. Lapeyre had invented a mechanical shrimp peeler in Houma, Louisiana. Such machines cut processing costs from eight dollars per barrel to four dollars and eliminated much waste. In 1951, the Lapeyre family firm introduced a cleaner; in 1953, a separator; and in 1954, a deveiner ("Technology for Shrimps" 1956; Becnel 1962).

The price of shrimp reached historic highs in 1953 when the shrimping grounds expanded farther into the gulf and more large trawlers were constructed. There was also an increase in the construction of bay shrimp boats (Bureau of Fisheries *Report* 1953, 187). Shrimp boats from Key West, Florida, and Brownsville, Texas, were based at Coden and Bayou la Batre (*MR* 3 August 1953).

As the price of shrimp attained new highs in 1953, more canneries used shrimp-peeling machines. In the mid-1950s, modern plants were built to process shrimp with deveiners, graders, and peelers, and to package frozen shrimp (Bureau of Fisheries *Report* 1956, 230).

To insure an even steadier supply of shrimp, processors began to import them. The next year the price of shrimp collapsed because of heavy imports. By the middle of the year, trawler owners who were in debt for boats they had purchased when prices were high were unable to meet operating expenses and payments on their boats. Maintenance, repairs, and crews were reduced throughout the shrimping fleet. People began canceling orders for new shrimp boats (Bureau of Fisheries *Report* 1954, 193; *MR* 4 September 1954). The boom in vessel construction slowed down in 1955 (Bureau of Fisheries *Report* 1955, 241).

The 1956 shrimp catch decreased in volume but increased in value. A number of independent trawlers began to purchase navigational aids previously available only to large operators (Bureau of Fisheries *Report* 1956, 230).

Since 1955 shrimpers in Texas had been experimenting with double rigs, towing two smaller nets rather than one larger one. In 1957 when the news spread concerning their 15 percent to 30 percent increases in catch, most gulf shrimpers converted their boats to double rigging. The memory of 1954's price fall inhibited boat building (Bureau of Fisheries *Report* 1957, 208).

In 1959 Graham Seafood, automated from unloading to canning, was the only remaining shrimp cannery in Alabama (*MR* 16 August 1959). Most of the oysters processed in Alabama came from Mississippi and Louisiana (*MR* 4 August 1976). In the place of the canneries a number of small oyster-processing operations sprang up to open oysters for the fresh-oyster market. They were subject to sanitation and refrigeration standards set by city, state, and federal regulation (*MR* 14 October 1943, 3 September 1961).

The history of the South Baldwin Bank's loan program reflects the history of shrimping in the gulf. In the mid-1950s the bank began making loans of $6,000 to $7,000 with two-year repayment periods for the purchase of forty-foot trawlers. During the mid-1960s it made loans up to $15,000 for larger boats with two-year repayment periods. By 1970 it had made a $35,000 loan for a sixty-five-foot boat with a four-year repayment period. It began financing steel-hulled boats in 1972 and lent up to $100,000 for a seventy-five-foot boat with a five-year repayment period (*MR* 30 January 1975).

As they wore out, small, individually owned boats had been replaced by large steel-hulled vessels, many of which were owned by fisheries as the earlier schooners had been. The 231 bay boats of 1962 had become only 129 in 1969 while large shrimp vessels increased from 168 to 506. The "changeover" provided optimistic figures. The United States Department of the Interior showed Alabama's seafood harvest in 1972 to be 40 percent higher than in recent years, and the director of the National Marine Fisheries Service predicted a good catch from the gulf in 1973. The Marine Resources Division of the Alabama Department of Conservation said the shrimp catch had set records for each of the past eight or ten years. The commercial landings of seafood had quadrupled from 1961 to 1972 (*Mobile Press* 15 January 1974, 6 July 1978).

New fishing technology and fishing grounds dramatically increased shrimpers' catching capacity, and processing technology and marketing kept up with the growth. Fisheries research was part of the process. The primary research goals were to identify and locate new fishing grounds and to learn about the biology of commercial species. Locating fishing areas was part of the program of expansion intended to bring more income to fishermen and more stable supplies to processors. The biological research was meant to supply the knowledge upon which to base management plans that would provide for the future of the fisheries.

The motor ketch *Atlantis* of Woods Hole arrived in Mobile in 1937. It had been doing exploratory work for the Bingham Oceanographic Foundation of Yale University (*MR* 16 March 1937) and the Woods

Hole Oceanographic Institution. It was also charged with exploring the gulf for shrimp "in an effort to increase the fishing range for the shrimp fleets in the gulf, and thereby increase their income" (*MR* 21 March 1937).

Founded in 1946, the Gulf States Marine Fisheries Commission was to determine the time and place of spawning, rates of growth, and time and places where the mature members of various species could be caught, biological knowledge to serve as the basis of fisheries policy which the commission hoped to make uniform for the gulf states (*MR* 22 July, 12 November 1950). In 1950 the U.S. Fish and Wildlife Service stationed its experimental fishing vessel *Oregon* at Pascagoula to map gulf waters and inform commercial fishermen of the best grounds and seasons (*MR* 15 January 1950). After its captain consulted with the Gulf States Marine Fisheries Commission, the boat's first voyage was to the western gulf to look for concentrations of tuna, snapper, and shark as well as shrimp (*MR* 16 April 1950).

In July of 1950, James McPhillips of Mobile's Southern Fisheries asked the U.S. Fish and Wildlife Service to search for new supplies of Brazilian shrimp as it was popular for canning. In August the Gulf States Marine Fisheries Commission requested the *Oregon* be used to test for Brazilian shrimp in the new shrimping areas some sixty miles off the coast with a full-sized, hundred-foot trawl (*MR* 7 August, 24 December 1950). That same year, along with the expanding fleet, the *Oregon* and the *Alaska* met the processors' desires for more exploratory research (Bureau of Fisheries Report 1950, 250).

When prices were high in 1952 and 1953 the *Oregon* continued its search for new shrimping grounds. After a collapse of the price of shrimp in 1954, the *Oregon* began to look for tuna (Bureau of Fisheries Report 1954, 193; *MR* 4 September 1954). The *Oregon* continued to search for red-shrimp grounds (*MR* 16 March 1955) and test different kinds of trawls (*MR* 6 July 1955).

Detailed research on shrimp biology to "provide sufficient knowledge to scientifically manage this industry and maintain production at the highest possible level" began in 1955. The *Oregon* continued tuna research and provided technical assistance to fishermen who wished to convert to tuna fishing (Bureau of Fisheries Report 1955, 241).

To insure themselves a supply of raw material, processors not only encouraged research to increase domestic production but also imported shrimp. In 1939, United States imports were a little over 3.7 million pounds, 4 percent of the 93 million pounds of shrimp consumed. The United States imported about 40 million pounds of shrimp in 1954, sufficient to bring down significantly the price of domestic shrimp. Imports were 85 million pounds in 1958; they accounted for 107 million pounds in 1959 compared to the domestic catch of 142 million pounds (*MR* 23 February, 13 March 1960). Furthermore, at the end of 1959 there were 40 million pounds of shrimp, 20 percent of annual domestic consumption, in storage as surplus (*MR* 13 March 1960).

Imports and Unions

In 1947 Chester A. Delacruz of Biloxi, Mississippi, represented the Gulf-South Atlantic Oyster Canners Association, the National Shrimp Canners Association, and the crab-canning industry to warn the U.S. House of Representatives Ways and Means Committee against postwar imports of processed seafood from Japan, which he feared would be part of that country's national reconstruction program. He pointed out that Russia was preparing to export processed crab from waters fished by Japan before the World War II. In addition to requesting a tariff on canned oysters and crab, Delacruz introduced a statistical table from the Fish and Wildlife Service to document the growth of Mexican shrimp imports from half a million pounds in 1936 to more than twelve million pounds in 1946. Suggesting that cheaper production in Mexico would double in output the next year, he requested an import quota on Mexican shrimp (U.S. Congress 1947, 1726–27).

In 1954, after imports of shrimp caused a collapse of the high prices of 1953, Representative Willis of Louisiana—where shrimp boats were idled by low prices—enlisted the support of gulf coast congressmen for legislation to impose a 35 percent duty on imported shrimp (*MR* 6 August 1954). The directors of the National Shrimp Congress called for legislation in 1959 to curb the importation of shrimp. They suggested that domestic supply and record imports might create an oversupply. The large supply of domestic and imported shrimp had caused a drop in price of twenty to thirty cents per pound of shrimp. Wholesalers and distributors were waiting for even lower prices as the volume of imports increased. A U.S. representative from Florida introduced legislation to impose a 35 percent duty and import quotas on foreign shrimp. Twenty-seven other congressmen had submitted similar bills (*MR* 12 August 1959, 13 March, 12 August 1960).

The low price of Alabama shrimp in 1959 was attributed to imports. Shrimpers reported catching a lot of shrimp, but the price of ten to sixty cents per pound at dockside made it difficult to make any money. Small operators said they had been forced out of business and large operators said the shortage of storage facilities limited their incomes. By 1960 shrimp imports were considered a problem. George Allen, chief of the Seafood Division of the Alabama Department of Conservation, said shrimp from forty nations had flooded inland markets and cut off demand for gulf shrimp (*MR* 20 January 1960).

In 1960 Andrew W. Anderson, assistant director of the Bureau of Commercial Fisheries, Department of the Interior, argued before the House of Representatives Subcommittee on Fisheries and Wildlife Conservation against legislation to exempt fishermen from antitrust legislation in the same way farmers were exempted so they could form cooperative associations without being found in violation of such laws, a position shared by processors. When a representative suggested that imports depressed domestic prices for seafood, Anderson agreed but said that his agency helped fishermen by trying to move gluts of domestic seafood via the school lunch program and talking to restaurant owners, episodic solutions to perceived short-term crises rather than long-term relief of a systemic problem (U.S. Congress 1960, 75–90).

One of the reasons there was no tariff was an agreement with Iceland that allowed its seafood into the United States tariff-free as part of another agreement under which the United States could keep a military base in that nation. Another representative pointed out that the Development Loan Fund had made uncollectable loans to promote shrimping in Pakistan, whose imports helped to depress the prices of domestic shrimp (ibid., 84–86).

In 1961, Representative L. F. Sikes of Florida again introduced a bill to impose a duty on shrimp. There was testimony that the importation of frozen shrimp depressed domestic prices (U.S. Congress 1961, 11–51). In spite of many initiatives since, no such legislation has passed.

More recently, techniques for farming shrimp have been developed in many countries. From 1975 to 1985, shrimp cultivation was Ecuador's second most important industry. Ninety-five percent of its product was exported to the United States to generate $225 million in foreign exchange and 150,000 jobs (Meltzoff and LiPuma 1986; Barnes 1986). Research and development in Taiwan has enabled Asian shrimp farmers to increase greatly their production. While Japan provides a market for much Asian pond-grown shrimp, half of all Chinese shrimp is exported to the United States. Because of the bountiful supply of shrimp, many argue that it will never again be a luxury food but has become a common item of consumption. Research in Indonesia, India, and Thailand has increased production of pond-raised shrimp in those countries. Vietnam and the Philippines also contribute to shrimp production. In such countries a sophisticated processing industry has developed along with industries to supply the shrimp farmers with the ingredients for their enterprises (Handley 1989a, 1989b; J. Moore 1989). The pressure from imports can only grow in the future.

Increasing shrimp imports had two consequences. On the one hand, they tended to suppress the price of domestic shrimp. On the other hand, imports freed packers from dependence on local shrimpers. At the same time, shrimpers were going into debt for larger boats to bring in the increased catches from farther out in the gulf. They became more dependent on processors for their livelihoods. Shrimpers had to catch and bring in shrimp to sell to processors who had many alternate foreign sources of supply. Shrimpers had to make their trip expenses and enough to pay interest and principal on their loans, as well as make an income for their families. Since they were operating near the edge, and since packers were not dependent on them for raw material, shrimpers lost bargaining power and finally the unions collapsed. Fishermen's organizations surfaced from time to time afterwards, not to negotiate with packers but to lobby for or against various government programs.

Both the inside and gulf fleets were idled in 1951 when Bayou la Batre's two canneries, McPhillips Packing and Graham Seafood, closed and refused to pay the thirty-five dollars per barrel the AFL-affiliated Mobile Bay Sea Food Union asked for small canning shrimp. Packers could buy Louisiana shrimp for less (MR 25 August 1951). The stoppage lasted only four days until the parties agreed to prices of thirty to fifty dollars per barrel, depending on size (MR 29 August 1951). In Texas, the Rio Grande Shrimpers Association, an independent union that cooperated with the Texas Fishermen's Association, proposed stopping shrimping for two weeks to allow sufficient frozen shrimp to be consumed so that better prices would prevail. William Estes, president of the union, said the stoppage would not be a strike but an effort to let shrimp grow larger while smaller ones were used on the market. He argued that market prices were so low that shrimpers' income had been cut as much as 21 to 30 percent (MR 6 September 1951).

There were disputes over prices in Mississippi from mid-April to early May, from mid-August to early September, and in late September. All Alabama shrimping ceased from mid- to late August because of a price dispute. Texas shrimpers stopped operations for three weeks in September. There were disputes between union and nonunion fishermen in Pascagoula (Bureau of Fisheries Report 1951, 183). There was a stoppage of about four weeks in Mississippi over shrimp prices (Bureau of Fisheries *Report* 1952, 187). In 1954 there were no price disputes (Bureau of Fisheries *Report* 1954, 193).

Legal interpretations began to define fishermen as firms, forbidden under antitrust legislation from acting together to set the prices for their goods. Rather than seeing them as workers who worked for packers or processors, judges began to rule that when fishermen organized into unions they were colluding to fix prices rather than bargaining for wages. As early as 1946 a federal grand jury had indicted a fisherman's union, the CIO-affiliated International Fishermen and Allied Workers of America Local 36 of Los Angeles, with conspiracy to fix prices of fresh fish. William C. Dixon of the antitrust division of the Department of Justice said it was the first time a price-fixing charge had been brought against a union. The indictment declared the union members were not laborers but independent businessmen who sold their catches independently. Their attempts to negotiate prices with processors and dealers were interpreted as a conspiracy to prevent buyers from receiving their normal supply of fresh fish (*MR* 4 August 1946). In 1955 the government charged that the Gulf Coast Shrimpers' and Oystermen's Association violated the Sherman Antitrust Act by fixing prices for seafood in Mississippi.

Bill Simpson of Simpson's Canning Company testified for the defense that a fisherman or a packer would open negotiating meetings by stating why he felt the price should be changed. Then the two sides would discuss the matter until they agreed on a price. Leon Strong, secretary of the union, testified that the membership of the association agreed on the prices, which were then submitted to the packers. At the request of packers, the association established a price committee in 1952 to negotiate with them. Strong stated that "if the packers didn't like the price, they would shut down and throw everyone out of work until the association got together again and set a price they [the packers] would agree on" (*MR* 26 January 1955).

The judge found the union in violation of antitrust legislation, fined the association twenty-five hundred dollars, and sentenced three of its officers to nine-month jail sentences. He said the case was vital to the shrimping industry, to the packers, and to the fishermen. When the defense asked for a new trial, he argued that there was no employee-employer relationship between fishermen and packers but a joint-venture relationship (*MR* 28 June 1955).

The WPA's 1941 description of Alabama said: "In the past, abundant, cheap labor and tax exemption were the major attractions offered to outside capital. . . . Plentiful, unskilled labor . . . has done much to sustain a low wage scale. In an unending circle, there is an annual migration from farm to mill and from mill to farm, especially in the textile industry" (Federal Writers Project 1941, 72–73).

In the 1975 revision of the work, this passage is deleted along with a discussion of the violation of the civil rights of labor organizers and sympathizers during the 1930s. Instead, there is a discussion of Alabama's "right to work" law, passed in 1963, which has had the effect of inhibiting union formation: "Labor-management conditions are exceptionally good in Alabama. Continuously fewer man hours are lost due to work stoppages than in most other states. There have been no really serious Labor-Management conflicts in a number of years" (Walker 1975, 65–66).

The union movement in Alabama was rendered ineffective, and once again "abundant cheap labor" was advertised as an advantage to industry in the state. By 1981, although there were various organizations of fishermen, shrimpers, and oyster catchers, because many of them were centered on and devoted to specific issues and had episodic leadership and transient membership it was possible for a Sea Grant economist, William Hosking, to observe that "never before have these shrimpers really managed to get together on anything" (*MR* 7 September 1981). Even the memory of the unions had disappeared.

Hard Times

The increasing size of shrimp boats and their catches and the conversion from an inshore to an offshore fleet occasioned a short-lived optimism. Threats to fishermen came from several directions. The remaining oyster resources were increasingly unavailable because of more frequent and spreading pollution. The costs of fuel, interest, and operating expenses for shrimpers increased greatly at the same time that imports of foreign shrimp were flooding the domestic market. Sport fishermen and the allied tourist industry continued to pursue their interests, which often conflicted with those of fishermen and exacerbated their other problems (U.S. Congress 1956, 94–97).

The early 1970s were a period of rapid growth for Gulf Shores on the eastern side of Mobile Bay. Sport fishing has increased because the area is attractive to retirees and tourists. The town passed an ordinance to forbid trawling or other net fishing in Little Lagoon, inside the municipal limits. Shrimpers of the east shore did not like the law. They had sought and received an attorney general's opinion that it was invalid since the state regulates fishing in state waters. When the municipality was planning its shrimp-boat parade as part of its annual shrimp festival, shrimpers refused to cooperate unless the ordinance was revoked (*MR* 14 September 1975). John Ray Nelson, owner of Bon Secour Seafoods with its own fleets of boats and trucks, said: "Why this is one of the oldest professions. I could quote you a passage from Matthew about the Sea of Galilee and some men that were called to become apostles. There wasn't a sports fisherman in the whole bunch" (ibid.). The shrimp boats did not participate in the festivities (*MR* 2 October 1975).

The year 1974 was bad for shrimpers. Seven or eight processors went out of business in Bayou la Batre and sixty or seventy fishing boats of the three-hundred-vessel Bayou la Batre fleet were sold. Though shrimp were plentiful, it did not pay to catch them because diesel fuel was expensive and the price of shrimp was low (*MR* 25 May 1975).

Boat owners supplied fuel, nets, supplies, and half the cost of ice and received 60 percent of the price of the catch. The crew paid for food and half of the ice and received 40 percent of the price of the catch. The shrimp boats cost between $100,000 and $200,000. If the boats were mortgaged, an owner would lose a great deal if he could not pay operating expenses. The crew would lose their incomes as well (ibid.).

In 1975 processors and shrimpers formed the South Baldwin Seafood Association. Members met with legislators and local office holders to discuss problems of increasing costs of nets, cables, fuel, and labor; poor shrimp prices; and imports. They suggested seeking government subsidies for fuel, relief from sales tax on their gear, and import duty on shrimp. Arguing that sportsmen's catches of undersize shrimp with sixteen-foot trawls reduced the commercial catches, they discussed the conflict and the laws that allowed it. The association elected four seafood executives, Harold King, Donald Nelson, Max Lawrenz, and Thomas Lee Mills, to represent its interests in Washington and Montgomery (*MR* 2 January 1975). The group's members petitioned their congressmen for assistance to control imports, to fund federal programs for high-school-level education to meet industry labor needs, to enact subsidies for the industry, and to establish federally funded low-interest loans (*MR* 23 January 1975).

Costs of production rose by 150 percent in the course of a year and the price of seafood remained stable or declined. Processing plants were idle. The majority of newcomers to the industry were leaving. The news from Bayou la Batre in the winter of 1975 was that "the boats don't go out from here much anymore. Fishermen sit idle or else occupy themselves with odd jobs on stymied vessels. The seafood capital of Alabama is in trouble" (*MR* 16 February 1975).

One of Alabama's United States representatives, Jack Edwards, requested that President Gerald Ford include fishermen in a program to provide fuel rebates to food producers to compensate for import tariffs and other measures designed to conserve fuel. The Office of Management and Budget also worked with the Small Business Administration to increase funds for nonphysical disaster loans (*MR* 19 February 1975).

Different people understood the situation in different ways. Shrimpers thought about how the high fuel prices and interest rates affected them and others like them. The effects would depend on the total expenses of operating the boat, including debt payments, fuel costs, and crew costs. Donald Nelson, a Baldwin County shrimper, suggested that a person who was in debt for his boat, engine repairs, and gear would have a hard time paying it off. People who had been shrimping for a long time were not hurt as much as those who had entered recently (*MR* 27 February 1975). He continued:

> It has reached the point with a lot of shrimpers that it's not doing them a favor to lend them money. A lot of people in the industry are caught up in this situation.
>
> The person who has been in shrimping for a long time isn't hurt as bad as the recent investors. We are in the position of just having to wait this out. And that's exactly what I plan to do. If there's a shrimping industry after this year, I'll be a part of it. (ibid.)

This view suggests that those who would survive bad times would be those with the least debt load, those who could operate on their own terms without having to make payments to a lender. Others saw the situation in terms not so closely tied to the economies of boats and households.

Some suggested that the influx of boats financed by doctors and lawyers as tax write-offs had added to the fishing pressure on shrimp. When Mexico closed its territorial waters to shrimpers, there was less area to fish and more boats, including the "tax boats." In 1980, Charles Lyles, executive secretary and director of the Gulf States Marine Fisheries Commission, made a statement characteristic of this viewpoint: "For American shrimpers, we're entering a period where the most capable will stay in business and make money, while those who are less capable, or don't have the capital to spend on $1.05 per gallon diesel fuel, are just going to be forced out of the business" (*MR* 9 January 1980). Thomas Bush, chairman of the Louisiana Shrimp Association, echoed this view when he said "the nature of shrimpers is that they are very free enterprise–oriented. While they may not like the present situation, they're going to be more inclined to battle it out in the water and let the most skilled fisherman win than try to exclude others through laws . . ." (ibid.).

The first view is that potential success depends on a shrimper's debt situation. People estimate their assets and needs and try to use their resources to produce an annual income to meet their needs. Their needs include a good income by local standards, the ability to replenish their holdings such as boats, nets, and gear, to invest in future production, and to repay debts (Durrenberger 1984). The comment by the shrimper shows this point of view because it takes into account the difference in needs between those with debts to pay off and those who are debt free.

The second view—that success depends on skill—does not rest on the same understanding of the economy of fishing. It takes no account of the assets and needs of the fisherman but suggests only that the skillful or efficient survive while the less skillful fail.

There is a close parallel to these two orientations in discussions of agricultural policy. Farmers understand that their ability to withstand hard times depends on the financial organization of their farms, whether they own their land and equipment outright or are in debt for them. Agricultural economists, on the other hand, argue that the "efficient" or "skilled" farmers survive hard times while the "inefficient" or "unskilled" farmers are weeded out. This view was put to a severe test in the farm crisis of the 1980s when those farmers whom the agricultural economists had singled out as efficient and progressive, heavily in debt for farm expansion programs, were the most vulnerable and began losing their farms (Durrenberger 1986).

In 1980, shrimpers faced the same problems that had troubled them in 1975, and worse. The price of fuel was so high that many captains stayed in port or made only short trips. Shrimpers adjusted to high fuel prices and began going out again only to find more boats on the water. Interest rates were 18.25 percent. Because of high costs of fuel and operation, shrimp prices were up and restaurants had begun to cut back their purchases. American shrimpers could not compete with the prices of imported shrimp. Only 40 percent of shrimp sold in the United States were from domestic shrimpers (*MR* 19 March 1980).

Bayou la Batre shrimpers formed an organization called the Bay Shrimpers Association and elected Grady Seaman its president. They expressed to the director of the Conservation Department, Dick Forester, their objections about the sixteen-foot-trawl regulations that allowed bait boats to shrimp whenever they wanted to. The shrimpers claimed the sixteen-foot trawlers disturbed the immature shrimp and reduced the catch of larger boats. They argued that if smaller boats were allowed to shrimp, everyone should be able to do so and that penalties for out-of-season shrimping were too mild to be effective deterrents (ibid.). One shrimper suggested:

> We need to band together nationwide, much like the farmers did. When they started voicing their opposition to what was going on with their particular situation the government stepped in and helped them out. Now those same farmers who drove their rigs to Washington are able to get federal money at something like three percent interest.
>
> If we get together with them and the truckers and voice our opinions as a group we might be able to get something done. (ibid.)

In the spring of 1980 about half of the approximately three hundred shrimp boats of Bayou la Batre were idle. Shrimpers argued that they could not afford to operate their boats at the high cost of fuel and low price of shrimp. Processors and dealers had little shrimp to process. The owner of a forty-foot boat said, "The catch doesn't pay for the fuel" (MR 23 March 1980). Victor Gonzales of the Star Fish and Oyster Company said: "Years ago a shrimper was from 30 to 40 feet long and had a 100 to 150 horsepower engine. In the last five years everybody has tried to outdo everybody else. These new boats have great big GM engines that burn 30 to 40 gallons of fuel an hour. At today's prices, that's about $50 an hour" (ibid.).

Some fishermen supplemented their incomes by catching oysters, and some of them were hired by or contracted with the Conservation Department to reseed damaged oyster beds. A Bayou la Batre fisherman and marina operator said "this helps the fishermen out quite a bit in terms of being able to put some money in their pocket," but, he added, some oyster catchers would take the newly planted oysters. One problem, he argued, was that the department had too few people to enforce the laws and "too many chiefs and not enough Indians." He concluded that the problems were that there were too many boats on the water, interest rates were too high, and the Department of Conservation did not enforce the rules sufficiently (MR 23 April 1980).

Because the oysters were destroyed by the floods and hurricanes, they provided no alternative to shrimpers. The Bay Shrimpers Association of Bayou la Batre met with the city council and asked council members to request the governor, Fob James, to help them get federal aid. The shrimpers said Texas fishermen were getting as much as fifty thousand dollars per boat to help them until the shellfish situation improved (MR 26 April 1980). One fisherman told the council: "For the last three years, I've worked real hard and put everything I made in a boat and it looks like if we don't get any help, I'm going to lose that boat" (*MR* 26 April 1980).

United States Senators Howell Heflin and Donald Steward and Representative Jack Edwards asked the Small Business Administration to provide low-interest loans to shrimpers under its Economic Injury Program (*MR* 7 May 1980). By the end of May the director of the SBA offered loans at 7.375 percent under the provisions of the Hurricane Frederic loan declaration. He said this was the only money he could make available under the Economic Injury Program (*MR* 28 May 1980). He said, "If we had to go through the process of working up an entirely new declaration it would be far too time consuming to do anybody any good" (ibid.).

Under the hurricane program, it would take about a month to process applications and provide loans to fishermen. The Bay Shrimpers Association president, Grady Seaman, was disappointed. He said association members were seeking assistance similar to that the Texas Small Business Administration provided Texas shrimpers who got federal aid after flooding destroyed their 1979 shrimp crop. He thought similar conditions and the high fuel prices and interest rates were analogous conditions as they made it difficult for Alabama shrimpers to make a living. It was not just a consequence of the hurricane, the shrimpers insisted. The Small Business Administration agent said his office did not have funds to do what the shrimpers wanted and that the program he outlined was all he had to offer (ibid.).

In October, to protest bad conditions, nine shrimp trawlers from Georgia and Florida circled for twenty minutes under a drawbridge in Georgia to back up traffic on U.S. Route 17. They said that Mexico's closing its waters had created a glut of shrimpers on the east coast of the United States and caused a decline in harvests when equipment and fuel costs were increasing to drive fishermen out of business (*MR* 6 October 1980).

The wives of Bayou la Batre shrimpers joined with wives of shrimpers from Georgia, Florida, Mississippi, Louisiana, and Texas in an organization named Save Our Shrimpers. They sent telegrams to President Carter and the Secretary of Commerce to ask for assistance and made it clear that their support in the upcoming election was contingent on the politicians' response. The women requested a dollar-a-pound price support system, a 20 percent import duty, and a monthly quota on foreign shrimp. One of the group's members, Sharon Auld, said the shrimp catch for 1980 was down 35 percent and the price was down 27 percent; she noted that owners of 57 of 418 shrimp boats

financed through the National Marine Fisheries Service were behind
in their mortgage payments (*MR* 26 October 1980). About 90 percent
of vessels in Bayou la Batre were purchased with Marine Fisheries
Service guaranteed mortgages (*MR* 7 September 1981). Speculating
that 200 boats would be repossessed in the next two years, Auld
observed that the Small Business Administration loan program was
inadequate, and added: "We've muddled through before, but this year
we're muddling through the good season. What are we going to do
when the bad season comes?" (*MR* 26 October 1980).

Auld said the women were organizing because the men were busy
fishing (ibid.). About fifty of the women met to reject a 12.2 million
dollar loan and grant program announced by the Department of Commerce. They argued that they could not borrow their way out of debt,
that they needed the subsidy and tariff program (*MR* 30 October 1980).
The group members repeated their ideas to Senator Heflin at a meeting
in Bayou la Batre (*MR* 5 November 1980). They took their campaign
to Gulf Shores to enlist the women there and ask them to assume their
share of the costs of maintaining a lobbyist in Washington D.C. (*MR*
7 November 1980).

Other vehicles for developing publicity for the industry included
the local ceremonies and celebrations centered around seafood. When
the Protestant clergymen of Bon Secour distinguished between "civic
celebration" and "religious service," they suggested that in addition
to whatever religious or ritual connotations blessings of the fleets may
have had, the more elaborate of them were also civic celebrations. The
function of publicizing the seafood industry, its boats and fishermen,
became increasingly important and elaborated as processing plants
relied more on shrimp, fishing boats became larger, debt grew more
burdensome, and the industry turned more to the government for
regulation, research and development, and relief.

Echoing the contrast Carmer (1949) had noticed between Catholic
Biloxi and Protestant Pasagoula, Bon Secour's Episcopalian minister,
Rev. J. D. C. Wilson of St. Peter's Church, said: "I hope the day will
not come when we in Bon Secour subordinate God to pleasures. . . .
[The blessing of the fleet] is no occasion for hilarity, but . . . it is a
sober recognition of the fact that nothing we do can prosper without
God's blessing" (*MR* 10 August 1953).

Not all communities followed his stern counsel. In 1956 Biloxi
sponsored a Shrimp Festival that lasted two days and "paid tribute
to the major industry along Mississippi's Gulf Coast" (*MR* 5 August
1956). The fleet blessing was "the only solemnity in the festival"
(ibid.). Thousands attended. There was a Shrimp Queen; a parade

of beauty contestants; a reception for guests, dignitaries, and newspaper reporters; and a parade of boats (ibid.). The importance and popularity of gulf shrimp were emphasized by all phases of the program (ibid.). Pascagoula joined the cities that blessed their fleets in 1956 (*MR* 12 August 1956). When the Dauphin Island Chamber of Commerce sponsored a blessing of a fleet of twelve commercial and ten pleasure boats in 1958, two thousand celebrants attended (*MR* 18 August 1958). Politicians such as legislators, governors, and lieutenant governors began to attend the celebrations (*MR* 7 August 1961, 4 August 1977). About five thousand people heard George Wallace promise to do "everything possible to put the fishing industry back on its feet" in 1962 at the Bayou la Batre fleet blessing (*MR* 6 August 1962). George Wallace was again among the twenty-five thousand people who attended in 1977 (*MR* 1 August 1977).

Such celebrations functioned as adjuncts to more direct lobbying efforts such as seafood dinners (*MR* 2 September 1961) to bring the seafood industry and its plights to the attention of politicians, policy makers, and the public.

With bumper crops from all of the gulf states, in 1981 there were too many rather than too few shrimp. Because the market was flooded, prices declined, and shrimpers had to work even harder to catch more shrimp to make less money (*MR* 16 August 1981).

Alabama fishermen suffered another economic setback the same year. Until then most fishermen had fit the definition of seafarers, people who worked on sea-going vessels. As seafarers, they were eligible to use the Public Health Service clinic in Mobile for their health care needs. In 1981 Reagan budget cuts closed the PHS hospitals and clinics. The Alabama Fisherman's Association with a membership of three hundred in 1981 was able to get group insurance for its members at better than individual rates (*MR* September 7 1981). This plan was comparatively costly and did not last long. Afterwards, fishermen were left with no source of health insurance.

Oysters

Since 1950, shrimp have been more important to Alabama's maritime economy than oysters, but oystering has not disappeared. It has remained a significant aspect of the seafood industry even though the large canneries have disappeared and the emphasis has shifted to frozen shrimp.

One consequence of the development of industrial shrimping was the increasing diversification of fishing. Instead of catching oysters part of the year and shrimping in the bay part of the year, shrimpers were increasingly turning to the gulf with large vessels, heavy investments in gear, and large debts. Some fishermen concentrated on catching oysters, and shrimpers turned to this resource when shrimping was unrewarding. Catch statistics show that their livelihood became more precarious as oysters remained unreliable. Whatever the consequences of dredging shell and pollution, the oyster catch has been quite variable since records were first kept (Swingle and Hughes 1976). It was because of this variability that the processors of the earlier period had begun to explore shrimp as a product.

This precariousness contributed to the politics of the fishery in the modern period in which shrimping predominates. When oyster catching was bad and oystermen's livelihoods were threatened by floods, storms, pollution, predators, water salinity, or other factors, they looked increasingly to the government for relief. Sometimes they demanded programs of shell planting or transplanting seed oysters from one area to another, a course they pursued as much for the income it provided as for its management and conservation potential.

The agencies of regulation were debated as the authority and expertise of the Conservation Department and its Seafood Division were challenged by a seafood commission appointed by the governor. There continued to be overlapping authorities among federal, state, and local agencies; various health departments charged with guaranteeing the quality of oysters impinged on one another, and the authority of the Seafood Division to regulate fisheries overlapped that of the health boards.

The legislature was still an important forum for policy debates as various factions fought for or against effective control of industrial and municipal pollution in the legislature. The courts were also an important arena as groups attempted to get what they wanted through judicial decisions. These decisions had to be based on scientific evidence, so technical data was at a premium for any disputant.

One Marine Resources Division regulator told me that his division had tried every imaginable program and combination of programs for oyster management by planting shells and transplanting seed oysters, and the history of the division bears this out. Not everyone has the detailed understanding of historical patterns evident in the *Alabama Marine Resources Bulletin*, published by the Marine Resources Division of the Department of Conservation and Natural Resources. If the people of this division must hear familiar arguments and disputes year after year, it cannot help them that some do not share their experience or memory of the past. In a 1987 discussion of the effects of shell dredging on oystering in south Alabama, one official said there was no evidence that there had ever been producing oyster reefs in Baldwin County, in Bon Secour, where his own agency had invested considerable funds and energy in oyster management for years.

Perhaps this was a rhetorical representation intended to manipulate media treatment of a political issue. Even in such a context, officials do not gain credibility if they indulge in obvious misrepresentations such as attributing political and economic power to the most powerless people in the fishing industry, oyster shuckers, and suggesting that policy is made at their behest, as did a past director of the division, George Allen (MR 30 May 1965).

Things have not always been as they are now. Bon Secour once supported a thriving oyster fishery. It no longer does. Regulation of water quality used to be a legislative responsibility. It no longer is, as the next chapter will show. While the explosive development of industrial shrimping resulted in economic successes and woes for shrimpers, other events ashore were beginning to affect the seafood industry. No longer were Alabama's waters free of pollution, making them ideal oyster-rearing grounds. The following chronology lists some of the events that affected the oyster industry during this period:

1943   Pollution is observed as a problem
1945   Sportsmen organize
1946   Dredging for shell starts
1949   Ineffective pollution law dominated by industry
1952   One-third of oyster areas closed
1956   Court stops dredging for one year
1957   With oyster-catcher support, revenues from dredging used for planting
1959   Pollution closes oystering between Cedar Point and Dauphin Island
1960   Flood damages oysters
1961   Flood damages oysters; pollution closes oystering between Cedar Point and Dauphin Island
1962   Thirty thousand barrels seed oysters planted in Bon Secour Bay
1963   Flood damages oysters; five thousand barrels seed oysters planted in Bon Secour Bay
1964   Flood damages oysters; pollution closes oystering between Cedar Point and Dauphin Island; fifteen thousand barrels seed oysters planted in Bon Secour Bay
1965   New shell dredge *Mallard* begins operations

1967	Low-oxygen die-off of oysters in Bon Secour Bay and Upper Mobile Bay
1971	Low-oxygen die-offs
1972	Health Department closes Mobile Bay; last private oyster beds in Bon Secour Bay
1974	Pollution closes Bon Secour Bay
1982	Dredging for shell ceases

Pollution and the Decline of the Oyster Industry

The Alabama Department of Game and Fish was organized in 1907 after ten years of organized support from sportsmen and conservation interests for modern legislation to protect fish, birds, and game. A 1912 article in the *Mobile Register* lauding the formation of the department said:

> The most vital question that is now absorbing the minds of the patriotic citizens of the American continent is that of the conservation of our natural resources. Perhaps no nation has ever been so abundantly endowed with all the necessities of mines and forests as have been the people of the United States; and also it is probable that the citizens of no nation have ever been so careless with their treasures and wasted their birthright, as have our people.
>
> The next generation will be made up of the little men and women now in the public schools of our state, and upon them devolve the real solution of the vital problem of saving from annihilation the remnant of the superb treasures with which the people of pristine times were so bountifully blessed. (*MR* 1 September 1912)

By 1922 the commissioner, I. T. Quinn, had organized his consultations with sportsmen. Representatives of local associations, such as the Mobile-Baldwin Game and Game Fish Protective Association, which had several hundred members, and the Alabama Fishermen and Hunters' Association, with 2,300 members, met with the commissioner to make suggestions about conservation (*MR* 3, 11 September 1922)

In 1943 Mobilians were warned against eating dead fish they might find. The Alabama Wildlife Federation identified industrial pollution as the cause of a fish kill, though it could not identify the source (*MR* 8 September 1943). The director of conservation said it was unfortunate that neither his department nor the health department had the authority to prevent industrial pollution (*MR* 9 September 1943). By the end of 1945, sportsmen were beginning to organize for environmental protection. The president of the Mobile County Sportsmen's Association, Albert J. Tully, argued for legislation to combat the high levels of pollution of rivers and streams around Mobile (*MR* 9 December 1945).

A law to control water pollution passed the Alabama legislature in 1949. It featured a "grandfather" clause to exempt existing offenders and established a fifteen-man Water Improvement Commission that was dominated by the polluting industries themselves. Its powers were limited to actions deemed to be economically feasible, scientifically possible, and practical. This law made very little difference because it simply put the offending industries in control of their own pollution. They deemed very little to be feasible, possible, or practical (*MR* 30 May 1965).

In a strongly worded article, Bill Ziebach used his "Out of Doors" column in the *Mobile Register* to suggest that Mobile was no longer a village, that industry had discovered that Mobile was a favorable locale for manufacturing, and that with industries would come a burden of impurities flowing into the bay and Mississippi Sound. Ziebach wrote, "There is one method and one method only which will prevent the eventual complete destruction of sea life in the waters of Mobile bay and its tributaries. That is a law—a law of local application, if not deemed expedient for other Alabama areas—with strength to deter unscrupulous persons from loosing harmful elements into public waters" (*MR* 18 June 1950).

A third of the oyster beds were closed in 1952 because of sewage pollution from Mobile, Pritchard, and Chickasaw (*MR* 8 March 1952). The northern reaches of Mobile Bay, Bayou Coden, parts of Portersville Bay, Bayou la Batre, and the Bon Secour River were permanently closed. The Mobile Bay Sea Food Union sent a delegation to Montgomery to protest the health department ban. Claiming that 90 percent of oysters came from the closed areas, this group retained its own biologist to test the water between Cedar Point and Dauphin Island (*MR* 9 March 1952). The state health officer told the delegation the waters would be tested daily and the conservation director promised to open the oyster reefs as soon as possible. They agreed that the correction of the problem in the long run would have to come from the polluting municipalities (*MR* 11 March 1952). The conservation and health departments devised a plan whereby oystermen would work in the winter and spring in those areas likely to be closed by pollution and then shift to uncontaminated reefs (*MR* 28 August 1952).

Also in 1952 the Mobile County Wildlife and Conservation Association developed plans for the prevention of future pollution. The group resolved to fight for effective antipollution legislation, to investigate current laws, to send a delegation to Montgomery to testify at state board meetings, to begin an educational program, and to study pollution around chemical plants and new industrial sites near Mobile. Association members affirmed they were not against industry but that "we cannot afford to see our rivers, streams and bays polluted as has been done in other areas." While they devoted most of their attention to chemical plants, they commended the Bayou la Batre Chamber of Commerce for its fight against sewage pollution in Mobile Bay (*MR* 11 September 1952). The Alabama Wildlife Federation and the Water Improvement Advisory Commission sponsored legislation in 1953 to increase the commission's authority to fight pollution of streams (*MR* 7, 26 August 1953).

The release of paper-mill effluent caused a massive fish kill in 1958 (*MR* 31 August 1958). In April of 1965 residents of Bayou Casotte, near Pascagoula, were concerned about a fish kill. A marine biologist attributed the cause to oxygen deficiency caused by waste materials dumped into the bayou from industrial and municipal sources. He said such fish kills had been regular annual occurrences since 1959 (*MR* 22 April 1965). Meanwhile, in Mobile Bay, a similar fish kill was labeled a "mystery" and biologists were checking for parasites (*MR* 20 April 1965).

While the Seafood Division's George Allen reported to the conservation commission that pollution was the major problem of the seafood industry in Alabama (*MR* 30 May 1965), one of the most hotly debated issues in the Alabama legislature in 1965 was antipollution legislation sponsored by the Alabama Wildlife Federation (The Alabama Wildlife Federation Bill, House Bill 132, Senate Bill 25). Interests from the paper, chemical, and other industries opposed the bill and offered no compromise on the issues of representation on the Alabama Water Improvement Commission and the removal of a "grandfather clause" to protect existing industry from antipollution requirements. Recognizing its economic benefits, proponents of the bill were not anti-industry, but they cited the unregulated cutting of timber early in the century, which resulted in economic loss, soil erosion, and blight, as an example of the need for conservation. Only through scientific management and replanting did the industry revive and survive. An article by John Spaulding of the Alabama Wildlife Federation explained: "The same condition now exists with water. If we continue to permit pollution, without adequate laws to control it, our rivers and streams will reach a point where it would be impossible for sportsmen to enjoy them or for additional industry to be attracted to the area" (*MR* 23 May 1965).

Industry and the industry-dominated Water Improvement Commission sponsored an alternate bill (HB 198) designed to delay any cleaning of Alabama waters. Both bills were based on the 1949 bill (*MR* 30 May 1965).

The bill the conservationists backed provided for the formation of a new ten-member water commission composed of the state health director, conservation director, state geologist, and representatives of municipal government, agriculture, fisheries, wildlife conservation, and industry. Within six months any polluting industry would submit a plan to the commission, and the commission would then have six months to consider the plan. The industries would have five years to put their plans into effect (*MR* 14 July 1965).

Industry interests formulated an alternate bill in the Senate Health Committee. It met some of the objections of the Wildlife Federation by giving it an additional member of the water commission and eliminating the grandfather clause, but the federation refused to accept it as an alternative to its bill (*MR* 29 July 1965).

Paper, chemical, and other industry interests claimed the AWF bill would cripple industry and offered a number of amendments to make the bill acceptable to industry and to "let us Alabamans continue to earn enough money to enjoy hunting and fishing," as one representative phrased it (*MR* 14 July 1965). Several amendments were debated before the bill passed the House in July of 1965.

There were twenty-eight pollution fish kills in Alabama in 1968. Nineteen were on the Dog River and most were in and around Mobile Bay. Governor Brewer warned that he might seek legislation to change the composition of the Water Improvement Commission if it did not act to insure that Alabama antipollution laws were enforced. Conservationists called for immediate action. The state sued two chemical firms. A suit against Monsanto was dropped after it gave the Department of Conservation a $20,000 gift. Industrialists called for an intensive study and asked that the Water Improvement Commission be left in authority. The Federal Water Pollution Control Administration held a public hearing in Mobile, and pollution was a newsworthy topic in other parts of the country as well. Some Alabama industries and cities began installing pollution control equipment (*MR* 5 June 1969)

In 1969, Wilson Gaillard of the Mobile County Wildlife and Conservation Association recognized such attempts to improve the situation and observed that "the time has come when water pollution must be stopped. It is no longer merely a few fish which are endangered. It is the health of our entire population that we are concerned about and we intend to work until dangerous pollutions are stopped!" (*MR* 25 May 1969).

In February of 1969 Buddy Smith, the *Mobile Register's* outdoors reporter, wrote:

> Here we go again. The annual closing of Mobile Bay and adjacent waters to oystering came just about on schedule.
>
> The State Health Department closed these waters to oysters because of pollution coming down the flooding rivers. The pollution is apparently getting worse instead of better. This is the first time I can remember Bon Secour Bay, Oyster Bay and Weeks Bay being closed.
>
> The current situation emphasizes the need for increased pollution abatement action by the state, federal agencies or whatever agency can get the job done the quickest.
>
> A lot of people are hard hit economically when they cannot tong oysters at this time of the year. (*MR* 23 February 1969)

The health department reopened Weeks Bay, Bon Secour Bay, and Oyster Bay in mid-March (*MR* 18 March 1969).

In response to objections of the oyster industry to frequent closures of the oyster reefs by conservation and health authorities, state legislators from Mobile County introduced legislation to abolish the Seafood Division of the state conservation department and to establish a nine-member commission to regulate the seafood industry. State and county health officers and seafood biologists conferred with members of the Mobile delegation and informed them that the state health department used federal standards and must close oyster beds when rainwater-borne pollution increased the harmful bacteria in oyster waters. Dr. Myers, the state health officer, suggested that one solution would be to relocate oysters from polluted areas to clean waters, but he said there were few such areas in Alabama. He said: "I have doubts if an absolutely safe shellfish can be grown any longer according to accepted health standards" (*MR* 25 June 1969).

Again in 1975 Alabama Senator Bill Roberts and Representative Bob Glass met with fishermen, oystermen, and others to discuss legislation to form a seafood commission to be appointed by the governor. The commission would consist of oystermen, shrimpers, fishermen, and processors who would make seafood regulations and thus control their own industry (*MR* 7 February 1975).

Concern for the quality of shellfish was neither new nor local to Alabama. Fifty years before, in 1925, processors and the Public Health Service started a cooperative program of shellfish-producing states to insure "shellfish as a safe marine food of high quality and in which the public has confidence." They produced administrative and technical manuals, evaluated state programs, and published a list of certified interstate shellfish shippers. The industry was to cooperate by using shellfish from safe areas, maintaining sanitary plants, and keeping records of and identifying shellfish they shipped. State and local health departments were to inspect and approve shellfish-growing areas and shellfish-handling plants. Each certified shipper was assigned a number with which they identified every package of fresh or frozen shellfish. The Public Health Service appraised state programs to insure their integrity (*MR* 28 February 1965).

Such a program was costly to administer and operate, and state governments were to bear the expense. When the Alabama Health Department suggested discontinuing oyster inspection to save money, the *Mobile Register* editorialized that it was vital to Mobile and Baldwin County seafood interests and should be continued (*MR* 21 August 1933). The United States Health Service sympathized with the oyster industry of Alabama but reiterated that inspection was a state responsibility (*MR* 27 August 1933). The Alabama Health Department found sufficient funds to pay an inspector to check oysters according to the United States Health Department regulations (*MR* 29 September 1933).

The establishment of the Gulf Coast Shellfish Sanitation Research Center on Dauphin Island in 1963 indicated the continuing concern with the health consequences of shellfish. The center is a division of the U.S. Department of Health, Education, and Welfare's Public Health Service and has a staff of chemists, marine biologists, microbiologists, sanitary engineers, food sanitation specialists, and technicians to serve South Carolina, Georgia, Florida, Alabama, Mississippi, Louisiana, and Texas (*MR* 28 February 1965).

In 1967 Governor George Wallace established the Mobile County Seafood Advisory Commission composed of individuals active in the seafood industry. In a familiar pattern, the commission condemned the Conservation Department and the department defended its policies as scientific and its staff as competent. During the next year the commission reported that pollution was a major problem for the oyster and shrimp industries. The report stated: "The Seafood Division of the Conservation Department is totally ineffective in that its equipment is in a shocking state of disrepair rendering patrolling and policing of the bay areas an impossibility. This department is headed by an unqualified and incompetent person, William Anderson, who has no background or experience in the seafood business" (*MR* 23 February 1968).

The report recommended removing Claude Kelley, director of the Conservation Department, because he had shown indifference to the needs of the seafood and sport fishing interests in Mobile County and supported shell dredging in Mobile Bay. The commission also recommended removing William Anderson from office and an investigation of his division.

Anderson retorted that the Alabama Department of Health, not the Seafood Division, closed the oyster reefs because of pollution and that his division had fought for clean water. He also said that his staff was "the most competent group of biologists in the Gulf Coast region," and that every person in his division was thoroughly screened before being hired (ibid.).

In response to a number of problems, the Alabama Fisheries Association had hired a lobbyist to communicate its woes to the legislature. Mobile Bay was increasingly polluted. Oystering was forbidden in many areas. Mud and freshwater floods hurt oysters. In 1967 low-oxygen die-offs of oysters signaled the end of oystering in Bon Secour Bay and upper Mobile Bay. More low-oxygen-level die-offs of oysters occurred in 1971. There had been a history of closing areas for taking oysters and of violent protests of oyster catchers. Likewise there was a history of suits against shell dredging that had been going on in Mobile Bay since 1946; appeals for federal disaster aid in the wake of freshwater floods; and requests for money to plant shells (*Mobile Press* 15 January 1974).

In 1971 Miller Johnson of Coden, representing the Alabama Seafood Protective Association, protested the planting of seed oysters to the director of conservation and the governor. He said that several years earlier there had been abundant oysters on the White House Reef. Then, people were allowed to use the oysters as seed oysters and damaged the reef. He wrote: "Up to approximately 15 years ago, the oyster tongers could make a good living on any reef in Mobile Bay. Today, resulting in mismanagement through our Conservation Department, it is impossible to make a living on the Alabama oyster alone. Today, 75 per cent of the income of the people in this area is coming from out-of-state oysters" (*MR* 4 February 1971).

Shell Dredging and the Decline of Oysters

Starting in 1946 dredges mined the bottom of Mobile Bay for oyster shells to make lime for cement and other uses (*Mobile Press* 17 January 1974). Dredging ceased in 1982. In 1956 Southern Industries was dredging White House Reef with Conservation Department permission. A. J. Wegmann of the Mexican Gulf Fisheries of Alabama, which represented about two hundred oyster catchers, claimed the dredging would ruin the reef and petitioned Mobile circuit court judge Claude A. Grayson to enjoin Southern Industries from dredging. Oystermen testified that White House Reef was the source of all the spawn for other reefs. Oyster catchers testified they had found live oysters close to the dredging site.

James McPhillips, president of the canning company of the same name in Bayou la Batre, was the first defense witness. He testified that his company, like Bay Towing and Dredging, which was dredging, was a subsidiary of Southern Industries. He opined that the northern part of the reef was covered with silt and therefore dead (*MR* 19 September 1956). The court ordered cessation of dredging, but after about a year the operations resumed at a "safe distance" from White House Reef, according to a biologist from the Seafood Division, which stood to gain about fifty-seven thousand dollars from the contract at a royalty of ten cents per cubic yard of shell removed (*MR* 21 August 1957). Oyster catchers supported the program when the Seafood Division told them the revenue from dredging was to be used to promote oystering by planting oysters (*MR* 29 September 1957). This source of revenue remained the mainstay of the division's shell-planting and transplanting program (Swingle and Hughes 1976).

In May of 1965, Southern Industries Corporation's dredge *Mallard* began operation in the northern part of Mobile Bay. It was 200 feet long, 50 feet wide, and drew 6 feet of water. Designed to dredge shell from up to 55 feet below water at a rate of 1,000 cubic yards an hour, it could dredge, wash, process, and separate the shell by size. Its 18-inch dredge pump had a capacity of 27,500 gallons a minute and could recover an average of 400 tons of shell an hour (*MR* 24, 25 April 1965). It could load a 190-foot barge with 800 to 1,000 tons of shells in two hours. The mud and spoil stirred up by the dredging process settled within 100 yards of the operation, so keeping the dredge 400 yards from living reefs was deemed sufficient protection for the oysters. Conservation department officials checked the location of the dredge whenever it was moved to insure it did not damage reefs (*MR* 1 August 1965). Representatives of the owners said they created jobs and wasted nothing in the process (*Mobile Press* 17 January 1974).

The president of the company met with Ralph Richards of the Alabama Fisheries Association and with the Conservation Advisory Board, Gulf States Marine Fisheries Commission, and Department of Conservation Seafood Division to offer the firm's equipment and resources to a program to increase oyster production (*MR* 23 April 1965). Richards said, "With the shell industry, the fishing industry, the Fisheries Association and Department of Conservation working together, Mobile Bay can be a world leader in oyster production" (ibid.).

The Mobile Area Chamber of Commerce formed a seafood committee composed of three seafood processors, the chairman of Southern Industries Corporation, and the head of the State Docks to promote and expand the oyster industry of Alabama. Houston Foster of the State Docks was named chairman and said: "We feel that some concrete program should be established to save the oyster industry. We will work closely with the Seafoods Division of the State Department of Conservation to do whatever is necessary to restore the oyster industry in this area" (*MR* 20 May 1965).

R. H. Radcliff, chairman of Southern Industries, said the committee was a constructive approach to bring the oyster back to "its former production." He said that for the first time fishermen and representatives of the dredging industry could talk together and that Southern Industries would try to help the oyster industry (ibid.). To offset the effects of its dredging an area off Point Clear that was good for planting oysters but had no oysters on it, Southern Industries dredged twenty-one thousand barrels of oyster shells from under six feet of mud in northern Mobile Bay and placed five thousand barrels in Bon Secour Bay and the balance off Point Clear in Mobile Bay (*MR* 23, 30 May 1965).

The Save Our Bay Club was formed as environmentalists began an opposition movement (*MR* 19 February 1972). Radcliff began a series of projects costing more than $142,000 to determine whether dredging was harmful. Environmentalists cited declining seafood catches. The Environmental Protection Agency, United States Army Corps of Engineers, Marine Resources Division of the Alabama Department of Conservation, and Gulf South Research Institute all concluded that there were no harmful effects. Biologists even said the stirred-up silt might nourish rather than harm marine life. The environmentalists retained their own biologist who argued that dredging could be deleterious in such an ecologically delicate place as Mobile Bay with its problems of pollution, poor oxygenation, and insufficient water circulation (*Mobile Press* 17 January 1974).

Attorney General Bill Baxley sued in federal and state courts to halt dredging in July of 1972. He argued that the Corps of Engineers should file environmental impact statements before approving dredging. In Alabama court he alleged that the dredging was a public nuisance and violated water standards. Baxley criticized the state department of conservation, which had authorized the dredging, for failure to prevent dredging of live oysters. He contended the money the Seafood Division received prevented it from admitting or controlling the dredge's damage, and he argued, "The Radcliff Shell dredge is chiefly responsible for the devastation of Alabama's once famous oyster resources" (MR 21 July 1972). He argued that Radcliff paid $138,016 to the state, 95 percent of which went to the Seafood Division and 5 percent to the Land Management Division, and pointed out that 48 percent of the Seafood Division's budget came from shell dredging (ibid.).

Walter Tatum, a biologist of the Conservation Department's Seafood Division, charged that Baxley's information was inaccurate and said: "We feel that data we have does not support the allegations of the attorney general's office. Mr. Baxley did not check with us before bringing the suit" (MR 12 August 1972). He said dredges had not strayed onto live reefs "in recent years" and had not caused any serious pollution problems (ibid.).

Baxley answered that "statements recently made by two employees of the Seafood Division of the Department of Conservation to the effect that no live oysters are being killed by oyster shell dredging operations in Mobile Bay constitute an out-and-out lie" and were an attempt to perpetrate a fraud (MR 12 September 1972). He alleged shell dredges deliberately and willfully dredged live oyster reefs and destroyed marketable oysters (ibid.).

Each side paraded biologists as expert witnesses to its conclusions (ibid.). The Corps of Engineers held a public hearing on whether to renew the dredging permit, and the Baldwin County Circuit judge refused to enjoin Radcliff. The Radcliff permit was to expire in January, and the complaint was based on the Corps's issuance of the permit without a proper environmental impact statement. The case was continued beyond the time of the permit and was therefore moot. The state court declined to enjoin against dredging (MR 6 October 1972).

There was considerable bitterness, and environmentalists accused Bill Anderson of the Conservation Department of manipulating figures (*Mobile Press* 17 January 1974). Attorney General Baxley maintained that experts had said the dredge was not monitored as it was supposed to be. There was no legal recourse as long as Radcliff and the Department of Conservation agreed to their contract that provided between $200,000 and $580,000 to the budget of the Marine Resources Division (ibid.). A *Mobile Press* article concluded: "Does dredging harm the bay? The answer depends on whom you ask" (ibid.).

In 1987 the one remaining reef available to oyster catchers, Cedar Reef by Dauphin Island Bridge, was once again closed because of pollution. Biologists at the Alabama Department of Conservation and Natural Resources suggested the oysters had declined because of Hurricanes Elena and Juan in 1985, and because of predation from oyster drills. A biologist at the Marine Resources Division said he expected the 1987 harvest to be low, and added, "It's a natural problem. Prior to the hurricanes, we saw a great many oysters" (*Montgomery Advertiser* 8 November 1987). Another biologist blamed oyster drills and salinity. Others attributed the decline to the dredging of oyster shell for thirty-five years, from 1947 to 1982, during which the Marine Resources Division received about $8 million in royalties, a significant portion of its operating expenses.

James A. Allen, who was an oyster inspector and then enforcement supervisor for Alabama's salt waters, said:

> It was political. The dredging companies made a deal with the state of Alabama. They wanted the shell and that was it. They would dig up live shells to get it. We fought the thing, but I was just one of the little guys fighting. You couldn't fight big industry and the administration. That was the political end of it. They weren't going to stop dredging—there was too much money in it. There have always been hurricanes and drills, but the oysters always came back. The natives here—the old-timers who made their livelihood out of the seafood and oyster industry—will tell you the mother reefs in upper Mobile Bay spawned the oysters. (ibid.)

Mark Van Hoose, an oyster biologist with the Marine Resources Division, discounted the effects of industrial dredging and said, "We've only had three reefs in the last 20 years that ever amounted to anything anyway. You hear all about these people catching a lot of oysters, but I never saw that documented. We've never seen any evidence of there being any major producing reefs in Baldwin County" (ibid.).

Cathy Donelson of the *Montgomery Advertiser* documented recorded catches from Bon Secour Bay greater than those from Mobile Bay in 1965 and 1966, and a decline of Bon Secour oyster harvests from 266,700 pounds in 1967 to 10,000 pounds in 1972, when harvesting of oysters more or less ceased (ibid.).

The Seafood Division's Walter Tatum suggested there was no "good answer to the situation," and mentioned low dissolved oxygen, fresh water, oyster drills, and sewage disposal from upriver as factors that may have affected the reefs (ibid.). He concluded: "I'm not going to tell you the shell dredge was the one responsible for it. The shell dredge has been gone out of Mobile Bay for six or seven years now and we certainly haven't made any recovery of the oyster reefs since then" (ibid.).

Leasing Programs

In 1955 there were but few productive private and leased reefs in Alabama (*MR* 26 May 1955). The leasing of oyster beds was controversial. The Mobile Bay Sea Food Union asked the Mobile circuit court to enjoin Earl McGowin, the state conservation commissioner, from granting Will Henderson the right to lease forty-five acres of oyster beds in Portersville Bay, because the proposed lease would be "an abuse of the discretion of the director in that Henderson would be in a position to gather all the oysters from this specific bed and it would take many years to develop the beds to the stage they now are" (*MR* 1 January 1955).

A state senator and Bert Thomas, the former conservation director, joined in the protest (ibid.). McGowin then announced that the department was negotiating with Henderson to lease his 1,800 acres of oyster property in Portersville Bay and open it to public tonging (*MR* 4 January 1955).

George Allen said that the Seafood Division did not have sufficient funds to develop new oyster bottoms or increase production on existing ones. He therefore suggested leasing bottoms that were capable of producing oysters but that were not in production. People or corporations could lease a minimum of 40 and a maximum of 640 acres in one area. He said the program required no legislation as the state had leased oyster bottoms from time to time, but that there had never been a leasing program (*MR* 24 February 1960).

Most leases then and in the past were to seafood-processing firms and there had never been many individual leases, but the Seafood Division encouraged them. Some large eastern firms offered to lease all available acreage, but their applications were refused as "no one should have all available areas under lease," Allen said. Lessees could get licenses to take seed oysters from public reefs and reseed leased areas once every three years. There was a tax of three cents a barrel on seed oysters. Seafood processors usually planted their shells on their own leases for cultch after returning a third of them to public reefs. The Seafood Division estimated expenses for a ten-acre lease would be about ten dollars for a lease at the minimum price and about five hundred dollars for 200 barrels of shells. Two men could plant the area in a month at a rate of 75 barrels a day with a boat that could carry 50 barrels of shells. Oysters could be harvested near the end of the second year. At the end of three years there should be about 6,000 barrels of oysters which would bring about five dollars per barrel. The division argued that experience in Mississippi and Louisiana indicated the possible success of individual oyster leases (MR 17 September 1960).

Allen said that oystermen could not see any advantage to leasing and developing their own leases as long as the public reefs were available, and he attributed the unpopularity of the oyster-leasing program to this outlook (ibid.).

The Graham Seafood Company of Bayou la Batre obtained a permit to dredge seed oysters from the deep White House Reef in Mobile Bay. It was allowed to dredge twenty thousand barrels of oysters to plant on bottoms the company had leased from private holders of riparian rights. The permit was challenged by Jimmy Collier, president of the Alabama Seafood Protective Association. The Seafood Division reviewed the permit and concluded that it was legal under laws passed by the 1959 legislature (MR 8 October 1960).

Allen held that in order to accommodate the demands of canning plants, the legal minimum size of oysters had to be reduced from that mandated by regulations. To keep the processors operating, the legal size would be reduced on the first of January, in mid-season. As a consequence, the reefs were depleted of sufficient small oysters to insure the next season of oyster growth. He argued that "the state feels that if the industry is permitted to develop its own beds it would eliminate the problem of supplying small oysters from public reefs and there would be large oysters on the public beds during the entire season," adding that the White House Reef was difficult to harvest by tonging and that dredging helped to cultivate reefs (ibid.).

In 1962 Leo Kuffskie started planting seed oysters he purchased from the state. With his forty-seven-foot shrimp boat he dredged and transported to his 23.5-acre lease in Bon Secour Bay 3,500 barrels in 1963 and 1,000 barrels in 1964 (MR 5 February 1965). Kuffskie had an additional 21-acre lease from the state, and a 16-acre riparian lease in Bon Secour Bay. When he was not planting or harvesting oysters, he shrimped. His wife and daughter opened the oysters for sale in his retail shop. Norman Wallace had a 4-acre oyster lease. In a 1965 suit the two men claimed a Brown and Root Company dredge working on the Intracoastal Waterway in 1963 caused silt to cover and harm oysters on parts of their leases, and they requested damages (ibid.).

Jack Mallory, a University of Alabama marine biologist, and George Allen said Kuffskie's program was a model to be emulated (MR 21 February 1965). Allen said that there had been an increase in the number of leases of private oyster reefs in the early 1960s (MR 23 May 1965).

Shell Planting and Transplanting

In 1960 with decreased Seafood Division revenues from dredging and increases in personnel, a vigorous enforcement effort, added equipment, and a new division office at Gulf Shores, there were no funds for oyster-shell planting, even though the legislature had authorized the expenditure of $100,000 for that purpose. Allen noted, however, that the law required replanting a third of shells removed on public reefs and that last year's harvest of 9,000 barrels of oysters would indicate, he assumed, that 3,000 barrels of shell had been replanted. The 52,000 barrels of oysters landed by April of 1960 should have produced 17,000 barrels of shells for replanting (*MR* 3 April 1960).

In addition to pollution, insufficient cultch for spat to settle on may inhibit oyster production. Large reefs may be covered with mud by the action of floods or hurricanes. Since 1914 the Seafood Division or Marine Resources Division has attempted to maintain producing oyster beds by planting shells (Swingle and Hughes 1976).

Although it does not agree with other sources on all points, table 4 summarizes the oyster management activities and harvests during most of the period under discussion as presented by the Alabama Marine Resources Laboratory.

In 1956, 1957, and 1958 the Seafood Division planted 100,000 barrels of seed oysters (*MR* 24 August 1958). In 1960 and 1961 floods washed fresh water and pollution into the bay, damaging the oyster reefs. The Seafood Division planted 153,000 barrels of shell and seed oysters in 1962 (*MR* 13 January 1963). Until 1963 when the oyster harvest improved, some oyster catchers lost their boats and had problems keeping their houses. In 1962 many oyster processors got their oysters from Louisiana. Even with the improved catch in 1963, processors were still receiving up to 75 percent of their oysters from that state. The Graham Seafood Company in Bayou la Batre was purchasing Mississippi oysters for canning. There was a call for a reduction of the legal size of oysters from two and five-eighths inches as canning plants required smaller oysters (*MR* 20 January 1963).

The next year floods killed the oysters as thoroughly as in 1961. A Seafood Division biologist said a new planting program would hasten recovery (*MR* 26 May 1964). There were damaging floods again in 1965 and another planting program (*MR* 7 January 1966). In 1966 the harvest was better and Biloxi processors sent freight boats to Alabama's reefs to purchase small "steam" oysters for canning. Hurricane Betsy had damaged Louisiana and Mississippi reefs and most of the oysters had been coming from Texas. Hundreds of oystermen worked

Table 4. Oyster Shell Planting, Transplanting, and Harvests

Year	Barrels of Shell Planted	Barrels of Seed Planted	Pounds of Meat Harvested
1943	(no data, ND)	(ND)	(ND)
1944	92,426	0	(ND)
1945	0	6,000	1,605,700
1946	12,743	19,040	(ND)
1947	15,000	18,950	(ND)
1948	25,000	40,000	1,531,200
1949	63,215	33,409	1,585,800
1950	0	40,713	2,070,300
1951	40,000	0	2,191,400
1952	17,749	54,000	1,842,000
1953	2,431	0	1,449,700
1954	0	7,500	739,300
1955	97,707	0	1,580,600
1956	0	40,000	769,900
1957	0	50,000	1,291,200
1958	0	59,860	457,600
1959	0	0	894,800
1960	23,534	15,000	1,169,300
1961	70,000	0	508,500
1962	115,000	39,839	442,700
1963	60,000	30,000	995,400
1964	65,000	36,000	1,005,300
1965	60,000	65,698	492,400
1966	50,000	60,000	1,304,500
1967	11,400	8,660	2,087,900
1968	46,470	0	1,211,800
1969	105,325	0	480,700
1970	51,296	0	279,000
1971	61,982	0	250,000
1972	117,346	0	1,069,515
1973	3,157	0	590,118
1974	167,330	5,451	732,776
1975	162,259	0	(ND)

Source: Swingle and Hughes 1976

Cedar Reef for canning oysters to sell to the freight boats for instant cash. In 1966 no canneries were operating in Alabama (MR 24 April 1966). There was still a raw-oyster trade, though it relied increasingly on oysters from Louisiana, Texas, and even Chesapeake Bay as the supply of Alabama oysters was insufficient and undependable.

In 1960 the oyster program was allocated $9,750. The Conservation Department contracted with about 120 oystermen in Baldwin and Mobile counties to tong seed oysters and plant them in designated areas. Each man was given a quota of about 120 barrels at sixty-five cents per barrel. The Seafood Division checked each load to verify the volume of oysters planted. Allen saw the program as a stopgap to provide harvestable oysters for the September season (*MR* 15 May 1960). Seafood Division enforcement officers patrolled the oyster reefs to enforce culling regulations; the required size was now two and three-fourths inches rather than two and five-eighths inches (*MR* 30 August 1960).

During 1962–63 oystermen whose production had been affected when pollution forced closures sold the Seafood Division 15,000 barrels of seed oysters which they planted in Portersville Bay and Grand Bay. During the summer of 1963, they planted 30,000 barrels of shells in Grand Bay and Portersville Bay. In 1964 they planted 10,000 barrels of seed oysters. When the Cedar Point Reefs were closed again in 1965 because of pollution, oystermen moved to Grand Bay, which had been planted after 1961, and were able to keep working during the season.

In 1964, 15,000 barrels of seed oysters were planted at Bon Secour River Reef. They produced 50,000 barrels of oysters. At that time Bon Secour Bay was not subject to the freshwater influxes or pollution that affected parts of Mobile Bay (*MR* 30 May 1965). Oyster harvesting between Cedar Point and Dauphin Island was banned because of pollution in 1959, 1961, 1964, and 1965. Influxes of fresh water killed 96 percent of the oysters in 1961 and 85 percent of the oysters in 1963 in that area. After the 1961 disaster the Seafood Division recommended two programs to rejuvenate existing oyster beds and to develop new reefs in areas not subject to pollution and freshwater influxes (ibid.).

The Seafood Division conducted a program of planting seed oysters during cold weather and oyster shells in hot weather. For the task they used a self-propelled steel-hulled barge they designed and had built at Master Marine shipyard in Bayou la Batre. Dredges loaded the barge to its 1,000-barrel capacity, and the seed oysters were washed overboard as the barge moved across the reefs. The seed oysters were planted in Heron Bay and Portersville Bay as well as Grand Bay in Baldwin County. Allen estimated that three barrels of oysters could be harvested for each barrel of seed oysters planted. Between October 1964 and the end of January 1965 the department planted about 15,000 barrels of seed oysters and 30,000 barrels of shells. The department also contracted with Jimmy Collier of Dauphin Island to dredge and plant 40,000 barrels of seed oysters on public reefs at forty-nine cents per barrel (*MR* 31 January 1965). The department reported that it planted 56,149 barrels of seed oysters in the fall-winter season of 1964–65 (*MR* 14 April 1965).

Shell Bank Reef in Bon Secour Bay was "just about gone" in 1962 when the Department of Conservation dredged off the remaining oysters and planted 30,000 barrels of seed oysters. In 1964–65 it produced 90,000 barrels of oysters and was the main source of oysters for the industry. In 1963, 5,000 barrels of seed oysters were planted in Bon Secour Reef. Hurricane Betsy buried some of the oyster reefs in silt and damaged them (*MR* 14 September 1965). Ten years later, after pollution caused Bon Secour Bay to be closed to oystering, Wayne Swingle, director of the Marine Resources Division, announced a program to cultivate the oyster reefs of Bon Secour Bay by dredging them to turn them over and expose existing shell to improve the set of spat. He pointed out that in the past the reefs had been planted with seed oysters from other areas (*MR* 9 February 1975).

At the end of February 1972, after the health department had closed Mobile Bay to oystering, W. F. Anderson closed the Mississippi Sound in order to plant shell west of the Dauphin Island bridge. Tonging would interfere with planting and he argued it was the peak of oyster-spawning season and time to close oystering. Nolan Ladnier of Dauphin Island asked Judge William Bollng to enjoin Anderson from doing so (*MR* 31 February 1972).

The judge refused to issue the injunction because all reefs except Cedar Reef had been closed due to pollution and because Anderson had based his decision on scientific reasons. The shell planting would endanger tongers if harvesting continued. Oystermen said oysters had finished spawning and scoffed at Anderson's expertise (*MR* 1 June 1972).

In 1973 the oyster harvest was good and William Anderson and his staff of biologists credited the shell plantings and research. Anderson attributed past low oyster production to unfavorable natural conditions and reiterated that the dredge had no effect on oyster reefs (*MR* 19 February 1973). Floods and attendant pollution once again caused oystering to be closed in April of the same year. The Alabama Seafood Protective Association requested that President Nixon declare Mobile Bay a national disaster area. Doody Peters, the spokesman for the group, argued that if the president could declare upstate farmland a disaster area because of the flooding, he should do the same for the bay. Twenty-five oystermen marched on a picket line in front of the federal building in Mobile. On the fifteenth of March, thirty oystermen were arrested for tonging in closed waters. The oystermen said the waters were not polluted and claimed that if the water were too polluted for oystering it should be too polluted for swimming (*MR* 13 April 1973).

Governor Wallace, U.S. Representative Jack Edwards, and Lt. Governor Jere Beasley promised support to the industry and efforts for relief programs (*MR* 14 April 1973). Wallace sent a representative to Bayou la Batre to meet with oystermen (*MR* 16 April 1973). The same group of oystermen protested in front of Mobile's Unemployment Compensation Agency office with 150 supporters. They applied for disaster unemployment compensation and while some received aid, others in similar situations did not (*MR* 7 June 1973).

Early in 1974 Alabama allocated twenty-five thousand dollars to the Seafood Division to plant shells. The emergency funds were to be used to employ oystermen—out of work because of closures— to plant the shells. Officers of the Seafood Division met with oystermen to discuss the program. Meanwhile a representative of the governor said that personnel would help oystermen sign up for food stamps. Members of the South Alabama Seafood Association displayed signs that alleged "communist tactics," requested a federal investigation of oyster reef closing, alleged discrimination against oyster catchers, urged fighting pollution and getting rid of the shell dredge, and referred to Watergate (*MR* 8 January 1974). The program started late in January as oystermen began tonging oysters from Dauphin Island Bay and planted them in Portersville Bay for four dollars per barrel (*MR* 27 January 1974).

In 1977 Doody Peters, president of the South Alabama Seafood Association, which had a membership of about 120, asked Hugh Swingle, the director of the Marine Resources Division, to revise the system of planting oysters. Peters favored a system of hiring oyster catchers to plant oysters at four dollars per barrel of seed oysters with a ninety-barrel quota per oyster catcher. Swingle replied that such a system had been tried in the past and proved inefficient. Peters claimed that oystermen knew best where oysters would grow and were out of work for up to half a year because of pollution and floods. The planting would give them jobs, "so they won't be handing us food stamps, welfare and all that jazz" (*MR* 25 August 1977). Swingle said oystermen were consulted under the contract system in which the department solicited bids for the planting and let contracts to one bidder (*MR* 25, 31 August 1977).

Early in February of 1979 oystering was again closed because of pollution (*MR* 3 February 1979). Doody Peters had delivered the vote for Fob James when he ran for governor, and when Peters complained about closings, James visited the area and heard about water testing and the importance of restoration of funds for shell plantings (*Birmingham News* 8 February 1979; *Montgomery Advertiser* 25 February 1979).

Lazarus Johnson spoke for another group of oyster catchers to say, "We don't need the Department of Conservation if the Department of Health is going to tell them everything to do. They (Health Dept.) are running the seafood business" (*Mobile Press* 3 February 1979).

In a 1965 report, George Allen, chief of the Seafood Division, said a continued planting program would provide sufficient oysters to meet the demand as long as pollution did not extend into new reefs outside the then polluted limits (*MR* 30 May 1965). The report said "there is little hope" of help against the threat of pollution "expected under the existing law." Allen urged support for new legislation then under consideration.

He suggested that experience in other states indicated that a system of private reef operation provided the best results for many oystermen and that his department was attempting to make areas available for private oyster reefs (ibid.). In 1965 1,606 acres of Baldwin County were leased. Reefs in Mobile County were used as producing public reefs and were not available for leases. The Conservation Department estimated that about five hundred acres under private riparian rights had been leased for oyster production. George Allen's report suggested that there was a trend that would continue until all private nonproductive bottoms would be under individual oyster cultivation.

Allen pointed out that oyster shuckers were paid by the pound of oyster meat and therefore did not like to open small oysters. Attributing them with undreamed-of political and economic power, he concluded that oyster shuckers would demand the large cultivated oysters so they could produce more pounds of oyster meats for less effort (ibid.).

Bon Secour Seafood operated riparian bottoms and leased beds from about 1910 until the mid-1950s. The company quit growing oysters because it could not depend on local oysters to supply their demand due to chronic scarcity of seed oysters and frequent closing of the beds by the Department of Health. Some growers continued until the 1960s. There have been no private beds since 1972. Some former growers said that effluent from the Gulf Shores sewage treatment plant destroyed their beds in Oyster Bay. They also said oyster theft was a problem (*MR* 21 November 1985).

The Food and Drug Administration proposed strict rules requiring that each fisherman, purchaser, and processor maintain records on where and when the oysters were harvested and sold, and who bought them. Wayne Swingle said the measures were designed to protect the public from polluted oysters but said that the Alabama standards for shellfish were "super safe." There could only be problems, he added, if oysters were illegally harvested from polluted waters (MR 9 October 1975). The department would have to enforce the regulations, and Swingle said it did not have the funds to do so. He said the regulations would cripple the oyster industry. The FDA announced a delay in the regulations (ibid.). By the end of the year, the FDA planned to delay its program, but not to change it. It said a series of shellfish poisoning outbreaks around the country made it evident that the fifty-year-old cooperative program with the states was not adequate to assure public safety (MR 6 December 1975).

The state board of health investigated the problem of high coliform oysters being shipped from Louisiana for processing at seven establishments in Bayou la Batre. In the meantime processors were not given licenses to transport oysters out of Alabama, depriving them of their greatest source of revenue, out-of-state sales, while the board of health tried to determine whether the oysters were from polluted waters or were contaminated by poor refrigeration, poor transportation procedures, or low-quality handling and shucking (MR 10 October 1975).

In the winter and spring of 1979, floods damaged oyster reefs and Hurricane Frederic disturbed them and covered them with sand and silt. William Eckmayer of the state Conservation Department said federal aid would be used to plant shell on 668.6 acres for cultch (MR 2 January 1980). The planting of about 120 acres was finished by the end of June (MR 28 June 1980). In 1980 Bon Secour Seafood was getting half of its oysters to process from Chesapeake Bay in Maryland and Virginia and nearly half from Texas, and some from Louisiana, but none from Alabama (MR 2 November 1980).

In November, Hugh Swingle announced a grant from the federal Economic Development Administration to hire Mobile County oystermen to move oysters from Dauphin Island Bay to other areas for harvest within a few weeks. Only oyster catchers who had 1978 or 1979 licenses were eligible, and they had to provide boats with bins. Marine Resources Division would measure the bins to determine their volumes and fishermen would be paid four dollars per barrel with a limit of twenty-five barrels per person per day (MR 5 November 1980).

Doody Peters of the South Alabama Seafood Association wanted Governor Fob James to explain why no state funds had been made available to oystermen to reseed the depleted reefs and whether the governor would recommend any federal assistance for the seafood industry. The mayor of Bayou la Batre contacted the governor's office to try to get him to meet with disgruntled oystermen and shrimpers (*MR* 30 April 1980). James scheduled, then canceled a visit to Bayou la Batre (*MR* 7 May 1980).

Affecting about a thousand oyster catchers and forty to fifty oyster-processing houses, Hurricane Elena of 1985 destroyed 90 percent of harvestable oysters, 89 percent of all oysters, and 85 percent of the spat at Cedar Point Reef (*MR* 7, 11 September 1985). The U.S. Economic Development Administration and the Alabama Department of Conservation provided funds for a New Orleans firm to place 14,457 cubic yards of clam shell on the western edge of Cedar Point Reef (*MR* 24 September 1985). Master Wayne, Inc., of Coden entered the low bid of $2.73 per barrel to relocate sixty-five thousand barrels of oysters to be dredged from middle and upper Mobile Bay and placed in Portersville Bay near Coden. The bid specified two or more oyster dredge boats or barges to dredge oysters and spread them evenly. The Marine Resources division would measure the oysters and insure that there would be five hundred barrels dredged daily. State Senator Bill Menton of Irvington said it would quickly replenish the oyster stock and put the oystermen back to work (*MR* 28 December 1985). Roland Nelson, president of Save Our Shells, said there were insufficient oysters for seed oysters and that the reefs were destroyed when the state sold the rights to oyster-shell deposits under the reefs (*MR* 21 November 1985)

It is clear that oyster management is not simply a matter of managing oysters and oyster reefs. It can also be a significant source of income for oyster catchers, one they especially seek in bad years when their incomes are low. Such programs therefore have a welfare dimension to them. Of course, it is complex and difficult to manage a number of individual oyster catchers, so it is much simpler to do the oyster-shell planting or transplanting by contract to a single contractor or for the Marine Resources Division to do it itself. In any case, year after year there are familiar cries of indignation, accusations of incompetence, and counteraccusations of ignorance. Year after year, pollution closes the oyster reefs. Year after year, the same debates about dredging, shell planting, and corruption are recycled.

Alabama is certainly not unique among the gulf states in this. The same debates have gone on in Mississippi, Florida, and Texas. Hepburn (1977) details the history of the oyster industry and its relation to the local economy of Cedar Key, Florida. People had tried to cultivate oysters there from the last decade of the nineteenth century, but failure was attributed to theft of the cultivated oysters. Within a decade after the turn of the century, two canneries depleted the oysters. Local oystermen were hostile to planting programs of the early twentieth century, though some were carried out near Apalachicola. There were some planting programs during the Depression years of the thirties, some in connection with the Works Progress Administration. After studies, there were further rehabilitation programs in the 1950s. Nonlocal enterprises using nonlocal labor harvested oysters in the mid-sixties for processing in nonlocal plants. In spite of replanting programs started in the early seventies, the relative contribution of oysters to the value of the marine fisheries of Cedar Key declined to 1975.

The once thriving oyster industry of Florida's Apalachicola Bay has died because of politicians operating in league with developers to allow increased building, sewage pollution, marina development, as well as changes in salinity and spoil dumping from navigation projects. As the shucking houses closed down in 1989, five hundred families moved from the county where 90 percent of the people had made their livings from the bay (Stimpson 1990).

Red Snapper and Finfish

As industrial shrimping took off, other branches of Alabama's fishery contributed a smaller and smaller portion of the value of the total catch. In 1964 the Star Fish and Oyster Company, long owned by the Gonzales family, had expanded and operated a fleet of ten deep-sea diesel-powered fishing schooners worked by about a hundred fishermen. It shipped fresh and frozen seafood to most of the United States (Gonzales 1964).

The last of Mobile's gulf-plying hand liners sailed in August of 1987. The Star Fish and Oyster Company is still in the Gonzales family and there are still two snapper schooners moored to the dock at the Star Fish and Oyster Company of Mobile. However, one is being repaired and refitted as a recreational boat and the other is simply retired. Nearby, the site where the company built the last of the boats is still visible.

Arthur Gonzales, a descendant of the founder of the company, attributed the end of the snapper fishery to several factors. The costs of production were up as it took longer at sea and more provisions to get a good load of fish. There was a problem with liability and insurance. The Jones Act made the company liable for accidents on its boats, so the company had to give up legal ownership of its own boats, but federal courts would not allow it to hide ownership with dummy corporations. The company had maintained that the seamen were employees of the vessels' captains, not of the company. The courts had held that seamen could sue the company for liability, that they were not employees of the captains of the vessel but of Star Fish and Oyster. The company could no longer deliver sufficient tonnage to insure the boats itself.

Gonzales said the forty-hour workweek also contributed to its demise. There were three railroad lines out of Mobile. Star Fish and Oyster could get an order for twenty-five pounds of fish, put it on the train on Friday, and an agent would meet the train on Saturday to receive it. Along the way, agents would meet the trains at each stop and check the ice, but with the forty-hour week there was no Sunday work and no one to meet the trains, no one to take care of a fragile cargo like iced fish, so there was no satisfactory way to ship small quantities of iced fish to small communities.

Today, trucks from Mexico have replaced the schooners that fished the Campeche Banks; airplanes have replaced the trains. Star Fish and Oyster still processes fresh fish, but the market is once again regional and local. The company no longer maintains its own fleet; it gets fish from trucks as far away as Brownsville, Texas.

In a 1974 review of the seafood industry in Mobile Bay, Sandra Baxley, writing for the *Mobile Press*, suggested that the future would be brighter for fish than for shrimp, crabs, or oysters because the number of bay shrimp boats had declined year by year, the crab catch had diminished each year since 1968, and oyster tonging was routinely halted by the health department closings of polluted waters. Meanwhile, catches of fish from Mobile Bay quadrupled from 1961 to 1972. While mercury poisoning was a problem in the delta, fish withstand low levels of oxygen better than crabs or oysters (*Mobile Press* 16 January 1974).

The Department of Conservation closed certain areas of Alabama's waters to net fishing in 1982. It was responding to considerable pressure from sport fishermen, who sent 1,292 letters to the department to urge such regulations as opposed to the 304 letters commercial fishermen sent. The sport fishermen thought the regulations were too lax while commercial fishermen thought they were too constraining and charged that the Conservation Department had bowed to political pressure. Sport fishermen charged that net fishing hurt the catch of speckled trout, 93 percent of which was caught by sport fishermen. Conservation Department studies indicated that the population of speckled trout was increasing rather than decreasing (*MR* 28 April 1982).

The regulations went into force on the first of May and seafood dealers requested an injunction to stop their enforcement. At the hearing on the injunction, Hugh Swingle testified that he took "sociopolitical" factors as well as the biology of the fishery into consideration when he recommended regulations as a compromise between the claims of sport and commercial fishermen. When asked whether his decision had been political, he said that "politics, unfortunately, plays a large role in a lot of things." He saw the regulations as an equitable and fair allocation of a resource. Dr. Lewis Cardinal, of Montgomery, a sport fisherman of fifty years and member of the Conservation Advisory Board, also admitted to taking political factors into account in his decision to favor such regulations. He added that he did not like gill nets. When confronted with the finding that 93 percent of speckled trout were caught by sport fishermen, he expressed a lack of faith in marine biologists and their studies (*MR* 15, 19 May 1982).

Marine biologists testified that there was no evidence for overfishing and no biological reason for the regulations, but added that there were not enough data to make a purely biological assessment of the speckled trout crop (*MR* 15 May 1982). Commercial fishermen and fish dealers testified that the regulations would deprive them of income (*MR* 19 May 1982). The Mobile County circuit judge who heard the case upheld the regulations without comment (*MR* 22 May 1982).

This was not the first clash between sport fishermen and commercial fishermen. As early as 1925 the Izaak Walton League opposed trawling, arguing it would destroy gulf fishing. It wanted commercial fishing in Mississippi, Louisiana, and Alabama regulated as a unit and sport fishing opportunities promoted (*MR* 15 August 1925). In 1956 L. D. Young, director of Louisiana's Wildlife and Fisheries Commission, wrote to the U.S. House of Representatives Merchant Marine and Fisheries Subcommittee:

> We believe that the policies of the Fish and Wildlife Service reflect emphasis upon recreational values, a dignification of recreational values at the expense of industrial values, while all the country has prospered; the fisheries have declined.
>
> Public thinking as influenced by the publicity-minded policies of the Fish and Wildlife Service have caused fish to be regarded as golf balls instead of items of commerce and industry, and the activities of fishermen is some form of outlawry. We in Louisiana believe that the outlook of the

fisheries is not promising so long as their administration remains buried in a branch of service whose primary objective is to appease the constant clamorings of the organized recreationalists. (U.S. Congress 1956, 95)

The tension between sport and commercial fishing has increased in recent years since sport fishermen have supported turtle excluder devices (TEDs) as a means of saving endangered species of sea turtles.

In this period, "science" gained legal legitimacy as the foundation for fisheries policy. Judges decided disputed cases on the basis of "scientific" evidence. Where one side could convince a judge of the "scientific" basis for its stance, it was likely to win. Where the two sides were about equally supported, as in the case of the conservationists versus the proponents of the dredging of oyster shells for construction material, the battle became more explicitly economic and political. In some cases, apparently, management decisions were virtually "all politics."

5

Recent Events: Science, Power, and Politics

The system of industrial shrimping and freezing is still operating. Whereas union negotiations were once customary, now the folklore and common sense of biologists, regulators, and shrimpers alike have it that shrimpers are too independent to cooperate on anything. Little has transpired in recent years to suggest that this is incorrect. Only from an historical perspective can we appreciate that when shrimpers were operating in another system, they behaved differently, according to a different logic that was itself determined by their different relations with processors.

I analyze recent events not because they are unique but because they all exhibit common patterns that are shared by similar events in many contexts from inland cities to federal bureaucracies. From an analysis of the common patterns, we can understand how this system is operating today.

In the past, various factions lobbied state and federal legislatures to represent their interests, as the accounts of previous systems have indicated, and there were appeals to courts. The current system of regulation is a recent development. It relies on bureaucracies to regulate processes, technical experts to formulate policy according to scientific findings, public hearings to assess reactions, and the reformulation of policy in response. The technical experts and administrators see themselves as neutral, operating only on the basis of scientific evidence. They come to be their own interest group, representing their own career interests and jealously defending themselves against challenges to their authority and expertise from any quarter. Those who do not like the result appeal it to a series of courts that make final rulings on the basis of their understanding of scientific findings.

Since science has become the foundation of policy, science itself has become political. One is tempted to speculate that the recent

development of "postmodern" approaches in some social sciences—
a fashion that suggests that because science is a cultural construct,
based on cultural knowledge, it is just another story, one among a
number of equally legitimate stories—is a consequence of the de-
valuation science has undergone in the process of its politicization
and a response to the defensiveness of technicians in bureaucratic
positions of power. When two opposing sides can demonstrate the
scientific virtue of their positions, when what are perceived to be
opposites can both be "true," then anything can be admitted, as "post-
modernists" advocate.

To analyze this system of decision making is necessarily to question it, to indicate that it is a product of its time and culture. This is
best done from the perspective of anthropology, which can see this
as one system among many, one way to do things determined by its
context and history, rather than from the perspective of resource management, which is a formulation of the process itself. Thus, I approach
this topic as an anthropologist, to describe cultural regularities and
patterns apparent in unique events, each of which is at the same time
a recognizable kind of event, a category of event. Though they are
fairly recent, the various phases of the "management process" are
now considered to be customary and regular; they are often specified
by law and encoded as "rational" in management science. Thus it is
necessary not to take the stance of assuming such practices are "natural," but rather to stay outside them to be able to understand them as
cultural constructs of a particular historical period and place.

Policy not directed at fisheries continues to determine the conditions for fishing. Oystering depends on unpolluted waters as places
where oysters can grow and live. Water-purity policy determines the
conditions for oystering: Municipalities and industries discharge various effluents into coastal waters. The policies that regulate these discharges determine the conditions for oystering. The price of shrimp
is determined by imports and imports are regulated by policy that
addresses foreign policy rather than fisheries. Even the fate of endangered species affects shrimping.

Because modern shrimping is so efficient and because more people
have entered the fishery, it has drawn even more attention from conservationists and sport fishermen. When an association between the
reports of mortality of certain sea turtles and shrimping was suggested, a lengthy policy debate followed, with inevitable results.

Turtles, Environmentalists, and Shrimpers

In 1978, marine turtles were classified as coming under the purview of the Endangered Species Act. Charged to protect them at sea, and hoping it would be attractive to shrimpers to eliminate unwanted by-catch of jellyfish, finfish, and trash as well as turtles, the National Marine Fisheries Service (NMFS), a branch of the National Oceanographic and Atmospheric Administration (NOAA) of the Department of Commerce, developed and tested a turtle excluder device (TED). The NMFS TED is a wire cage about three feet on a side, with a top hinged at the front. A chute composed of bars runs from the bottom front to the top back. The motion of the water through the trawl is supposed to wash any sizable object such as a turtle or fish that enters the front of the box up the chute and through the hinged top to freedom. The shrimp are supposed to continue through the bars of the chute into the bag of the trawl behind it (Edwards 1987; Taylor et al. 1985).

Because only widespread voluntary use of the devices could head off expensive legal confrontations with environmentalists determined to support the enforcement of the Endangered Species Act, NMFS promoted a voluntary TED program in 1983 (Fee 1987). By January 1986 it was clear that the voluntary program had failed (Edwards 1987, 37). "The shrimping community . . . not only refused to welcome this gift but, after a close look, sent it packing. Baffled environmentalists were at once puzzled and irritated. Shrimpers, it seemed to them, were not only ambivalent about the welfare of the turtles, but also apparently indifferent to their own opportunities" (ibid.).

In August, a National Oceanic and Atmospheric Administration administrator, Tony Calio, summoned representatives of the gulf shrimp industry to Washington for a briefing on proposed regulations to require TEDs. Two days later, the Center for Environmental Education, a private environmentalist group, informed the Department of Commerce it intended to sue NOAA and NMFS to have all shrimp trawlers equipped with TEDs by January 1987. The next week, on 29 August, Calio invited representatives of the shrimping industry to participate in mediation of the TED issue with conservation groups.

Jay Johnson, the assistant general counsel for the National Oceanic and Atmospheric Administration, who was involved in negotiating the TEDs rules, reports that the meetings were for gathering and presenting data. Everyone, he says, agreed that any means should be used to prevent the extinction of Kemp's Ridley sea turtles and the decimation of other species. A secondary consideration was to minimize adverse affects on the economics of the shrimp industry "as much as possible." They heard about every turtle sighting and capture that had been recorded. Johnson recalled, "And NMFS continued to supply information throughout the negotiation process. The government took no other role, nor did we indicate what we wanted in the way of the regulation—except that we wanted an immediate solution. And for that reason, we just stood back and let the environmentalists and the industry have a go at each other" (1987, 236).

Representatives of four shrimping associations and two shrimpers, one lawyer, and one former government bureaucrat spoke for shrimpers. The former head of the United States Justice Department's wildlife and natural resources section, a former staff director for the House of Representatives' Merchant Marine and Fisheries Committee (both lawyers who represented the Center for Environmental Education), a representative from the Monitor International Fund for Animals who had worked in the State Department, and an agent from Greenpeace presented environmentalists' positions.

Even though shrimping industry representatives were involved in the decision, the associations and shrimpers repudiated the agreement (Johnson 1987). Johnson admitted there were doubts about whether TEDs save turtles, whether turtles were caught in shrimp nets, and whether shrimpers lost shrimp, but he said they used the best data that existed (ibid., 238).

Frank Patti, a shrimper, fleet owner, and processing-house owner in Pensacola, Florida, characterized the NMFS data Johnson called the "best available" as "quasi-scientific and semi-factual" (Patti 1987, 15). He pointed out that of 6,030 boats shrimping in the gulf, only 865 or less than 15 percent were represented in the negotiation, while larger groups were not invited to participate. He noted that "all the groups are very localized, and no central core group exists to represent all the shrimpers. We certainly were not able to put together the type of think tank that the environmentalists assembled. In fact, it has been almost impossible to find a good environmental lawyer to represent us, since most of these special attorneys are on retainer to an environmental group or are on the staff of one" (ibid., 34).

This is Patti's description of the process Johnson described:

> The representative shrimpers went to the meeting prepared to negotiate in good faith on behalf of their members' welfare and the well-being of the turtle. The proceedings began, and while the industry spokesmen were in private caucus, Dr. Tony Calio, administrator of NOAA, told them that if they did not come to terms with the environmentalists in the meetings, he would hand down a federal mandate requiring TED use on all vessels, in all waters, 365 days a year.
>
> This ultimatum totally stripped the shrimpers of all bargaining power.

Instead of the administration providing unbiased mediation, they intimi-
dated the industry representatives and forced them to yield. The shrimpers
then did what they could and attempted to cut the best deal possible,
allowing for restriction of seasonal TED use. (ibid.)

After four meetings from October to early December a report was
issued. A forty-five-day period of public hearings on TED regulations
began in February 1987 (Fee 1987). It became clear in these hearings
and in other contexts that NMFS technical personnel and shrimpers did not agree in their interpretations of the results of using TEDs
(Blanchard 1987).

Edwards (1987) spoke with shrimpers who had used TEDs on the
Atlantic, Texas, and Louisiana coasts where the original "shooters"
had been developed to eliminate unwanted by-catch. He supposed
that such shrimpers would see an advantage to TEDs beyond federal
regulations, but found that the devices caused decreased catches. A
Texas shrimper said: "I've never been able to make them quit losing
shrimp. That doesn't mean there aren't some people that can, I just
was never able to." A Louisiana shrimper said: "I just wanted to see
how they worked. I thought they had something better than mine. I'm
always in favor of any kind of improvement, and if theirs were better
than mine, I was going to pull theirs" (Edwards 1987, 39).

Edwards writes, "Far more apparent is the host of widespread complaints about the NMFS TED, criticism based on sincere efforts to
make it work. The device is now widely branded as both impractical
and dangerous" (ibid.).

Patti reported the outcry among shrimpers against the promulgated
regulations in public meetings. "Thousands of shrimpers have shown
up at TED meetings, and thousands of others support them but were
not able to attend. (They must fish in the daytime, when the meetings
are held.) A large number of shrimpers are publicly militant about
the use of TEDs and plan direct defiance of the rules at whatever
cost. The militant faction is quickly growing and will soon reach the
boiling point. Only the removal of the TED requirements will defuse
them now." Patti continued, in a letter to his senator: "These shrimpers do not wish to defy the law. They are honest, hard-working and
law-abiding, but required use of the TED will destroy the only way
they have of making a living. Many families have been shrimpers for
generations. Most shrimpers are not fleet owners but rather single-
boat owner/operators barely able to make a decent living. Many times,
a trip will not even pay fuel and crew costs. Many of these people
are uneducated and are not able to understand or fight government
regulations" (Patti 1987, 34).

In 1985 the legislation that authorized the Endangered Species Act expired. For three years, the program had been supported with emergency appropriations while the act was debated. In November 1987 the Merchant Marine and Fisheries Committee of the United States House of Representatives voted against an amendment to delay the requirement. The chairman of the committee opposed the amendment because of "the practical politics of the thing as I read it. The environmentalists, who we have to contend with whether we like it or not, . . . would not agree to the . . . amendment. So to get a bill through, we had to take this position" (MR 20 November 1987).

The amendment to delay TEDs was supported by representatives from Florida, Texas, Alabama, and Louisiana. The Texas and Louisiana representatives told the committee that NMFS data were from the Atlantic, where conditions are different from the gulf. They argued that TEDs would reduce catch, require extra fuel and higher insurance rates, and that the combined effects of these consequences would be to put many shrimpers out of business. The amendment failed on the House floor, when the House approved reauthorization of the Endangered Species Act by a vote of 399 to 16.

Alabama's Senator Howell Heflin put a hold on legislation to renew the Endangered Species Act in the Senate so it could not be brought to the Senate floor without informing him in time for him to offer amendments and raise objections. Such a "hold" acts as an informal agreement with the Senate majority leader to delay action on a bill. Environmentalists remained opposed to amendments that would establish a precedent for congressional action to overturn administrative decisions.

The attorney general of Louisiana filed a lawsuit against the U.S. Department of Commerce on behalf of the state in which he sought a judicial review of the TEDs regulations. He held that the regulations were not supported by data, were arbitrary and capricious, and that NMFS failed to follow administrative procedures. He also charged that the regulations were impossible to enforce, deprived shrimpers of their livelihoods, and had negative economic consequences that created an undue burden on the state and shrimpers.

Shrimpers from Florida to Texas continued to request that NMFS conduct local studies. NMFS officials said they would sponsor more workshops to explain to shrimpers how to use the devices. The Alabama Sea Grant Extension Service held workshops in February 1988 in Bon Secour and Bayou la Batre to help shrimpers cope with the regulations, which were to go into effect on 1 March of that year.

As the implementation deadline approached, shrimpers and processors reiterated estimates that they would lose between 25 and 50 percent of their catch, and that the regulations had nothing to do with turtles but were meant to eliminate trawling to protect finfish for sport fishermen. Such estimates were common in the media. In my visits with shrimpers in western Florida, southern Alabama, and southern Mississippi, I heard the same story repeatedly: Shrimpers would lose up to half of their catch; they could not survive if they were forced to use TEDs; someone was trying to drive them out of business.

There were few federal agents to enforce the new regulations, and some state agencies were approached for help. The Louisiana legislature passed a law that state agents could not help federal agents enforce TEDs regulations. Officials applied to the state attorney general for a ruling as there was a contradiction between federal and state laws. The attorney general and the Concerned Shrimpers of America sued to reverse the TEDs regulations. A U.S. district court judge found against them, and the attorney general said he would appeal. In late April, a U.S. district judge in New Orleans granted a stay on enforcing federal TEDs regulations until the attorney general's lawsuit was resolved.

On 7 June 1988 the president of the National Audubon Society urged Senator Heflin to remove his hold. He said: "Sen. Heflin is holding the Endangered Species Act hostage, protesting the requirement that American shrimp fishermen use special devices to prevent threatened and endangered sea turtles from drowning in shrimp trawls" (*MR* 8 June 1988). Heflin said figures the environmental groups had provided showed that shrimpers cause only about 1 percent of turtle deaths and injuries.

Alabama environmentalists started a letter-writing campaign urging Heflin to stop blocking the renewal of the Endangered Species Act. National environmentalist groups reported that thirty-nine (of one hundred) senators signed a request that the senate majority leader move the bill. An Audubon Society wildlife specialist maintained that TEDs "were one of the most thoroughly studied efforts put into regulations under the act and it's time for Heflin to back off." A member of the Mobile County Audubon Society agreed, remarking, "I don't know why he's being so reluctant." The executive director of the Alabama Conservancy concurred, saying, "It's ridiculous that he's holding up the Endangered Species Act. He's repeatedly given us [environmentalists] problems," and calling Heflin an obstructionist on environmental issues. He grouped strip miners, timber interests, and shrimpers in the same negative category and said Heflin sided with them (*MR* 15 June 1988).

The next day, the Mobile newspaper reported that environmental groups had "flayed" Heflin. A spokesman for the Center for Environmental Education (a party to the original TEDs negotiations) held a press conference in Washington at which he charged that Heflin was factually wrong, incoherent, and presented no alternatives to save sea turtles. Heflin responded that his data came from governmental and environmental group sources and maintained that TEDs imposed unfair economic hardships on shrimpers. He called for further testing before the regulations should be enforced, and concluded "that all the data being used in this discussion is suspect and therefore a full study should be conducted by unbiased researchers" (*MR* 16 June 1988).

Heflin's office argued that passage of the bill would not change anything very much. The bill had been held up for two or three years, endangered species provisions would continue under existing law, and the Department of the Interior had received funds under the present arrangements. Environmentalists countered that the new bill would provide more adequate funding and increase funding for state agencies (*MR* 19 June 1988).

The National Marine Fisheries Service reported that within a week after shrimping season opened on 8 June 1988, five dead sea turtles were found along the Alabama gulf coast. Under the Endangered Species Act, accidental catching of an endangered species is illegal. An Orange Beach, Alabama, resident announced that if TEDs regulations were not enforced, he would sue the federal government for failing to enforce the Endangered Species Act.

Early in July, lawyers for the Justice Department and the Center for Environmental Education urged the U.S. Circuit Court of Appeals to revoke the April injunction that blocked enforcement of the TEDs regulations. One of the judges pointed out that it was the middle of the shrimp season and shrimpers would have to start using the TEDs overnight. A Center for Environmental Education lawyer replied that there was no surprise, that the regulation had been on-again and off-again for ten years and that shrimpers had the TEDs ready for use. A lawyer for the Louisiana attorney general's office repeated that TEDs reduced shrimp catches and did not protect turtles. The U.S. Justice Department lawyer replied that he was being selective in the studies he cited and maintained that other studies had shown that shrimp trawling is dangerous to the turtles and that TEDs reduce shrimp catches only 5 percent. The assistant attorney general of Louisiana contested this finding and argued that the TEDs law discriminated against shrimpers because dredging and beachfront building kill more turtles than shrimpers do.

On 11 July the federal appeals court affirmed the lower court's dismissal of the Louisiana attorney general's lawsuit that challenged the TEDs law and ordered shrimpers to begin using them on the first of September. This decision, issued without opinion, revoked the stay on the TEDs enforcement.

Jackie Taylor, president of the Alabama chapter of Concerned Shrimpers of America, said she did not expect shrimpers to accept the court decision without a struggle, but that the decision was now in the political arena rather than the courts. She suggested that a test of the effectiveness of the law would be for shrimpers to refuse to use the devices, but she hoped that the TEDs requirement could be removed. She contended that "it's going to be a war in the Gulf of Mexico" and that shrimpers saw the regulation as an injustice that would destroy their industry (MR 13 July 1988).

Meanwhile, in Washington, Senator Heflin and the chairman of the Senate Environmental Protection Subcommittee worked on a compromise agreement that permitted nongovernmental scientists to conduct studies of endangered turtles and the effectiveness of TEDs to determine whether the turtles were actually endangered, whether TEDs were effective, and how TEDs affect shrimp catches. Enforcement of the TEDs law would be delayed until May 1989. With such a compromise, as an amendment, Heflin removed his hold on the Endangered Species Act, and it was voted on in the Senate. The agreement was similar to the one rejected in the House of Representatives earlier in December.

At a meeting of the Alabama chapter of the Concerned Shrimpers of America, Mrs. Taylor announced that shrimpers were happy with Heflin's compromise amendment since it was what shrimpers had been asking for, and she announced the shrimpers' support for the amendment (MR 14 July 1988). Senator Mitchell of Maine, chairman of the Senate Environmental Protection Subcommittee, accepted Heflin's amendment and the Senate passed it on 25 July.

Shrimpers showed their appreciation of Heflin's efforts on their behalf by sponsoring a reception for him in Bayou la Batre. About a hundred people attended, including Tee John Mialjevich, president of Concerned Shrimpers of America, who presented the senator a plaque on which he was called "the shrimper's number one friend" (MR 24 August 1988).

John Fitzgerald of the Defenders of Wildlife said that Senator Heflin's amendment would "cause the death of a number of sea turtles" and suggested that the studies mandated by the amendment would show that the animals are seriously endangered. Senator Heflin opined that the turtles would be found not to be endangered and that other measures would preserve them more effectively than TEDs would (*MR* 29 July 1988). The Endangered Species Act with the Heflin amendment passed both houses and President Reagan signed it. TEDs regulations were delayed.

Senator Heflin's press secretary told me that while the senator's stand on TEDs had won him friends among shrimpers and may have made enemies among environmentalists, the environmental groups agreed to the compromise amendment so they would offer no political opposition. He suggested that while it is impossible to keep everyone happy, politics is the art of compromise, and that the Heflin amendment was a good compromise for turtles, shrimpers, and environmentalists.

In November 1988 a representative of the National Audubon Society visited Bayou la Batre and went for an overnight trip on a shrimp boat with a semiretired shrimper. The representative visited local members of the Concerned Shrimpers of Alabama and said he had developed a new appreciation for shrimping, that it "is not a job, it's a way of life" (*MR* 2 November 1988).

Stating that they had had little say in the TEDs matter, shrimpers argued that they should help make laws since others do not know about their work. When they were represented at all, it was by processors, not fellow fishermen. The Audubon man said he "got a feel for the [shrimpers'] inherent mistrust of National Marine Fisheries" and that shrimpers hoped that studies done during the delay period would result in "a fair shake from an unbiased body"; but he added that he was sure studies would indicate the necessity of TEDs. Shrimpers hoped the studies would prove the added gear was unnecessary (ibid.).

In early April 1989, about thirty-five hundred shrimpers gathered at a mass meeting of Concerned Shrimpers of America in Thibodaux, Louisiana. Shrimpers and speakers alike expressed confidence that they would be vindicated. The new studies by objective (rather than NMFS) scientists would show that shrimpers did not catch turtles. The scientists would see that the bottom was mud, not sand, as the bottoms had been where the original tests were done. The scientists would be able to observe the 30 to 50 percent decrease in catch the TEDs caused. Shrimpers in this and other contexts indicated that they thought the scientists would collect new data, make new studies, and observe them in their working conditions. They were convinced that scientists of the American Academy of Science would tell the truth and the truth would help the shrimpers. Their faith in science and its power seemed almost religious. None of the speakers at the mass meeting said anything different.

Tee John Mialjevich, president of Concerned Shrimpers of America; the attorney general of Louisiana; Representative Billy Tauzin; Governor Roemer of Louisiana; and others addressed the meeting. The governor said that state wildlife agents should boycott TEDs laws until studies showed conclusively they worked. He said he would take the issue to Washington and "tell George Bush to read my lips." Congressman Tauzin said, "We are going to win this war eventually. A fishing family deserves to live every bit as much as a farming family" (*New Orleans Times-Picayune* 9 April 1989).

In another context a Texas shrimp-boat fleet owner said, "We feel like when the study comes back from the National Academy of Sciences, it'll prove what we've said all along—that Texas shrimpers don't catch any turtles off our coast" (*Corpus Christi Caller-Times* [hereafter CCCT] 25 July 1989).

Unbeknownst to shrimpers, the "studies" were to be only reviews of studies NMFS had already completed. A committee was to be appointed to review the methodology of the studies to find whether any were biased. Several fisheries administrators expressed the conviction to me that there had been no biases and that the findings would be vindicated. The shrimpers and the bureaucrats had in mind two quite different processes.

Under threat of lawsuits from conservationists, after the year had passed and even though the review had not been started, NMFS began to enforce its previous TEDs regulations. In July 1989, the Coast Guard announced it had been instructed to enforce the regulation.

The gulf states—Florida, Alabama, Mississippi, Louisiana, and Texas—open their shrimping seasons at different times. Shrimpers gather for each opening hoping for quick and relatively easy catches for at least a few days before the shrimp become scarce and more difficult to catch. As the season remains open longer and the supply of shrimp diminishes, boats must trawl longer to fill their nets and trawl more to fill their holds. Shrimpers from the other gulf states had converged on Texas ports for the opening of the Texas shrimp season.

On 22 July 1989, a week after shrimping season opened in Texas, angry shrimpers drew their boats into lines to block egress from and access to ship channels at Galveston, Port Arthur, Port Aransas, and Brownsville, Texas, and Cameron, Louisiana. Among the shrimpers were some from Coden and Bayou la Batre, Alabama. At Aransas Pass, Texas, 150 or more shrimp boats overwhelmed the Coast Guard and caught its cutters in the blockade. The Coast Guard attempted to break the blockade by blasting boats with water and cutting their anchor cables, but the attempt failed. About 200 boats blockaded the

Houston and Galveston ship channels. Some of the boats surrounded the ferry boat from Galveston and forced it to stop (*Dallas Morning News* 23 July 1989).

Sport fishing boats were held inside their ports or not allowed back in. This disrupted two weekend fishing competitions, interrupted charter boat operations, costing them their income for the weekend, and turned some sport fishermen against the shrimpers. While some large offshore oil-rig service boats and tenders ran the blockade, other boats were delayed.

Hoping the shrimpers would "take it as a victory of some sort and . . . relax a little," the Coast Guard broadcast the news that gulf coast congressmen would meet with the Secretary of Commerce to negotiate a resolution (CCCT 23 July 1989). The blockade broke up about noon the next day when the Coast Guard promised that negotiations would be held. Shrimpers vowed to return to the blockade if negotiations were unsuccessful.

Shrimpers were as surprised as anyone else at the success of their spur-of-the-moment blockade. One shrimper said, "This is the first time in thirty-something years that the Texas fishermen have been together on anything" (CCCT 24 July 1989). Vietnamese and American shrimpers from all gulf states joined in the blockade. No organization such as Concerned Shrimpers of America had orchestrated the action. It literally developed overnight as shrimpers expressed their outrage to one another on their radios (Cooper 1989).

A delegation of senators and representatives from the coastal states met with Robert Mosbacher, Secretary of Commerce, and urged him to suspend the regulations. Representative Billy Tauzin, a Democrat from Louisiana, had discussed the matter earlier with Mosbacher and suggested that the regulations might lead to violence. During the blockade, Tauzin and others requested Mosbacher's help. "I told him he could help if he wanted to. But he says his lawyers were telling him he was on shaky ground, that he'd be sued if he modified the regulations. I said, 'So get sued, let the courts decide' " (ibid., 3). Mosbacher met with two dozen congressmen from the region and with representatives who had discussed matters with shrimpers in Galveston (CCCT 30 July 1989).

The Coast Guard said it would file no charges against shrimpers. The Secretary of Commerce agreed to suspend the regulations again for forty-five days. After that time, until the National Academy of Sciences study was completed, shrimpers would be allowed to keep their nets in the water no longer than ninety minutes at a time instead of the usual three hours, short enough not to drown turtles. This announcement made shrimpers as happy as it made environmentalists angry (*CCCT* 25 July 1989).

Mosbacher is from Houston, Texas. After he suspended the regulations, a political scientist at Rice University, in Houston, said, "It seems pretty political to me, Texas fishermen appealing to a Texan for help" (*CCCT* 30 July 1989).

A National Marine Fisheries Service representative said that shrimpers were getting the wrong idea, thinking they would not have to use TEDs. He said they would have to use the devices eventually because economics were not to be a consideration in the salvation of endangered species (*CCCT* 25 July 1989).

Within two days the National Audubon Society called for a shrimp boycott to protest the gulf fishermen's refusal to use TEDs. No one thought such a boycott would have any impact on shrimpers, if for no other reason than that most shrimp consumed in America is imported. An Audubon Society spokesman criticized the Secretary of Commerce for responding to the blockade and said it was outrageous, goonish hooliganism (*CCCT* 27 July 1989). Local Audubon Society leaders on the gulf coast repudiated the national society's call for a boycott (*CCCT* 28 July 1989).

The National Wildlife Federation sued the Secretary of Commerce immediately, claiming that his proposal had no scientific basis and offered no protection to the turtles. Federation lawyers argued that he had responded only to the threats of violence and that shrimpers would not comply with time limits on their trawling since it would be costly to them. They said that the secretary's suspension of the regulations was illegal (*CCCT* 3 August 1989).

The federal judge ruled that the Commerce Department would have to implement some rules to protect turtles but did not specify what the rules were to be. If the department did not prepare new regulations, shrimpers would be required to use TEDs. The Department of Commerce said it would use trawling time limits. Environmentalists were pleased that the judge recognized the danger to turtles but displeased that he did not mandate a return to the TEDs regulations (*CCCT* 4 August 1989). The Commerce Department submitted new rules allowing a 105-minute tow instead of TEDs. This would allow 90 minutes to tow the nets and 15 minutes to drop and retrieve them (*CCCT* 5 August 1989). There would be a 105-minute fishing period, a 30-minute break, then another fishing period, alternating through the day. Anyone fishing in the break times would be in violation of the law (*CCCT* 8 August 1989).

The National Wildlife Federation was in court again charging that the fishing-period scheme did not protect turtles. The courts refused to overturn the Secretary of Commerce's procedure until September, when the time needed to promulgate rules had elapsed (*CCCT* 31 August 1989). Early in September, the Commerce Department announced that shrimpers must use TEDs. The department found that the time limits were ineffective and the shrimpers did not comply with them (*CCCT* 6 September 1989).

When President Bush visited New Orleans, four hundred to five hundred shrimpers demonstrated to request his intervention. They wanted the requirement suspended until the National Academy study was completed (*CCCT* 10 September 1989).

Each side appealed to science. The shrimpers were convinced that impartial scientific study of the issues would vindicate their position that they were not the major threat to turtles and that TEDs did not work nearly as well as some people claimed. Environmentalists cited "scientific" studies by biologists. It was not immediately apparent how many of these studies were done by biologists directly or indirectly connected to the environmental movement, such as those the Gulf Coast Conservation Association retain and pay.

The bureaucrats made repeated reference to "scientific studies" that showed that TEDs did not reduce the shrimp catch by more than some 10 percent. One fisheries official confided to me that some of the tests were based on numerous short tows because the biologists wanted to be sure to have a large sample to make the study appear statistically legitimate. Having witnessed the data collection, he reported that the "scientists" were more concerned with making their study appear to meet the criteria of statistical soundness than anything else. Therefore they made many short pulls of about twenty minutes rather than few long pulls of three hours or so to simulate the usual operating conditions of shrimp trawls.

I interviewed a number of shrimpers in 1989 in the months just before the disturbance of the blockade. They were part of a random sample of Vietnamese and American shrimpers, not individuals I had heard about or identified on other grounds. I talked to some shrimpers who were angry about almost everything, including TEDs, bureaucrats, and imports. Others were self-possessed, unflappable, cool headed, and, while recognizing the effects of events on them, more indifferent to those effects. All—Vietnamese and Americans alike—indicated that TEDs were their major concern and a major problem to them, but some had actively participated in the process of testing TEDs. Reports from shrimpers who cooperated with biologists in making the studies agreed with the fisheries bureaucrat.

Some shrimpers had conducted their own TEDs tests or had participated in field tests with NMFS biologists. One who had conducted independent tests under many conditions of weather, bottom, and depth showed me log books and reported that this volunteered data had been rejected. One who had participated in NMFS field tests said that the results of observations made under working conditions had been systematically discarded and disregarded. He told me that an NMFS observer had accompanied him and under normal working conditions he lost 20 to 25 percent of his catch. He said, "I never got the TED to work. I tried to get the results of the study they did with me. They didn't use my results. They did it to make the numbers look right."

He explained that a trawl is a funnel with a bag at the end. The TED lengthens the narrow end of the funnel and changes the flow of the water. The stream of the water through the trawl forces fish, trash, and shrimp to the inner surfaces of the bag. As things accumulate on the inner surface of the bag, they line it and impede the flow of water; the water begins to flow through the narrow end of the funnel rather than through the bag. The bag begins to act as a parachute. For the first twenty minutes or so, the TED does not make any difference. After that, when the bag begins to act as a parachute, much of the catch is propelled through the opening of the TED. Thus short pulls are not representative of actual working conditions, and NMFS observers have not accurately reported experience under true working conditions.

The National Academy of Sciences committee was charged to assess the scientific adequacy of NMFS studies regarding TEDs. The studies reportedly amounted to several "piles of paper three feet high." They were to review "scientific and technical information on conservation of sea turtles and causes and significance of turtle mortality, including that caused by commercial trawling. . . . The resulting report will be used by the Secretary of Commerce to assess the effectiveness of and need for regulations requiring the use of turtle-excluder devices (TEDs) by commercial shrimp-trawlers" (Magnuson et al. 1990, vii).

The study mentions a number of problems in assessing the consequences of TEDs for shrimping as well as their effectiveness for preserving turtles. The committee pointed out the problem of relying on data generated by short towing times, the variability of bottom conditions, and the complications introduced by trash and plants (ibid., 94). Turtles eat jelly fish and plants that resemble plastic debris that is discarded into coastal waters. The committee noted the effects of ingestion of plastics but was unable to quantify them (ibid., 84).

Committee members recognized the effects of shore-side human activity associated with beach development on the high mortality of turtle eggs and young turtles (ibid., 3, 84). Since natural mortality is high for eggs and young turtles, the chances of a single individual contributing to the next generation are small. The longer an individual survives, the more likely it is to contribute to the next generation. Hence it is more important to protect older juveniles than eggs and young turtles (ibid., 3). Since these older and larger turtles are the ones affected by shrimping, and the ones with higher reproductive value, the committee focused its attention on their preservation.

The report enumerated five sources of evidence that convinced committee members that shrimp trawling is a major source of mortality for this age category: the relation between mortality in trawls and the length of tow time; the coincidence of the shrimp season with turtle strandings in Texas and South Carolina; the relation between declining turtle populations and high shrimping effort on the Atlantic coast; the quantification of mortality in shrimp trawls; and the relation between turtle stranding and the timing of shrimping in North Carolina (ibid., 66–74).

The committee observed that "even if individual fishermen catch few turtles, the size of the shrimp fleet and the effort exerted result in a collective catch that is 'large,' although not all sea turtles that are caught in shrimp trawls necessarily die as a result" (ibid., 66). It identified "the incidental capture of turtles in shrimp trawls as the major cause of mortality associated with human activities" (ibid., 85) and recommended the mandatory use of TEDs (ibid., 9).

David White (1989a) presents data to show that gulf coast shrimpers' perceptions of their catch rate and turtle mortality are realistic and reasonable. He concludes that shrimpers would be satisfied with regulations—even if they are not in their interests—if they "make sense" and are "fair." He writes, "In the present instance, this would require (a) convincing them that turtles are in fact endangered, (b) presenting them with evidence that their activities are a significant threat, and (c) demonstrating that all culpable parties (whether beachfront developers, or foreign countries) are being proportionally burdened with responsibility for setting things right" (77).

There is little in the National Academy of Sciences report or the makeup of the committee to comfort shrimpers. Many of the ten members of the committee were associated with institutions that receive Sea Grant funds. One member represented the Florida Audubon Society, but no members represented the shrimping industry. The committee finding strongly supported the policy NMFS had adopted and suggested there were no alternatives. Though the report recognizes numerous other sources of sea turtle mortality, it only obliquely acknowledges that a reason to control shrimpers is that they are more easily controllable than real estate developers, foreign governments, and sea-litterers.

The experience of shrimpers with NMFS personnel and other fisheries bureaucrats did not inspire their trust. When I was interviewing shrimpers, many would ask initially whether I was a biologist, and a number expressed hostility toward biologists. Various levels of policy-making bureaucracies have provisions for "public input." At least, there is usually some provision for publication, and a waiting period for public comments. There are often hearings. Consensus among fishermen and even fisheries bureaucrats is that such periods have little impact on policy once it is formulated. Based on their experience, fishermen take the stance of "what is the point, no one will listen." M. E. Smith (1988) has pointed out occupational barriers and Meltzoff (1989) has discussed cultural impediments that prevent fishermen from participating meaningfully. In the specific instance of TEDs their opinions have not been taken into account. They therefore see the regulation as unfair.

That some fisheries bureaucrats and scholars agree with shrimpers' perceptions suggests that shrimpers are not simply being disagreeable because of their structural position or their stake in the matter, though that may well shape their rhetoric.

As it happened, it was less important to convince shrimpers of anything than to convince judges and administrators. This example of policy concerns the kind of gear shrimpers must use and affects them directly. Other policy decisions have equally severe consequences for fishermen even though those decisions do not directly regulate or even concern fishing. Policies that affect the quality of coastal waters determine the area, extent, and kinds of fishing.

Municipal Sewage and Water Pollution

The permanent population of Gulf Shores is about 2,500, but it has to be prepared to provide services for up to 100,000 people at peak recreational seasons when its condominiums, hotels, and even recreational-vehicle camping sites are full. In 1985 the Governmental Utility Services Corporation of Gulf Shores began building a $3.8 million sewage treatment plant to discharge as much as three million gallons of treated water per day. The corporation had to apply to the Alabama Department of Environmental Management (ADEM) for a permit to discharge the treated water into the Intracoastal Waterway.

The plant could operate under an administrative order until ADEM reached a decision on a permit to limit biochemical oxygen demand (BOD) and other characteristics of the discharged water.

Rick Wallace of Sea Grant explained (*MR* 10 December 1987) that biochemical oxygen demand (BOD) is a measure of how much oxygen bacteria consume while they break down the organic material in the discharged water. He went on to note that "a discharge with a high BOD has lots of organic material in it that will feed a lot of bacteria which in turn will consume oxygen to the point that less oxygen is available for shrimp, crabs and fish." ADEM permits set limits on a number of characteristics of discharged water at levels "which it is believed will not degrade the receiving body of water." He concluded: "The bottom line is that BOD and TKN [another measure] are indicators of how well sewage has been treated before it is discharged. When we pump more sewage into our streams, bayous and bays than they can assimilate, then we generally end up with a reduction in our desirable renewable resources and a loss of highly prized aesthetic values." The plant began discharging treated wastewater on 3 December 1987.

The levels in the draft permit, which recommended a BOD of two milligrams per liter during the summer and 15 milligrams per liter for the winter, were based on a 1984 ADEM study. Gulf Shores city experts proposed a revision to four milligrams per liter in the summer because it would cost another $2.2 million to modify the plant to meet the stricter requirement. Cost was a primary consideration as the community was not eligible for Federal Environmental Protection Agency funding until the EPA finished its overdue environmental impact statement on sewage disposal.

Because of pollution problems evident in Perdido Bay, where the discharge of treated wastewater from a paper company, Champion International, was suspected of being a major contributor, the issues of BOD, dying bays, treated wastewater discharges, and administrative hearings were much in the news and on the minds of environmentalists of Baldwin County when Gulf Shores applied to lower ADEM's standards. The town council of Orange Beach, a community on Perdido Bay, passed a resolution urging ADEM not to relax its standards for Gulf Shores.

On 18 November 1987, biologists and environmental officials held a symposium in Lillian, Alabama, a community on Perdido Bay, to discuss the problems of the bay. Biologists from the Dauphin Island Sea Lab discussed various findings and suggested that marine life in the bay might improve if they could find and correct the cause of oxygen depletion. The next evening in nearby Fairhope, the president of the Perdido Bay Environmental Association discussed signs of pollution in the bay at a public meeting sponsored by the League of Women Voters of Baldwin County.

Officials of Orange Beach called a meeting on 6 January 1988 to oppose lower standards for Gulf Shores. The chairman of its utility board moderated. An ADEM representative said the difference in standards was insignificant. A Baldwin County Commissioner suggested ADEM was inconsistent in requiring different standards for different communities. The next week Gulf Shores held a public information meeting at which the ADEM spokesman reiterated that the change in standard was insignificant and that ADEM would issue the permit unless it received testimony and data to show the reduced standards would be detrimental.

More than two hundred people attended ADEM's hearing on 26 January 1988 concerning its proposal to lower standards for Gulf Shores. Most speakers opposed the plan, and a lawyer for the private sewage company that serves Orange Beach said the company would sue ADEM to recover the million dollars it spent to bring its plant into compliance with the more rigorous standards. Citizens and officials both suggested the lowered standards would lead to pollution of the Intracoastal Waterway and adjacent Perdido and Bon Secour bays. The ADEM representative said the reduction in standards "is really not going to affect the bays on either side of the waterway" (*MR* 27 January 1988).

An assistant chief biologist for the state conservation department's Marine Resources Division opposed the permit and said: "I don't and you don't understand the water quality dynamics in the Gulf Intracoastal Waterway. And yet you are willing to sacrifice the health of that water body and perhaps the health of those multitudes of individuals who utilize that body of water for recreation, when it is not necessary" (ibid.).

In February a coalition of environmental groups, the Council of Concerned Communities, accused Alabama Senator Perry Hand of Gulf Shores of a conflict of interest because his engineering company had performed contract services for the community of Gulf Shores. The group accused him of accepting payment from the city to influence ADEM's decision to reduce the stringency of its permit because his firm helped the Gulf Shores utility board prepare and present engineering data to the ADEM staff. The assistant director of the Alabama state Ethics Commission said Hand had disclosed the relationship and that he had not appeared before ADEM. Hand said the environmentalists did not know the law and made false accusations.

In mid-February the Council of Concerned Communities organized a motorcade to Montgomery to request that the permit not be issued. According to a letter from one of the participants, the group received short shrift from Hand and Governor Guy Hunt in Montgomery, but it did meet with Attorney General Don Siegelman's staff.

Subsequent ADEM studies indicated that a BOD of four would not degrade the water quality of the intracoastal canal, and the permit was issued. The chief of ADEM's water division in a 1991 interview said that the initial water-quality standards are generated from abstract models that do not take into account local conditions or cost effectiveness criteria. One of the largest contributors to poor water quality was a seafood processor that has since discontinued operations in the area. ADEM's local tests since have indicated no deterioration of water quality.

Industrial Pollution

On 19 October 1987, Gert Becker, the president of a German firm, the Degussa Corporation, hosted Alabama's Governor Hunt, Lieutenant Governor Folsom, and Congressman Callahan of the First Congressional District at the unveiling of a new chemical plant in Theodore. The governor said he would continue to operate with his motto: "Alabama is open for business." Callahan said Degussa exemplified "the type of industry that we're trying to attract" (*MR* 20 October 1987). After an hour of speeches, guests and plant employees were treated to a seafood buffet.

The Mobile Board of Water and Sewer commissioners recommended the construction of a pipeline to discharge up to twenty-five million gallons of treated industrial and domestic sewage per day from the Theodore Industrial Park, where the new chemical plant is located, into Mobile Bay. ADEM conducted studies of potential effects of such discharges in 1976. The Fowl River Protective Association, a property owners' group, and the South Alabama Seafood Association argued that these studies were inadequate and that the effluents would deprive the water of oxygen and endanger the nearby oyster reef, and they challenged ADEM's permit in Mobile County circuit court. Judge Kendall ruled that ADEM failed to consider the threat to the oyster reefs and sent the permit back to ADEM for "such further consideration and proceedings as the agencies below may deem necessary or appropriate in light of this order" (*MR* 31 December 1987).

The president of Degussa said the pipeline is vital to the company's future expansion. He commented, "I think the question is not 'will it be built,' but 'when will it be built'" (ibid.). The Board of Water and

Sewer commissioners argued that the industrial potential of Mobile could not be realized without the pipeline, and it encouraged the Chamber of Commerce and other groups and industries to support its effort to construct one. Toward the end of January, the board voted to appeal the decision to the Alabama Supreme Court, and the Alabama Environmental Management Commission, parent organization of ADEM, joined in the appeal. The board and the Mobile Area Chamber of Commerce filed a motion requesting the judge to reconsider.

Late in January, the attorney for the Fowl River Protective Association proposed eliminating the five million gallons per day of domestic sewage from the pipeline by processing it at another site. The water board pointed out that this would overtax the facility, and that any expansion of industry or a homeport for the Navy would require additional sewage treatment facilities anyway. In 1986 ADEM found that the facility's discharge exceeded specified concentrations for BOD and suspended solids.

By mid-March the circuit judge denied the motion to reconsider his ruling, and the water board voted to appeal it to the Alabama Supreme Court. At the same time two developers approached the board with requests for sewage treatment for a light industrial and a residential complex on the west side of Mobile Bay. The board said that ADEM had reported fecal coliform levels of 900 parts per million in the Dog River, many times greater than the Alabama Health Department's standard of 100 parts per million. Leaking septic tanks were blamed for such high levels. ADEM was to conduct its restudy of consequences of wastewater discharges from the Theodore pipeline during the appeal period so it would be completed if the circuit judge's order were upheld.

Four days after the announcement of the appeal, a West German chemical company, Kay-Fries, announced that the company was considering expanding the facility at Theodore. The plant manager said, "If the pipeline were there, I think the decision will be made quicker. That's a factor we have to consider" (*MR* 26 March 1988).

There were several letters to the *Mobile Register* on both sides of the issue. One appealed to technical knowledge:

> The Theodore treatment system and outfall [from the pipeline] into the bay is proposed as a solution to pollution that is now occurring in the Theodore area. This treatment system and outfall have been conceived and designed by highly qualified chemists, engineers, biologists, physicists, ecologists, medical doctors and computer experts. It has been designed with all known safeguards, automatic and manual, to prevent a failure.
>
> The plan has been approved by the Mobile Water and Sewer Board

with direction from its expert technical staff, by the Environmental Protection Agency and the Alabama Department of Environmental Management, which is no longer controlled by politics or industry but has a dedicated, technically trained staff and enforcement power.

Now, we find that a judge, who probably didn't know what stratification water was until he heard it in the courtroom, has delayed the project by sending it back to the Alabama Environmental Commission, which has no technical staff. . . .

When will the citizens of Mobile and Baldwin counties wake up and not allow a few amateur environmentalists with no technical data delay a project that can only improve the environmental condition that currently exists. . . . (*MR* 13 February 1988)

An answering letter on 27 February quoted the studies presented in a symposium called "The Natural Resources of the Mobile Bay Estuary" to the effect that, "The relationships between treated sewage outfall and health of the bay oysters are complex and poorly understood. There is a critical need to evaluate the accuracy and sufficiency of existing data. . . ." The writer said further that it was not a few amateur environmentalists who were involved, but "a distinguished and independent group in the scientific community, along with the lay public [who] are trying to prevent the further degradation of our beautiful and very complex Mobile Bay."

Another writer objected to the assessments on homeowners to build the new pipelines, and wrote, "I sometimes feel after reading the papers the state of Alabama should erect new signs on our borders: 'Welcome to Alabama, you are free to dump your wastes in both our land and water resources' " (*MR* 29 February 1988).

A letter of 14 April 1988 agreed that Mobile needed new industry but said the pipeline was not the solution: "Mobile's economic ills go far beyond any outfall pipe and the fact is that, if the outfall is constructed as proposed, it would further deteriorate Mobile Bay, which is the economic heart and soul of the city of Mobile."

A *Mobile Register* editorial (27 April 1988) suggested that the pipeline would promote public health by removing the threat of septic tanks. The editorial continued, "This represents one more valid argument in favor of the outfall line [pipeline] which is being blocked by self-styled environmentalists who have no supporting scientific or technical arguments on their side."

Offshore Drilling

The Alabama Department of Conservation and Natural Resources has a State Lands Division, which is responsible for oil and gas leases.

Money from the leases and a 20 percent royalty on production is paid into a trust fund, the income from which goes into the General Fund of the state. Any offshore drilling site has to be approved by the U.S. Army Corps of Engineers, the state conservation department, and the state oil and gas board. No well can be closer than a mile to the southern beaches of Dauphin Island or Baldwin County, or closer than a half mile to the beaches of the Mississippi Sound or Mobile Bay. Oyster reefs are located in three tracts in the middle of Mobile Bay. From 1981 to late in 1987 no drilling was allowed within a half mile of living oyster reefs. This requirement would have made one drilling structure impossible. The Conservation Department removed the requirement and agreed to evaluate each proposal individually. The department's policy is to encourage locations as far as possible from reefs and not to permit the location of rigs on reefs or dredging of reefs.

Mobil Oil leased such tracts between Dauphin Island and Fort Morgan, in the southern part of Mobile Bay, in 1968 and discovered gas in 1979. It took the company nine years to get a permit to drill under the Alabama Oil and Gas Board's rules, and then only with a $55 million surety bond. Alabama has a "zero discharge requirement," so Mobil had to pay $20,000 per month to haul rainwater ashore and between $2 and $4 million per well to haul drilling waste ashore. In late October 1987, a Mobil official addressing the American Society of Mechanical Engineers in Mobile said:

> We encountered nothing but hostility over and over and over here. It has been an emotionally draining experience for us. . . . It's really to the company's credit that we stuck with it. We were not accustomed . . . to being treated in this manner.
>
> It was a poker game. We were in the game, and we couldn't afford to get out.
>
> We have taken a lot of verbal abuse that we do not think is justifiable.
>
> It shows a lack of farsightedness. . . . we need relief from the rainwater discharge. . . . I don't think there's anything we can do to hurt the environment. . . . We have to make a profit. If we have to, we will walk. (*MR* 28 October 1987)

When Exxon returned some of its leases to the state late in 1987, an editorial in the *Register* (29 November 1987) suggested that one reason for their return was "the antagonistic political climate in Alabama toward the oil and gas exploration industry."

In 1981 Shell Offshore Inc. had leased a tract directly south of the Mobil wells, outside Mobile Bay, in the gulf, about five and a half miles south of Dauphin Island, just inside the three-mile boundary that differentiates state waters from federal waters. Under the terms of the lease, the company had to start drilling by 12 October 1987. After a two-year review ADEM issued it a permit to discharge drilling wastes, a reversal of the previous zero discharge policy.

The Baldwin County Commissioners appealed this decision to the Alabama Environmental Management Commission (AEMC), ADEM's parent agency, which voted to revoke the permit, but at Shell's request it reconsidered, and then reversed its decision. Thus, Shell held the first ADEM drilling permit that allowed discharge of wastes into the gulf. AEMC set up a committee to monitor discharges.

Among other tasks, ADEM regulates landfills, hazardous waste haulage, and other waste disposal matters. An Alabama law of 1981 established a Solid Waste Management Act for Mobile County. The county requires permits on some of the activities regulated by ADEM, and by October 1987 had issued some two thousand permits under the act. The county's Solid Waste Management Act gives it power to regulate all solid and semisolid waste generated in Mobile County except sewage. With the support of Alabama's attorney general, the Mobile County Commissioners denied Shell permission to discharge drilling wastes. Within hours Shell had filed an appeal in Mobile County circuit court claiming that the commissioners had no authority to overrule an ADEM permit and that the Solid Waste Management Act applied to garbage, not drilling waste.

A dozen opponents and some proponents spoke at a special meeting of the commissioners. Shell's lawyers told the commissioners that studies had shown there was no permanent damage from drilling wastes and asked them to reject "emotional pleas." At a hearing the county commissioners maintained their power to regulate waste disposal and said the revocation of this decision would undermine their authority in other waste disposal matters. Shell argued that drilling-waste discharge was a water-pollution permit activity under ADEM's sole jurisdiction. The company further argued that the county commission and its Solid Waste Management Advisory Board lacked the expertise to evaluate applications like Shell's. The judge upheld Shell's claim that ADEM had exclusive power and the county had no regulatory power. Saying that ADEM had heard testimony from experts and had reviewed technical data during two years of review and decided that the discharge would cause no damage and that if there were any damage, he would rule on its amount, the judge refused the commissioners' request for bond from Shell.

The county commission and the Alabama attorney general appealed the circuit judge's decision and filed an appeal in the Alabama Court of Civil Appeals. The county argued that if drilling were delayed the "only harm to Shell would be economic, while the harm on the County's side would be environmental" (*MR* 10 October 1987). The commissioners moved for a stay of the judge's order. It was denied. Shell began discharging wastes immediately.

In the meantime, Shell had named the individual members of the Mobile County Solid Waste Management Advisory Board as defendants in a lawsuit against the county commission and requested $5 million in damages as the cost of operating under the no-discharge regulations. The county attorney interpreted this as an attempt to intimidate the individuals of the board, but Shell dropped the suit when they started drilling because, its attorney explained, the company would not lose the money at stake since they could discharge the wastes into the gulf.

Early in October a Baldwin County commissioner commented to me, "I'm just a layman, but we need to preserve the environment. Oil companies have so much wealth, they control all the processes." He used metaphors of money-filled hearing rooms. I asked, "Are you suggesting that oil companies bribe the people regulating the process?" "Yes," he answered without hesitation.

On 12 October an editorial in the *Mobile Register* said that the decisions were a victory for justice and common sense over emotional, unscientific and unstudied arguments of both the Baldwin and Mobile county commissions and concluded: "The irresponsibility of the Baldwin County Commission, however, has been matched by the Mobile County Commission, showboating Attorney General Don Siegelman and other politically motivated groups and environmental zealots who ignore scientific and technological evidence to try blocking a drilling program that is important to the economic growth of our entire area."

Baldwin County challenged AEMC's rehearing and reversal in Montgomery County Circuit Court. Shell appealed to the court of civil appeals, which prohibited the circuit court from deciding the issue and said the issues of the case should be presented to the circuit court on appeal of the permit's issuance. Baldwin County then appealed the civil appeals court's ruling to the Alabama Supreme Court.

The county challenged ADEM's permit in the Alabama Supreme Court on the procedural grounds that AEMC cannot rehear a case after it has voted on it, and two and a half months later the Alabama Supreme Court upheld the county and reinstated the original AEMC order. Shell had no permit to discharge wastes, but by then it was finished drilling.

At a meeting of the Baldwin County commissioners on 1 March in

Bay Minette, one commissioner said: "The problem was ADEM. They showed a lack of capacity for wanting to do a proper job. When the man who signs the application at ADEM doesn't even know where the well is, you've got a problem. You've got some dedicated people up there, but some of the folks over those people . . . they've got to go" (*MR* 2 March 1988).

In an attempt to get "science on its side," Shell Offshore provided funds for the University of South Alabama's Coastal Research and Development Institute and Dauphin Island Sea Lab to conduct preliminary research on the impact of the discharged materials on larval fish and fish eggs, but the research could not test effects of the rig in question because its discharges would be complete before the conclusion of the study.

The Coastal Environmental Alliance—a coalition of the Mobile Bay Audubon Society, the Mobile Bay Sierra Club, the Fowl River Protective Association, the Hollingers Island Community Association, and the Coastal Chapter of the Alabama Conservancy—announced on 17 December a boycott of Shell Oil Company. The president of the group said: "Shell Oil Co.'s dumping of drilling muds and cuttings into our state waters has opened the door for other petroleum companies to do the same. This poses a serious threat to the health and productivity of the Mobile Bay estuary" (*MR* 18 December 1987).

The president of the Mobile Bay Audubon Society supported the boycott and maintained, "If we continue to allow this dumping we don't know what it will do to the Mobile Bay ecosystem" (ibid.).

A *Mobile Register* editorial two days later said that experts had testified at numerous hearings that the discharge would do no harm, that such operations enhance rather than damage sealife, and that the environmentalists were more interested in publicity than anything else. It noted, "This is not all that surprising; the environmentalists have also chosen to ignore many other facts in a near-hysteric opposition to a project which most experts agree poses no threat to the environment" (*MR* 20 December 1987).

An Irvington man responded to the same editorial the next day: "Over the past 25 years or so, Mobile Bay has been the dumping ground for rapidly expanding chemical industry operations. This discharge of chemical by-products has been absorbed by the unique silts and clays of the bay bottom. The question is how much can the bay absorb, how much can the fish and oysters absorb, how much can 'us' absorb?" (*MR* 21 December 1987).

On 12 January, a priest from the Spring Hill Jesuit Community wrote:

The company "experts" and public relations staff assure us that this witches' brew of poisons is as harmless as a child's mud pies. The corporate lie is exposed by these two writers [of previous letters]. We should be grateful for their work.

We are reminded of the days when cigarette companies ran ads picturing famous athletes smoking to improve their game and health, and white-clad doctors assuring us that cigarettes add zest and health to life. (*MR* 12 January 1988)

On 19 April, Mobil's natural gas processing plant near Coden went into production to treat the gas from the wells in south Mobile Bay. After briefly telling of the history of Mobil's gas exploration and drilling from 1969, the trials and tribulations of court cases and delays, the *Mobile Press* editorialized: ". . . we congratulate Mobil for its perseverance over these many years and express our appreciation for the hundreds of millions of dollars poured into our economy by the industry exploration and development in our area waters."

Summary

Each of these four cases illustrates how policy is made and how it affects the fishing industry. Often the fishing industry is not the central concern of the policy, as with imports, environmental quality, and endangered species. These cases have common elements which I discuss in the next section in the context of the past, the evolution of Alabama's fishing industry to date, and its future prospects.

6

Past, Present, and Future: Rhetorics and Realities

The Past: Changing Systems

In each of the three periods of Alabama's seafood industry we see the interaction of different elements. Railroads are important to the first period but not the third. Canneries are central in the second period but not in the first or third. Each period is a different system with interdependent parts. As one changes, the others change until the whole system changes and a new period starts.

In the first period the volume of seafood depended initially on local demand and then on a wider market made accessible as the regional transportation system developed. Originally, the seafood industry developed in tandem with the cotton industry. As the United States removed Indians from Alabama, planters moved in with slave labor and Mobile became a cotton port. The transportation system developed to bring cotton from the interior to the port of Mobile. The wider the transportation network became, the larger the possible market area for coastal Alabama's seafood products. Poor white farmers provided a supply of cheap labor for cotton factories, and later for coal, iron, timber, and fishing industries. They scratched out their livings moving between poor farms and unskilled minimum-wage industrial jobs.

As railroads and steamboats penetrated farther to the north and local merchants began to produce ice in Mobile, fish merchants could pack seafood products for shipment to more distant destinations and they began to process fish and oysters for the inland trade. Then they started to fit out boats to seek red snapper in the Gulf of Mexico. They packed oysters to send by rail and riverboat to consumers as far from the coast as winter weather and ice supplies would allow. The following chronology outlines these developments in the era characterized by preservation with ice, transportation by rail, and experimentation with canning:

1814   Mobile fish market established
1850   Thirty-four fishermen, two oystermen in Mobile; sixteen watermen in Mobile County
1852   Railroad extends thirty-five miles
1858   Railroad extends 260 miles
1860   Seventy-one fishermen, thirty-seven oystermen in Mobile; forty-eight fishermen, fifty-seven oystermen in the rest of Alabama
1861   Railroad connects to Illinois Central
1870   First ice manufactured in Mobile
1890   First cannery in Mobile
1891   Legislature creates office of oyster inspector and levies ten-cents-per-barrel oyster tax
1896   First cannery in Bayou la Batre
1900   Eastern interests buy Bayou la Batre cannery
       Schooners fish for red snapper in gulf
1904   Second factory, at Alabama Port
       First shrimp caught for canning in seines
1909   Oyster Commission established
1912   Canneries close

We can see the increase in the number of Mobile's fishermen as the railroad gets longer and longer. We see also the first experiments with canning and the first seafood legislation, which had the consequence of shutting down the oyster industry because no one could make a living at it with such high taxes. Figure 5 outlines the main processes as relationships among elements of this system. As the cotton industry developed, the railroads increased in mileage. As railroads increased their mileage, the market area for seafood increased. With local supplies of ice and the increased market area, the demand for fish and oysters increased; there were more fish dealers as well as fishermen and boats, and the catch was larger. Figures 6 and 7 show the increases in value of fish and oysters that resulted from this process.

Toward the end of the nineteenth century some canneries were established on the gulf. The Alabama legislature put a heavy tax on oysters and oyster boats so that it became unprofitable to can, catch, or cultivate oysters. While the fledgling oyster-canning industry ground to a halt in Alabama until 1915 when the legislation was repealed, it continued to develop in Mississippi, especially at Biloxi. As the

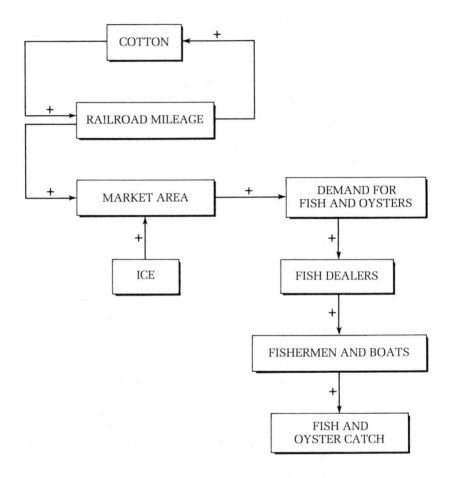

Figure 5. Phase 1: Regional distribution system, 1820–1915.

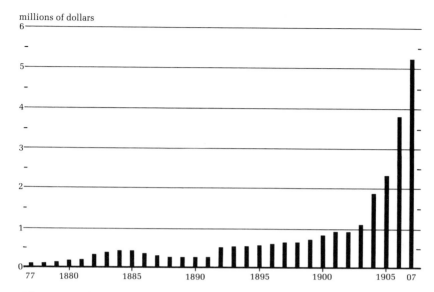

Figure 6. Value of fish in millions of 1967 dollars.

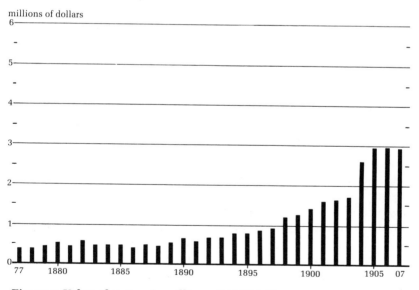

Figure 7. Value of oysters in millions of 1967 dollars.

problems increased in the oyster industry of Chesapeake Bay and the East, some eastern packers began to invest in facilities in Alabama. Local people began to catch oysters for the canneries. At first the factories imported "Bohemian" workers from the East. The supplies of oysters were undependable, and canneries tried to stay in operation by canning vegetables and shrimp.

Factories first used schooners to seine for shrimp in Louisiana's marshes. When fishermen tried to organize, the owners simply replaced them with unorganized independent fishermen. Attempts to organize failed until the predominant form of shrimping started to shift to trawling about 1918 when fishermen began to own their own boats and gear.

The following chronology charts the development of this process between 1915 and 1950, the period of industrial canning:

1915   Oyster Commission abolished
       Portersville Bay Cannery opens, imports labor from East Coast
1918   Introduction of shrimp trawls
1919   Legislature puts shrimp and oysters under Department of Conservation
1922   Five canneries in south Mobile County
1935   Gulf Coast Shrimpers' and Oystermen's Association labor union at Bayou la Batre strikes for better prices
1937   Woods Hole Oceanographic Institution ship *Atlantis* searches for shrimp off Alabama coast to increase fishing range
1940   Shrimpers' and Oystermen's Union in Bayou la Batre strikes. Bayou la Batre fishermen withdraw from union and form a local union
1947   Frozen shrimp begins to compete with canned shrimp
1949   Shrimp imports cause alarm among producers

The chronology shows that as canneries were established with outside and then local capital, there was a greater demand for a stable supply of seafood which encouraged the development of shrimping with trawls. In 1918 when it was introduced, trawling made the supply of shrimp more reliable. This increased the catch of shrimp and encouraged the canneries. Fishermen began to provide canneries with shrimp in the summer and oysters in the winter. The canneries were dependent on local shrimp and local labor, so factory workers and fishermen were in a favorable position to organize into unions to bargain for wages and prices. The canneries resisted this organization, but over a period of years, a system developed whereby the fishermen and packers could negotiate with each other for prices.

Sometimes there were strikes that lasted for days or even weeks, but the packers negotiated because they had no other source of raw materials. Figure 8 illustrates the relationships among variables of this system.

Processors began to organize on behalf of the industry not only to negotiate with fishermen, but also to sponsor advertising campaigns to build greater demand for seafood and to encourage increased government-funded fisheries research. This research effort began to affect gulf fisheries in 1950 when the National Fisheries Service stationed a research vessel at Pascagoula. The processors have benefited since from government-sponsored programs of research on marine biology, food processing, and allied subjects.

Shrimpers and biologists alike searched for new fishing grounds. The period of industrial shrimping began in 1950 with the discovery of unexploited regions in the Gulf of Mexico. The development of this period is outlined in the following chronology:

1950   Shrimp "rushes" in Gulf of Mexico
       Fleet expands number of large vessels
       Shrimping area expands
       U.S. Fish and Wildlife research vessel *Oregon* stationed at
       Pascagoula for shrimp research
       First blessing-of-the-fleet ceremonies at Bayou la Batre
1951   Price disputes close shrimping
1954   Some shrimpers are unable to repay boat debts
1955   Court case finds Shrimpers' and Oystermen's Association violates antitrust laws
       Bayou la Batre incorporates
1956   Shrimp processing and freezing mechanized
1957   Double-rig trawling spreads from Texas, increases shrimp catch 15 to 30 percent
1958   Influx of imported canned oysters discourages canning operations
1960   Imports seen as a problem to shrimpers
1961   Industrial and domestic pollution cited as reasons for decreases in oyster production

To exploit the resources of the gulf, shrimpers ordered larger vessels for the rougher and deeper waters and in the mid-fifties began dragging a trawl off each side of the boat to increase catches.

At the same time, with the development of freezing technology, processors began importing shrimp to even out their supply and make it more reliable. No longer reliant on local supplies of shrimp, they

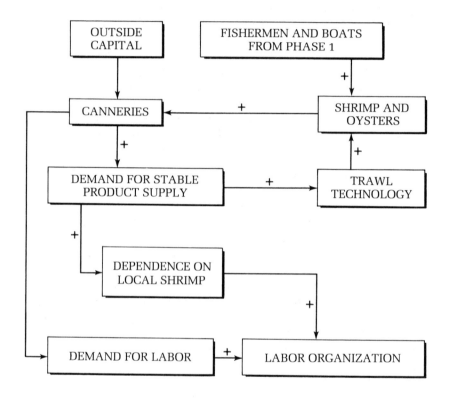

Figure 8. Phase 2: Industrial canning system, 1915–50.

were less dependent on local fishermen just when fishermen could deliver larger and more reliable catches. Shrimpers were in debt for the expenses of their new technological devices, more and more expensive and sophisticated each year as they incorporated new navigational aids and electronic equipment. The dependency relationship was turned around. Now shrimpers were dependent on processors to buy their catches so they could pay off larger debts and meet increased operating expenses. Fishermen began to lose their boats, now sizable investments, and more and more boats were once again owned by processors. Processors began to rely increasingly on foreign shrimp and were less dependent on local fishermen for their raw material. The unions lost influence. Figure 9 illustrates the relationships during this period.

In these years, biologists became much more involved in making fisheries policy at national, regional, and state levels. The rhetoric of fisheries policy became scientific, and the best defense for any policy was a scientific one. Sportsmen organized to support legislation to preserve the quality of the environment and to oppose commercial fishing.

The Present: Science and Policy

Experienced administrative personnel are acutely aware of the "politics" of any decision and understand better than anyone else involved the conflicting interests of various groups, the long-term objectives to assure the public good, the technical and legal requirements, the overt political considerations from politicians, the power of the press and public opinion.

Paredes (1985) has described the workings of the Gulf Coast Fisheries Management Council's Scientific and Statistical Committee (SSC), whose task it is to inform the council if the proposals it considers are based on the best available scientific data, whether the interpretations and analysis are appropriate, and whether the conclusions are scientifically warranted. The committee is concerned to maintain the scientific purity of the SSC and not contaminate it with political matters. Paredes conjectures that the possibility of court challenges to managerial measures is behind these procedural rituals. Indeed Leary (1985, 183), in his comment to Paredes's paper, verifies this when he says: "The use of the multidisciplinary, blue-ribbon panel of scientists as a review board has provided a position of strength in defense of plans and management regulations. Although there have been legal challenges to plans and the quality of data used, none have

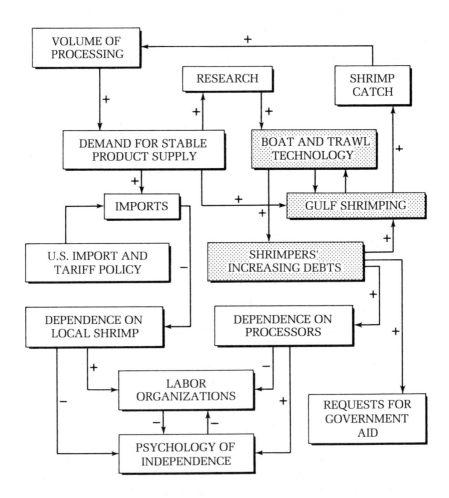

Figure 9. Phase 3: Industrial shrimping, 1950–present.

yet prevailed in court with respect to gulf fishery management plans. The system seems to work."

Leary's criterion for "working" is procedural purity that is defensible in court. This takes for granted the point that Acheson (1985, 183) makes explicit in the same context, that "it is impossible to promulgate any rules without causing some people to benefit and others to lose." While every administrator knows this from experience, it is just this experience which social scientists such as McCay (1985) describe when they point out that these matters of allocation and distribution effects, political issues, are often what anthropologists are most competent to talk about, and that the issue of "big guys against little guys" is beyond the committee's purview. It is not that anthropologists or social scientists are the only ones who have noticed this, but it is part of our subject matter, part of the data we try to understand, while it is not part of the subject matter of biologists.

There are other criteria for whether a policy "works." A biological criterion is the state of the stocks managed. An economic one is the level of prosperity of fishermen, processors, or whoever the policy is meant to benefit. A political one is the degree of acceptance or unrest that greets the policy.

In each of the examples of policy in the last section, the rhetoric of scientific analysis was highly valued (Miller 1987). Each disputing party, except shrimpers, had credible experts allied with it.

It appears that the TEDs matter has reached a conclusion. I do not think that any scientific study of any kind can have or has had any major impact in the process. The shrimpers do not have the power to make use of science. The environmentalists have used scientists and their evidence in their own rhetorical interests, not in any objective way. A "blue-ribbon panel" has put the seal of approval of the National Academy of Science on the policy. Now it remains but to assess the consequences of the new regulations.

Sport fishermen have been trying to outlaw trawling almost since it was introduced to the Gulf of Mexico. It remains to be determined to what extent the pressure to preserve turtles through the use of TEDs has been brought to bear by sport fishermen. Sport fishing groups have started calling for additional devices on trawls to exclude finfish so they will not be killed as incidental by-catch. It is certain that such finfish are not endangered species by any measure. Preservation is no motive for demanding such gear changes. Sport fishermen argue that the fish should be reserved for their entertainment. Shrimpers widely suspect that the main motive of such regulations is less to protect turtles or fish than to remove trawling from the Gulf of Mexico. There has been considerable controversy and litigation about the promulgation of fisheries regulations in the Gulf of Mexico (Shelfer 1987; Oertel 1987). Oertel writes: "As someone who represents the commercial fishing industry in Florida and confesses to such a bias, it is my impression that commercial fishermen want no more than a reasonable piece of the pie, while the recreational sector wants the entire resource for its exclusive use" (1987, 59).

The shrimpers' blockade in 1989 was on a weekend and interfered with fishing tournaments and charter-boat operators. The businesses that cater to sport fishermen lost most of a weekend's income (CCCT 23 July 1989) and sued some of the shrimpers, seeking restitution of losses (CCCT 10 August 1989). Sport fishermen and the enterprises that serve them were vocal in their opposition to the interference with their pursuits and, when I was in Port Aransas during the blockade, had no good word to say for shrimpers.

While shrimpers may gain some national-level support from a few local politicians such as those representatives and senators who come from areas with many shrimpers, especially coastal Louisiana, some parts of coastal Texas, and coastal Alabama, it is clear that at the level of national politics support for shrimpers is slight. Politicians can gain much greater political benefit by supporting environmentalists than fishermen. The cause of conservation has the aura of purity and virtue. Environmentalists castigated Alabama's Senator Heflin for his stance on TEDs (Durrenberger 1988). Most politicians can better afford to be against rather than for commercial fishermen of all kinds. Sport fishermen therefore have a much more powerful political hand than shrimpers at both state and national levels. As one fisheries bureaucrat put it in a conversation with me, the question is whether the Gulf of Mexico will be a recreational lake for the rich or a place to make a living. This is the proper context for thinking about the political and ideological consequences of the TEDs issue.

In the policy and courtroom discourse, science has ceased to have any objective value or use. It has become emblematic of the imputed purity, awareness, and progressiveness of environmentalists as versus the imagined pollution, ignorance, and backwardness of shrimpers. Environmental groups have sufficient funds to retain their own biologists and lawyers. They create science in their own service. Shrimpers have no scientists working for them to invent a favorable ideological atmosphere for commercial fishing. Because of the very nature and conditions of bureaucratic science, it serves policy ends (Mills 1959). The issues of methodology have become so complex that a committee of the Academy of Sciences had to be appointed to sort them out. The committee members did not do what shrimpers thought they would do. They did not collect new data or consult with shrimpers or observe them to learn of their working conditions. Nor did they delve into the sociology of knowledge to analyze the underlying assumptions that guided the collection and classification of data, the definitions of facts, the formulation of questions, and the ideological and political origins of such propositions (Durrenberger 1990).

Sport fishing even affects anthropological analyses. Pálsson (1989, 1) points out that many anthropologists "operate with a 'natural' model of fishing which emphasizes material context and ecological relations. Such a model draws attention to the adaptive significance of social organization, depicting the producer as an autonomous individual engaged in the technical act of catching fish. An alternative theoretical approach is needed which appreciates the differences between fishing economies and the social relations in which production is embedded." He relates the individualistic view to the fascination of the European leisure classes with the individualistic pursuit of mobile prey, terrestrial and aquatic. Fishing was for them, as it is for contemporary American sport fishermen, a nonsubsistence activity with recreational value. Pálsson goes on to quote Walton's *Angler* to exemplify this quality, and its nobility. While the contemporary United States has no hereditary aristocracy, there is a class of the wealthy and dominant who derive similar power and prestige from the pursuit of terrestrial and aquatic animals.

To be sure they are not the only ones who fish for sport. Some people fish to supplement their subsistence resources, and many who fish for sport are neither rich nor powerful. But it is the wealthy who are organized and who transform their desires into political terms.

There will be economic consequences of the TED regulations. Over the past years, the gulf shrimp fleet caught more shrimp to sell at higher prices. The number and size of boats increased and each boat increased its effort. The increase in shrimp catch was due to more and larger boats fishing more days.

From 1971 to 1977 the cost of fuel increased 208 percent and fixed costs (insurance, overhead, depreciation, interest) increased 149 percent. Proportional to catch, the costs increased 115 percent. The consumer price index, a measure of inflation, increased 50 percent. Net income depended on vessel size and material. Wooden vessels and medium-sized boats did better than larger, steel-hulled vessels (Gulf of Mexico Fishery Management Council 1981).

For some years, increasing shrimp prices offset increases in expenses, but in 1980 prices fell, causing a cost-price "squeeze." Fuel efficiency became an important concern in vessel design and construction. Boat size affects fuel efficiency. Medium-sized boats, from fifty-one to sixty-five feet long, had about twice the gross revenue per dollar of fuel expenditure as vessels larger than sixty-five feet. Medium-sized boats also fared better than small ones. Large wooden boats landed $7.65 worth of shrimp per dollar expended on fuel, while steel boats of equal size landed only $5.88 (ibid.).

In the past when the balance of prices and costs was favorable and shrimp prices were rising, investments in shrimp boats were more profitable than alternative uses for capital. When prices declined, shrimpers continued to operate as long as they could pay the costs of operating their boats. When they could not make enough to cover expenses, they tied up their boats. At that point, an owner would try to sell his boat, but, since shrimping was no more attractive to anyone else, there was no market for boats (ibid.).

By the late seventies "it [was] clear that the management of the shrimp fishery to achieve economic optimums would necessitate a drastic reduction in the amount of effort applied in the fishery, and hence a reduction in the number of vessels allowed to fish" (ibid., 3–84).

Since that time, the number of boats has not decreased but increased dramatically with the influx of Vietnamese shrimpers. Success during periods of high prices leads to investments, which have engendered losses during periods of price declines. The importation of shrimp has contributed to lower domestic prices for shrimp, and, while low prices may hurt shrimpers, they benefit packers and processors, so imports are not likely to be curtailed.

In 1980 the Secretary of Commerce issued a statement that the shrimp industry was in a critical situation because of increased fuel costs, declining demand, and depressed prices. He offered an assistance program of low-cost loans and research (Gulf of Mexico Fishery Management Council 1981).

United States shrimping inside Mexico's 200-mile limit was terminated in 1980. About 17 percent of Texas landings and 19 percent of its revenues were from Mexican waters. Most of the Mexican catch was landed at Brownsville and Port Isabel. Forty-seven percent of the landings at these two ports were from Mexican waters. For all gulf states, about 10 percent of effort and landings were in or from Mexican waters. Economists correctly predicted that the diversion of this effort from Mexican to U.S. waters would result in losses of income (ibid.).

In summary, imports result in lower prices and are not controlled.

Fuel and other costs have increased more than shrimp prices have. Because of the closing of Mexican waters and the influx of Vietnamese fishermen, more effort and boats were directed to a fishery that already had too many boats and fishermen working it. Such factors do not affect all shrimpers in the same way. They have different effects for those with steel rather than wooden boats, those who own larger or smaller rather than middle-sized boats, those who are in deeper debt for their boats, those who own one rather than several or many boats.

TEDs will not have the same effects for all shrimpers, but they will reduce everyone's catches. How much catches will be reduced is debated and may never be established with certainty. TEDs will increase everyone's fuel expenditures because they add to the resistance of the gear. The devices may be responsible for accidents and may have an impact on insurance rates, though this will be differentially felt as many owner-operators have no insurance since the rates are already prohibitively high for them.

It is certain, however, that given the consequences of increasing costs, decreasing or stable prices, imports, increasing effort, increasing numbers of boats, the entrance of new fishermen into the fishery, and the closure of the Mexican waters, TEDs will not benefit anyone in the shrimping industry—fishermen, processors, or dealers.

Assuming that TEDs will have some positive impact for turtles, Patricia Sharpe (1988, 105) asks the same question many shrimpers have: "Who pays for saving an endangered species?" As one shrimper put it, "Not one of those damn environmentalists would give 20 percent of his paycheck for a turtle" (*CCCT* 30 July 1989). Sharpe says that "in the midst of rhetoric about the ruination of the shrimp industry, it's easy to ignore that other businesses bear the cost of regulations that provide a public good, such as clean air or safe work-places . . ." (Sharpe 1988, 105).

This analogy is false on several grounds. First, it compares shrimp boats to large corporations. As the examples I have discussed show, corporations are much more powerful than shrimpers and often evade their responsibilities and their expenses or transfer the costs of cleaning up the environment to the public at large. Second, this analogy does not take into account the social costs of polluted air and water—the costs that appear in rates of cancer, respiratory ailments, and other environmentally caused health problems, and the impact of the expenses of lost work, health care, and shortened human lives. Unsafe working conditions have similar social costs.

One of the reasons TEDs regulations do not make sense to shrimpers (D. White 1989a) is that it is quite impossible to conceive of similar, parallel, or analogous social costs even if one or several species of turtles do become extinct. Because imports are such a large portion of the market that there is no possibility of passing the cost on to the consumer, it is these same shrimpers who, one way or another, will pay the price of protecting turtles with TEDs. Thus, it appears unfair to them (ibid.).

While the TEDs regulation is not likely to destroy the gulf shrimping industry, it will probably make a significant difference to some in the industry and alter the composition of the industry.

Sport fishermen who favor TEDs share interests with commercial fishermen when it comes to pollution. They have been determined in their pursuit of pollution control and environmental quality, issues of importance to both commercial and sport fishermen. Both benefit from unpolluted waters.

If a corporate group wishes to discharge wastewaters into Alabama waters, it must apply to ADEM for a permit. ADEM studies the matter, holds hearings, and issues a permit. At any point, other groups (including municipalities, special interest groups, environmental groups, and counties) may attempt to influence ADEM through persuasion at meetings or through administrative appeals to its parent body, the Alabama Environmental Management Commission; they also have recourse to the state's county circuit courts, civil appeals courts, and Supreme Court, other kinds of lawsuits, appeals to public opinion through letters to newspapers, editorials, and the employment of public relations specialists to make credible responses. Such groups may also have access to extra-processual means, as the anthropologist Paul Bohannan calls processes outside the legally constituted channels of decision making, appeals, and influence (1958), such as boycotts, demonstrations, blockades, attempts to capture press attention, and, it is sometimes alleged, bribery.

The rhetoric of the appeals is a cultural dimension of the process. Some argue that ADEM regulations are sufficient to prevent environmental degradation; others say that any interference with the environment is deleterious and to be avoided; still others believe that we do not know the ecological consequences of discharging treated wastewater and drilling wastes into estuarial and gulf waters and all discharges should be avoided. Some hold that if one has a permit for it, it is all right, whatever it is and whatever its consequences may be, because competent public officials would not issue a permit for actions that are against the public health and welfare they are charged to protect. Some argue the public officials are not competent; others, that they are negligent of their charge. Scientific inquiry becomes one component in this rhetoric, used by all sides, for their own purposes.

The consequences of the processes are more political than ecological. They shape the understandings and discussions of commercial fishing rather than the realities of fish in the sea, in the nets, at the markets, or on the tables. But these rhetorics, their application, and the forces that shape them contribute to the formation of policies that directly affect the realities of fishing whether it be via pollution or cleaning of waters, opening or closing of fisheries, legislation on endangered species, or the classification of imported versus domestic production.

Public bodies such as municipalities, counties, and state agencies are not monolithic. The TEDs issue pitted a single state (Louisiana) against the United States and shrimpers against NMFS and environmentalists. In just the four cases discussed in the last chapter we see municipality against municipality, one state agency against another, a state against the federal government, regulated fishermen against their regulators, as well as the classic model of corporations against environmentalists.

The League of Women Voters was established in part to combat corruption in government, and in Baldwin County it has also participated in environmental debates. There are several other environmental groups that have not come into this analysis because they have not been active in any of the cases: The Coastal Land Trust is a private organization to purchase gulf coast wetlands; Wildlife Rescue, Inc., of Gulf Breeze, Florida, not far east of the Alabama border, tries to save pelicans that become tangled in fishing line. In 1982 an Alabama chapter of the Gulf Coast Conservation Association was formed in Mobile. The group was formed in Texas, and Alabama was the second state to form a chapter.

These groups form coalitions with other environmental groups on national, local, and state levels to pursue common goals. The National Audubon Society is active in lobbying in favor of the Endangered Species Act and its TEDs regulations so adamantly opposed by shrimpers. At the same time, such groups favor regulations to preserve the waters and hence the resources that the oystermen and shrimpers rely on for their livelihoods. In the context of water quality preservation they are natural allies of fishermen, but in the context of the Endangered Species Act they oppose one another.

The TEDs case was complex as it involved state and federal levels of administration and legislation, as well as judicial review. First the Endangered Species Act was passed, a legislative act. Then various sea turtles were classified as coming under the purview of the act, an administrative act. NMFS was given the responsibility for protecting the turtles as an executive agency whose function it is to carry out legislation. Private groups threatened NMFS with lawsuits if they did not require the use of TEDs. After token negotiations, NMFS promulgated a TEDs policy under this threat of judicial action. Legislators attempted to change the law. One attempt failed, but another succeeded for a time. A court stayed the enforcement of the administrative orders at the behest of a state agency, and another court upheld the rules and the rules were enforced.

Legislation, administrative practice, and judicial review all contribute to the formation of policy in a set of complex relationships, which figure 10 illustrates. In the legislative process, legislators at the state legislature, the U.S. House of Representatives, or the U.S. Senate represent what they see to be the interests of their constituents in a process that is recognized as intensely political. Given conflicting interests among those constituents, they must make some judgment about which interests to favor in their attempts to shape legislation. Senator Heflin and Representative Callahan of Alabama and other gulf states legislators have represented the desires of Alabama shrimpers against the desires of various environmental groups. The compromise amendment was supposed to satisfy both groups. Individuals with common interests can band together into special interest groups to advance their interests to legislators and attempt to gain legislative power for their points of view by any number of means or appeals to legislators.

The formulation of administrative procedures is similar whether it be at the level of city councils, the state, or the federal government. The administrative process does not represent interests in the same way but is conceived of as a technical process. The administrators see some problem that requires regulation. They call on experts, scientists and technicians, to define the issues and propose regulatory measures. The regulations are formulated in a technical rather than an explicitly political context. After the regulations are formulated, then the affected members of the public are invited to comment directly on the issue, to represent their own interests to the policy makers. As with fishery regulations from NMFS, the proposed regulations are, by definition and by law, formulated in terms of the best available scientific data. Thus control of scientific production and the definition of its questions and terms become important political weapons.

The third source of law is the courts, which have several functions. One is to insure that proper procedure is followed, for instance, adherence to scientific knowledge in administrative processes. Another

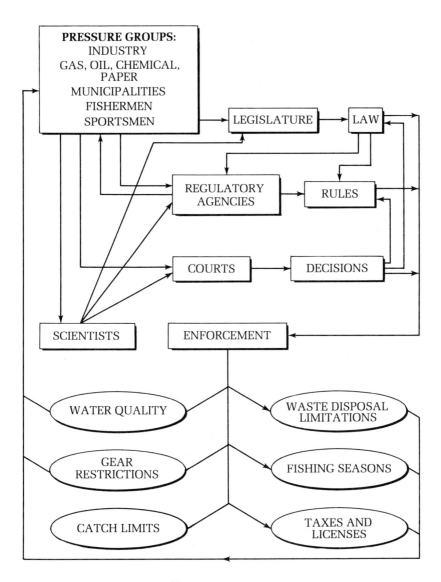

Figure 10. Contemporary policy process.

is to interpret such matters as areas of jurisdiction, to determine what branches of government have what powers.

In each of the three processes, the rhetoric of scientific analysis is highly valued. Shrimpers have reported their experience, but this does not have the impact of scientific findings, with the imprimatur of a university, a research facility, and a PhD researcher with Sea Grant funding. Shrimpers recognize this problem explicitly (Patti 1987).

Patti (1987) points to some of the reasons that fishermen are underrepresented in the rules-making process, and M. E. Smith tells the same story: Fishermen fish for a living. They do not make a living by going to meetings. Smith reports that when a New England skipper thought it necessary to attend New England Regional Fisheries Management Council meetings, "his crew grumbled at the lost fishing days, his wife nagged about decreased household monies, and the buyer to whom he regularly sold, complained about short landings" (M. E. Smith 1988, 36).

Given that the management process rests on scientific rhetoric, and that of all participants in this process, the fishermen have least access to scientific work and personnel, they are confined to "degrees of tokenism" or "nonparticipation" in their level of participation, as Kafka (1984) calls such relationships in Canada.

All cases entail two sides. This is not a trivial observation, because it is clearly possible for each case to have involved more than two sides, and in some countries, especially those with proportional representation, there are routinely many-sided debates and contests. The American adversarial process of policy making, however, makes two the maximum number of parties to a dispute, hence the saying that "politics makes strange bedfellows."

The opposing parties are not always "corporations" versus "environmentalists." ADEM, a state agency, and Gulf Shores, a municipality, were aligned against another municipality, Orange Beach, and a group of environmentalists that organized for the specific case. The Mobile Water Board, a municipal agency, and ADEM, a state agency, with the support of multinational corporations and the chamber of commerce, were opposed to environmental groups. A branch of a large multinational corporation, Shell Offshore Company, and a state agency, ADEM, were opposed to the county commissions of Baldwin and Mobile counties with the support of another state agency, the attorney general.

There seems to be agreement on the principle that the contested matters can be decided by appeal to scientific evidence. One rhetorical posture is to present one's position as scientifically justified while branding the other's as unscientific, emotional, and irrational even to the point of insanity. Each side of the TEDs issue argued its case on the evidence and said the other side lacked credible evidence. The *Mobile Register* referred in its editorials and reports to "emotional pleas" (TEDs), "environmental zealots who ignore scientific and technological evidence," "emotional and unscientific arguments" (the Shell case), and "self-styled environmentalists who have no supporting scientific or technical arguments" (the Theodore case).

This kind of characterization was obviously entailed in the Perdido Bay Environmental Association when a member said the group needed persuasive scientific evidence lest it be caught in a dead-end hearing. An ADEM representative said the agency would respond to data that would indicate the proposed reduced standards for Gulf Shores would be detrimental. Shell labeled the case against it as "emotional pleas," and said its opponents lacked relevant expertise. A judge accepted the scientific quality of ADEM's review, as it was based on expert testimony and technical data. Another judge questioned the scientific quality of ADEM's findings about the Theodore outfall line.

One question is, Which of the two sides has more compelling "scientific" evidence? Each side marshals its experts—those who agree with its premise—and may literally accuse the other of witchcraft as the Jesuit father did in his letter.

A second issue, similar to the first, is the credibility of the decision makers. A Mobile County circuit judge found that ADEM's study of the environmental consequences of the Theodore outfall line was insufficient and remanded the case for further study. A letter writer challenged a circuit judge's competence to decide environmental issues in this case. In the Shell case a Baldwin County commissioner suggested that ADEM staff or their supervisors were inadequate to the decisions they must routinely make. The environmentalists in the Gulf Shores case accused a local lawmaker of corruption.

In May 1988 the chief attorney for ADEM, who had worked for the agency since its inception in 1982, resigned and said that the agency's performance had deteriorated from moderately effective earlier to inadequate because politics influenced the regulatory process. He said that in the private sector he would no longer have to answer "political questions about whether taking enforcement action is going to result in layoffs of employees or whether the violator is a contributor to somebody's campaign . . . of (whether) the violator has some influence with political officials. I have experienced these things in my employment with the state of Alabama" (*MR* 16 May 1988).

The director of the agency denied most of these points and said, "We really have got a professional organization, and we are trying to make it better" (ibid.).

The two points of view mirror the rhetoric of those who appeal to the agency. It is political, biased, incompetent. It is professional, scientific, competent. It is the same for any key figure, a judge, an environmentalist, an environmental group, a corporation spokesman, a county commissioner.

A third dimension of the rhetoric entails prosperity versus stagnation. Prosperity and progress mean more people, more industry, more wastes to dispose of, as all three cases show. One side has the view that discharging treated wastes into coastal waters threatens the estuarial life of the bays, bayous, and sounds, and thus the seafood industry built on it. The other side argues that increased waste disposal is necessary to a future-oriented and prosperity-oriented community. Each side can label the other as antibusiness, antiprosperity, and antifuture.

This binary rhetoric fits the social model of two opposing sides. Each can easily place the other into its ideology as a representative of impurity or danger. Each side must be careful to represent itself as scientific, unemotional, future oriented, and incorruptible. The arguments are variants of a single purity/pollution dichotomy often discussed by anthropologists (Lévi-Strauss 1963, 1966; Durrenberger and Quinlan 1987; Douglas 1982), which can be expressed in the following way:

Purity	Danger (Impurity)
rationality	irrationality, emotionality
sanity	insanity, zealotry
science	folklore, superstition
competence	incompetence
stability	instability
pro-progress	anti-progress
cleanliness	corruption (political); pollution (environmental)
clean	dirty
moral	immoral
natural	unnatural; artificial; perverted

As each Alabama example shows, scientific expertise can be aligned with either side of a contest; a plausible scientific rhetoric can be constructed for any position. While science may be neutral, its uses are political (Pálsson 1989). The United States and Canada may be unusual in their growing conflicts, especially evident in the Gulf of Mexico, between recreational and commercial fishermen. In his review of the anthropological literature on fishing, Gísli Pálsson (1989) mentions fishing for use and fishing for exchange. We must now add a third category, fishing for pleasure. In this and other issues of allocation, the decisions are by their very nature political. Management decisions allocate a resource and answer the question of who gets what and how, and politics is the practice of making such decisions. An appeal to biology or economics does not make a decision better or more neutral.

In politics, the people with the power win, so winning is an exercise in trying to influence people, trying to gain power. The power of oil and gas companies is well documented, as is their ability to influence public officials (Edwards 1988a, 1988b).

There is a widespread distrust of politicians and the political process in Alabama. In a *Mobile Register* column headed "Politics Deserves Reputation," Mike Casey wrote:

> Many politicians always look at things through glasses that have dollar signs on the lenses. If the money is not there, the support is often not either.
>
> It comes in a variety of forms, including seeking drinks and dinner off a lobbyist who needs the legislator's vote and a legislator requesting campaign contributions from companies and associations when he faces no opposition and has virtually no campaign expenses.
>
> And what do you think might happen if the lobbyist refuses to pick up the dinner and drink tabs for legislators or refuses to give campaign contributions when they are sought. He'll likely be kissing votes good bye on a bill he wants passed.
>
> . . . Just as bad oysters keep some people out of a seafood restaurant, bad politicians keep good people out of politics. (MR 10 July 1988)

The public image of politicians cannot have been enhanced a few days later when the *Mobile Register* reported an FBI investigation of alleged bribery or extortion at every level of government in Alabama. An agent was quoted as saying that he sensed "a growing public resentment against unethical and illegal behavior on the part of government officials here in Alabama" (MR 27 July 1988).

Whatever the realities of the behavior of public officials, such reports suggest an underlying distrust on the part of the public which adds credulity to the rhetoric of corruption when it is used by any participants in a process. The important point here is not what politicians actually do or whether it is legal or ethical. The important point is how people think and talk about politicians.

There are many assumptions and little knowledge about the social, cultural, and economic structure of the fishery on the gulf coast. While the biology and life cycles of most species and even the consequences of fishing for their reproductive structures may be well known, we do not know the range, distribution, or frequency of different types of motives for fishing.

Fishing can be a part of a complex household economy that may also involve agricultural or industrial work. It can be an industrial job, a small business analogous to a farm, or big business.

Sociopolitical data are comprised of more than just the number of letters an agency receives on each side of an issue. Gathering such data does not mean simply making a politically motivated guess about policy. Where fishing is concerned, there are no sociopolitical data and few analyses upon which to base any policy or in terms of which to think about policy. Most policy makers are biologists and do not know what sociopolitical data are, how to collect them, or how to analyze them. Nor should they, because this is not, after all, the subject matter of biology.

Oysters, shrimp, and other seafood products are imported, processed, and shipped out. Much local seafood is frozen and marketed on the East Coast. Bayou Foods, which belongs to General Mills, had raw materials shipped in from New England, processed and packaged them in Mobile, and then shipped them to the northeast (*MR* 9 August 1988). The economic structures in place here are not simply local but national and international. Such a plant could be located anywhere. It has no relationship to the local seafood industry. As processors come to rely less on local seafood sources, they begin to approximate this extreme example.

Some processors attempt to pass Mexican shrimp as local shrimp by labeling it as a product of the United States under the concept that their handling of it in this country makes it a U.S. product, regardless of where it was caught or produced. Perkins (1987) labels this practice a deception. The U.S. Customs Service has seized shrimp in Bayou la Batre and Gulf Shores for this reason, but the Commerce Department argues that the practice is legitimate. A Bayou la Batre processor called the customs service "gestapo-like" in its procedure (*MR* 11 June 1988). Two federal agencies apparently operate with different policy assumptions.

We do not know the structure of capital and labor in the fishery. Who owns what and who works for whom? As David White (1977) shows of shrimpers in Bon Secour, captains have quite different motives and respond differently if they are hired and if they own their own boats. Maril (1983) shows how patterns of boat ownership affect the Texas shrimp fishery.

Not all shrimpers are alike. There are differences among the fleet owner, the absentee owner, the captain/owner/operator; between the owner who is in deep debt for a large "slab" in which he hopes to harvest royal reds far out in the gulf, and the bay shrimper in a small boat. There are differences between an independent, family-operated processing company and one that is part of a large corporation or some other large organization.

The problem is that while we are increasingly sophisticated in our biological and ecological knowledge so that we know the different breeding structures and recruitment structures of oysters, crabs, shrimp, and redfish, and the threats of overfishing and pollution to them, we remain ignorant of consequences of policy for fishermen of all kinds. This is as true of policy that directly affects fishermen, such as that concerning TEDs, and that which indirectly affects them, such as ADEM water-quality policies, and foreign trade policies.

In the same way that agricultural "science" serves the interests of and ratifies the basic tenets and assumptions of agricultural policy (Durrenberger 1984, 1986), the "science" of fisheries authorizes and confirms policy. C. Wright Mills (1959) analyzed the dynamics of science in the service of policy and showed how administrators define the questions. Having defined the questions, they have also defined the presuppositions that give the questions their importance and meaning, the paradigmatic assumptions of any "research" to answer them.

An example of scientific ratification of policy is the economic analysis of fishing boats based on the assumption that they are firms, as the courts have defined them in the cases that broke the unions. The economic analyses of the *Fishery Management Plan for the Shrimp Fishery of the Gulf of Mexico, United States Waters*, issued in 1981 by the Gulf of Mexico Fishery Management Council of Tampa, Florida, rest on such assumptions. As in agriculture (Durrenberger 1984, 1986), if one assumes the operating units are firms, one can develop such an analysis, but there is reason to doubt that fishing boats are firms in the classic economic sense. This ought to be a question, not an assumption. Policy-directed research takes it as an established fact.

The assumption has political consequences. Policy makers and shrimpers agree that shrimpers are such loners that they cannot engage in collective action for their mutual benefit. Icelandic fishermen are known for their independence. It is celebrated in folklore and literature (Durrenberger and Pálsson 1982, 1983a, 1983b, 1989). Icelanders at sea or ashore consider themselves to be autonomous. Halldor Laxness captured this psychology in his novels and entitled one *Independent People*, a label Icelanders wear with pride. In the eyes

of Icelanders and foreigners alike these people are notoriously individualistic. Yet in Iceland all fishermen, as well as farmers, workers,
teachers, and government employees, belong to unions.

The reason there are no unions in the gulf fishery has nothing to do
with the psychology of fishermen. There are no such groups simply
because they are against the law. To say that being independent-
minded is contradictory to collective action is to neglect the history
and ethnography of the gulf fishery. David White (1989b) shows the
importance of collective work groups in the gulf. Though they may
be ephemeral, such groups show that shrimpers are not inveterate
loners. To assume independence and rule out collective organization
is an important policy decision. If policy makers were to shed this
false assumption and dedicate themselves to changing the law, the
social reality would change as well.

One fisheries bureaucrat, discussing "important topics for social
science research" that his agency might fund, suggested the topic
"Why are shrimpers so conservative?" David White (1989a) shows
that the stereotype of the conservative shrimper is seriously mislead-
ing, as the history of rapid innovation in the shrimp industry shows.
The bureaucrat had built the assumption of the conservative shrimper
into his "objective research question" and only awaited its demonstration by some social scientist who would prepare a proposal and
"prove" the assumption.

The scientific questions about gulf fisheries remain largely unasked. They include questions about the political power of conser-
vationist groups, the co-opting of biologists by corporations and environmentalist groups through their funding practices, the role of
grant funds and the agencies that provide them to local institutions
that undertake coastal studies, the cultural analysis of conservation-
ist ideologies and the impact of those ideologies on the assumptions
of "scientific" work, along with questions about the nature of household production units and how they function in the fishing industry
(Durrenberger 1984), and the response of household production units
to various economic changes, including the dynamics of the transla-
tion of economic to political issues (Durrenberger 1987, 1988). One
of the reasons such central questions remain unasked is that fisheries
agencies with research funds do not see them as having any bearing
on "applied" research or policy, and do not even consider funding
projects that would study these questions, much less actually fund
them. Thus, when an event such as the shrimpers' blockade happens, the agencies are left puzzled and fall back on stereotypes of
conservative or violent or irrational fishermen.

When "science" becomes a form of rhetoric in the service of policy, it no longer has the status of a way of knowing things. It becomes, rather, a political weapon in the hands of those powerful enough to afford it.

The Future in the Gulf: Industrial Pollution, a Recreational Lake, or Commercial Fishing?

There are a number of possibilities for the future of the seafood industry in Alabama. To see what an unrestrained policy of "open door to business" and industrial growth could do in Mobile, Mobile Bay, and the Alabama shore, one need not speculate. Ecological processes are slow, and the effects of ecological damage are difficult to detect in the short term. The public becomes more aware of this each day as ecological disasters of decades ago are shown to have impacts on public health today. There is an instructive parallel in Japan.

Japan is praised for its rapid postwar development, for its managerial successes, for its industrial prowess. After World War II there was massive industrialization around the Inland Sea where there were special advantages: a calm sea with good ports, "infrequent natural disasters . . . , absence of heavy snowfall . . . , relatively heavy concentration of population, providing a ready source of industrial labor force" (Befu 1980, 335).

These are the same advantages Alabama offers to industry. In Japan between 1964 and 1967, 344 industrial plants for petrochemical processing, plastics, steel, shipbuilding, and automobile making were built close to the Inland Sea. Marshes and estuaries were destroyed and with them the spawning and nursery grounds of fish. The ocean bottom was dredged for sand to use for landfill and to deepen ship channels for deeper ocean going boats. "Disturbance of the ocean bottom . . . meant loss of a large quantity of natural resources." A petrochemical complex destroyed fishing as an occupation in several fishing villages. Inadequately treated industrial effluent has decreased levels of dissolved oxygen and several species of fish no longer exist in the Inland Sea (Befu 1980).

Another, alternate future for the Alabama coast is being written in the Florida Keys and other areas of Florida as they become recreational playgrounds for the rich or settlements for the retired (Meltzoff 1989). As the contradictions between sport and commercial fishing, between gentrified and working neighborhoods, between the sophisticated and the unsophisticated increase, there will continue to be political decisions about resource allocation between "fishing for exchange" on the one hand and "fishing for fun" on the other. While advocates of recreational fishing may join with commercial fishermen to avoid the Japanese Inland Sea future, they may envision a future different from the commercial fisherman's. They may see the gulf as a playground rather than an exploitable resource from which working people can extract a living.

Whether the future of Mobile Bay will reflect that of Japan's Inland Sea, Disney World, or Iceland's commercially used North Atlantic depends on the outcomes of innumerable policy decisions, decisions about who gets what. It is, as they say, all politics.

Epilogue

Early in March 1989 I got a call from V. M. Parker. He told me he had finally succeeded in getting some money from the oyster tag fees for the replanting of oysters. He said it had taken a long time and much effort, but that because he and the Save Our Shells group had stuck with it, they had got a contract to plant shells. The Seafood Division gave them the contract, but not without eight months of delays.

When I asked about the politics of the matter, V. M. speculated that since Governor Hunt is a Republican, as V. M. is, and the state legislators from south Mobile County are Democrats, the Seafood Division might have common cause with the legislators. They would not want Hunt or his administration to take credit for any oyster-planting program, so they might not move very quickly to implement such a program.

The contract called for the oyster catchers to move eight thousand barrels of oyster shell at a dollar a barrel. V. M. also told me the legislature had allocated a separate sum of money apart from oyster tax revenues to plant oyster shells but had provided no vehicle for spending the money, so while the money was available, there was no way to use it.

He concluded that he was glad that he had some experience in government as a legislator and a mayor and that the experience could be of some use.

References Cited

Acheson, James M. 1985. "Comments on Paredes, 1985." *Human Organization* 44:182–83.

Allen, Susan. 1990. "Adding Perspective to the News: A New 'W.' " *Anthro-Journalism* 2, no. 2: 3–5.

Alsobrook, David Ernest. 1983. "Alabama's Port City: Mobile during the Progressive Era, 1891–1917." Ph.D. diss., Auburn University.

Amos, Harriet Elizabeth. 1976. "Social Life in an Antebellum Cotton Port: Mobile, Alabama in 1820–1860." Ph.D. diss., Emory University.

Barnes, Jill. 1986. "Big on Shrimp Farming." *Nation's Business* 74, no. 7: 62.

Becnel, Thomas A. 1962. "A History of the Louisiana Shrimp Industry, 1867–1961." Master's thesis, Louisiana State University.

Befu, Harumi. 1980. "Political Ecology of Fishing in Japan: Techno-Environmental Impact of Industrialization in the Inland Sea." *Research in Economic Anthropology* 3:323–47.

Blanchard, Walton. 1987. "Setting Records Straight on TED Trials." *National Fisherman* 68 (June 1987): 7, 41.

Bohannan, Paul. 1958. "Extra-Processual Events in Tiv Political Institutions." *American Anthropologist* 60:1–12.

Brady, Donald W. 1979. "Water Resource Management through Control of Point and Nonpoint Pollution Sources in Mobile Bay." In Loyacano and Smith 1979, 31–73.

Brown, James Seay, ed. 1982. *Up Before Daylight: Life Histories from the Alabama Writers' Project, 1938–1939.* University, Ala.: University of Alabama Press.

Bureau of Fisheries, United States Department of Commerce. 1899– . *Report of the United States Commissioner of Fisheries.*

Burman, Ben Lucien. 1954. "Sailing with the Shrimpers." *Collier's* 134, no. 9 (29 October): 98–107.

Carmer, Carl. 1949. "The Seven Sisters." *Holiday* 6, no. 5: 98–105, 139–41.

Cooper, Christopher. 1989. "Gulf Shrimpers Attack TEDs." *National Fisherman* 70 (October): 2–4.

Copeland, Charles W. 1982. "Geology." In *Alabama Coastal Region Ecological Characterization*, vol. 2: *A Synthesis of Environmental Data*, edited by P. E. O'Neil and M. F. Mettee, 3–103. Washington, D.C.: United States Fish and Wildlife Service, Office of Biological Services, FWS/OBS-82/42.

Douglas, Mary. 1982. *Natural Symbols*. New York: Pantheon.

Durrenberger, E. Paul. 1984. *Chayanov, Peasants, and Economic Anthropology*. San Francisco: Academic Press.

———. 1986. "Notes on the Cultural-Historical Background to the Middlewestern Farm Crisis." *Culture and Agriculture* 28:15–17.

———. 1987. "Household Economies and Agrarian Unrest in Iowa—1931." In *Household Economies and Their Transformations*, edited by Morgan Maclaughlan, 198–211. New York: University Press of America.

———. 1988. "Shrimpers and Turtles on the Gulf Coast: The Formation of Fisheries Policy in the United States." *Maritime Anthropological Studies* 1, no. 2: 196–214.

———. 1990. "Policy, Power, and Science: The Implementation of Turtle Excluder Device Regulations in the U.S. Gulf of Mexico Shrimp Fishery." *Maritime Anthropological Studies* 3, no. 1: 69–86.

Durrenberger, E. Paul, and Bob Quinlan. 1987. "The Structure of the Prose Edda." *Scandinavian Yearbook of Folklore* 41:65–76.

Durrenberger, E. Paul, and Gísli Pálsson. 1982. "To Dream of Fish: The Causes of Icelandic Skippers' Fishing Success." *Journal of Anthropological Research* 38:227–42.

———. 1983a. "Icelandic Foremen and Skippers: The Structure and Evolution of a Folk Model." *American Ethnologist* 10:511–28.

———. 1983b. "Riddles of Herring and Rhetorics of Success." *Journal of Anthropological Research* 39:323–35.

———. 1989. "Forms of Production and Fishing Expertise." In *The Anthropology of Iceland*, edited by E. Paul Durrenberger and Gísli Pálsson, 228–46. Iowa City: University of Iowa Press.

Edwards, M. L. 1987. "Shrimpers Say All TEDs Have Drawbacks." *National Fisherman* 68 (July): 38–41.

———. 1988a. "Loss of Louisiana Wetlands Threatens Gulf Fisheries." *National Fisherman* 69 (July): 12–14.

———. 1988b. "Fighting Back: Halting the Flow of Refinery Discharge." *National Fisherman* 69 (July): 23.

Evans, Lawrence. 1938. "An Oysterman." Federal Writers Project Papers, #3709. Southern Historical Collection, University of North Carolina Library, Chapel Hill.

Federal Writers Project of the Works Progress Administration. 1939. *Mississippi Gulf Coast*. Gulfport, Miss.: Gulfport Printing Company.

———. 1941. *Alabama: A Guide to the Deep South*. New York: Richard R. Smith.

———. 1975. See Walker 1975.

Fee, Russ. 1987. "Turtle Excluders Rankle Shrimpers." *National Fisherman* 67 (April): 4–5, 32.

Fee, Russ, and Linda Buckmaster. 1991. " 'Best Available Science': How Good Is It, Really?" *National Fisherman* (February): 24–26.

Fisheries Report. See Bureau of Fisheries.

Fiske, Shirley J. "Anthropology and Marine Extension: Can We Make a Difference?" *Practicing Anthropology* 12, no. 4: 4–5, 8.

Gonzales, V. A. 1964. Letter dated 10 February to Emma C. Harris. Mobile Public Library Special Collections, Mobile, Ala.

Goode, George Brown. 1887. *The Fisheries and Fishery Industries of the United States*. Washington, D.C.: Government Printing Office.

Gulf of Mexico Fishery Management Council. 1981. *Fishery Management Plan for the Shrimp Fishery of the Gulf of Mexico, United States Waters.* Tampa, Fla.

Hamilton, Peter J. 1910. *Colonial Mobile: An Historical Study.* Boston: Houghton Mifflin.

———. 1911. *The Founding of Mobile: 1702–1718.* Mobile, Ala.: Commercial Printing Company.

Handley, Paul. 1989a. "Cultured Revolution: Once a Luxury, Shrimp Are Now a Low-Cost Commodity." *Far Eastern Economic Review* (5 October): 96–97.

———. 1989b. "Profileration of Ponds." *Far Eastern Economic Review* (5 October): 98–99.

Hartley, Helen S. 1938. "Shrimping on the Schooner Berney Geneva." Federal Writers Project Papers #3709. Southern Historical Collection, University of North Carolina Library, Chapel Hill.

Heath, Stevens R. 1979. "Shrimp Assessment and Management in the Mobile Estuary." In Loyacano and Smith 1979, 201–9.

Hedeen, Robert A. 1986. "The Oyster: The Life and Lore of the Celebrated Bivalve." Centerville, Md.: Tidewater Publishers.

Hepburn, Marcus J. 1977. "Cedar Key, Its Fisheries, and the Oyster Relocation Project: History, Analysis and Evaluation." In *The Cedar Key Oyster Relocation and Demonstration Project—1977. Final Report*, edited by Marcus J. Hepburn and Robert C. Glassen. Florida Department of Natural Resources.

Idyll, Clarence P., and Robert F. Sisson. 1957. "Shrimpers Strike Gold in the Gulf." *National Geographic* 111 (May): 699–707.

Ingersoll, Ernest. 1887. "The Oyster, Scallop, Clam, Mussel, and Abalone Industries." In Goode 1887, section 5, vol. 2, 505–626.

Isbell, Frances Annette. 1951. "A Social and Economic History of Mobile, 1865–1875." Master's thesis, University of Alabama.

Isphording, Wayne C., and George C. Flowers. 1987. "Mobile Bay: The Right Estuary in the Wrong Place!" In Lowery 1987, 165–74.

Jarman, M. Casey, and Daniel K. Conner, eds. 1987. *Conference on Gulf and South Atlantic Fisheries: Law and Policy.* New Orleans: Mississippi-Alabama Sea Grant Consortium, MASGP-87–013.

Jarvis, Norman D. 1935. *Fishery for Red Snappers and Groupers in the Gulf of Mexico.* U.S. Department of Commerce, Bureau of Fisheries, Investiga-

tional Report No. 26. Washington, D.C.: United States Government Printing
Office.

Johnson, Fred F., and Milton J. Linder. 1934. *Shrimp Industry of the South
Atlantic and Gulf States.* U.S. Department of Commerce, Bureau of Fisheries, Investigational Report No. 21. Washington, D.C.: United States Government Printing Office.

Johnson, Jay S. 1987. "Sea Turtle Mediated Negotiations: A New Approach."
In Jarman and Conner 1987, 234–38.

Jordan, Weymouth T. 1957. *Ante-Bellum Alabama: Town and Country.* Tallahassee: Florida State University Press.

Kafka, John. 1984. "Politics of the Bluefin Tuna Fishery: Prince Edward
Island." In Lamson and Hanson 1984, 205–34.

Lamson, Cynthia, and Arthur J. Hanson, eds. 1984. *Atlantic Fisheries and
Coastal Communities: Fisheries Decision-Making Case Studies.* Halafax,
Nova Scotia: Dalhousie Ocean Studies Programme.

Leary, Terrance R. 1985. "Comments on Paredes, 1985." *Human Organization*
44:183–84.

Lévi-Strauss, Claude. 1963. *Structural Anthropology.* New York: Basic Books.
———. 1966. *The Savage Mind.* Chicago: University of Chicago Press.

Lowery, Tony A., ed. 1987. *Symposium on the Natural Resources of the
Mobile Bay Estuary.* Mobile, Ala.: Mississippi-Alabama Sea Grant Consortium, MASGP-87-007.

Loyacano, Harold A., Jr., and J. Paul Smith, eds. 1979. *Symposium on the
Natural Resources of the Mobile Estuary, Alabama, May, 1979.* Mobile,
Ala.: U.S. Army Corps of Engineers.

Loyacano, Harold A., Jr., and Wolf-Dieter N. Busch. 1979. "Introduction." In
Loyacano and Smith 1979, 1–5.

McCay, Bonnie M. 1985. "Comments on Paredes, 1985." *Human Organization*
44:184.

Magnuson, John J., Karen A. Bjorndal, William D. DuPaul, Gary L. Graham,
David W. Owens, Charles H. Peterson, Peter C. H. Pritchard, James I.
Richardson, Gary E. Saul, and Charles W. West. 1990. *Decline of the
Sea Turtles: Causes and Prevention.* Washington, D.C.: National Academy
Press.

Malinowski, Bronislaw. 1948. *Magic, Science and Religion and Other Essays.*
Boston: Beacon.

Maril, Lee. 1983. *Texas Shrimpers: Community, Capitalism, and the Sea.*
College Station: Texas A & M University Press.

Meltzoff, Sarah K. 1989. "Politics of Conservation in the Florida Keys." In
Marine Resource Utilization, edited by E. Paul Durrenberger, Lee Maril,
and J. Thomas, 125–32. Mobile, Ala.: Mississippi-Alabama Sea Grant Consortium, MASGP-88-039.

Meltzoff, Sarah K., and Edward LiPuma. 1986. "The Social Economy of
Coastal Resources: Shrimp Mariculture in Ecuador." *Culture and Agriculture* 28 (Winter 1985/86): 1–10.

Mettee, Maurice F., and Patrick E. O'Neil. 1982. "Conceptual Model." In *Alabama Coastal Region Ecological Characterization*, vol. 2, *A Synthesis of Environmental Data*, edited by P. E. O'Neil and M. F. Mettee, 215–53. U.S. Fish and Wildlife Service, Office of Biological Services, Washington, D.C., FWS/OBS-82/42.

Miller, Marc L. 1987. "Regional Fishery Management Councils and the Display of Scientific Authority." *Coastal Management* 15:309–18.

Mills, C. Wright. 1959. *The Sociological Imagination*. New York: Oxford University Press.

Moore, Albert Burton. 1927. *History of Alabama and Her People*. Chicago: The American Historical Society.

Moore, H. F. 1913. *Condition and Extent of the Natural Oyster Beds and Barren Bottoms of the Mississippi Sound, Alabama*. Bureau of Fisheries Document 769. Washington, D.C.: Government Printing Office, Department of Commerce and Labor.

Moore, Jonathan. 1989. "The Hi-Tech Hatchery." *Far Eastern Economic Review* (5 October): 97–98.

Oertel, Kenneth G. 1987. "Commercial-Recreational Fisheries Litigation in Florida." In Jarman and Conner 1987, 59–64.

Oubre, Claude F. 1978. *Forty Acres and a Mule: The Freedmen's Bureau and Black Land Ownership*. Baton Rouge: Louisiana State University Press.

Owen, Marie Bankhead. 1949. *The Story of Alabama: A History of the State*. New York: Lewis Historical Publishing Company.

Pálsson, Gísli. 1989. "The Art of Fishing." *Maritime Anthropological Studies* 2, no. 1: 1–20.

Paredes, Anthony. 1985. "Any Comments on the Sociology Section, Tony? Committee Work as Applied Anthropology in Fishery Management." *Human Organization* 44:177–82.

———. 1991. "Anthropology and Marine Extension." *Practicing Anthropology* 13, no. 4: 2, 23.

Patti, Frank. 1987. "Insider Airs Shrimpers' Views on TEDs." *National Fisherman* 69 (June): 14–15, 34.

Peirce, Paul Skeels. 1904. *The Freedmen's Bureau: A Chapter in the History of Reconstruction*. The University of Iowa Studies in Sociology, Economics, Politics, and History, vol. 3, no. 1. Iowa City.

Perkins, Brian E. 1987. "Needs within the Commercial Seafood Industry." In Jarman and Conner 1987, 100–107.

Powell, Murella. 1976. Interview with Theo Savoy. Tape and transcript in the Biloxi Public Library, Biloxi, Miss.

Prine, Ila B. 1938. "Life in a Shrimping and Oyster Shucking Camp." Federal Writers Project Papers #3709. Southern Historical Collection, University of North Carolina Library, Chapel Hill.

———. 1939. "It Ruins Oysters to Wash Them." Federal Writers Project Papers #3709. Southern Historical Collection, University of North Carolina Library, Chapel Hill.

Rayford, Julian Lee. 1956. *Whistlin' Woman and Crowin' Hen: The True Legend of Dauphin Island and the Alabama Coast.* Mobile, Ala.: Rankin Press.

Rushton, William Faulkner. 1979. *The Cajuns from Acadia to Louisiana.* New York: Farrar Strauss Giroux.

Sass, H. S. 1950. "They Found a Fortune on the Ocean Floor." *Saturday Evening Post* 222, no. 47: 38–39, 168, 170, 173–74.

Sharpe, Patricia. 1988. "Better TED Than Dead." *Texas Monthly* 16, no. 6: 105.

Sheffield, David A., and Darnell A. Nicovich. 1979. *When Biloxi Was the Seafood Capital of the World.* Biloxi, Miss.: The City of Biloxi.

Shelfer, Charles. 1987. "The Florida Marine Fisheries Commission: Status of Spanish Mackerel and Redfish Litigation." In Jarman and Conners 1987, 48–58.

Smith, M. Estellie. 1988. "Fisheries Risk in the Modern Context." *Maritime Anthropological Studies* 1, no. 1: 29–48.

Smith, M. F. Jr., ed. 1984. *Ecological Characterization Atlas of Coastal Alabama: Map Narrative.* U.S. Fish and Wildlife Service FWS/OBS-82/46; Minerals Management Service MMS 84–0052. Washington, D.C.: U.S. Department of the Interior.

Stearns, Silas. 1887a. "The Red-Snapper and Havana Market Fisheries." In Goode 1887, section 5, vol. 1, 585–94.

———. 1887b. "The Fisheries of the Gulf of Mexico." In Goode 1887, section 2, 533–87.

Stimpson, Dee. 1990. "Apalachicola Bay—Development, Overfishing Wipe Out Oysters." *National Fisherman* 70 (January): 28–29.

Stout, Judy P. 1979. "Marshes of the Mobile Bay Estuary: Status and Evaluation." In Loyacano and Smith 1979, 113–21.

Swingle, Hugh A., and Edgar A. Hughes. 1976. "A Review of the Oyster Fishery of Alabama." *Alabama Marine Resources Bulletin* no. 11: 58–73.

Taylor Charles W., Anthony F. Serra, John F. Mitchell, and Rodney C. Sawyer. 1985. *Construction and Installation Instructions for the Trawling Efficiency Device.* NOAA Technical Memorandum NMFS-SEFC-71. Pascagoula, Miss.: U.S. Department of Commerce, National Oceanic and Atmospheric Administration, National Marine Fisheries Service, Southeast Fisheries Center, Mississippi Laboratories.

Taylor, Paul Wane. 1951. "Mobile: 1818–1851 As Her Newspapers Pictured Her." Master's thesis, University of Alabama.

"Technology for Shrimps." 1956. *Fortune,* September, 262.

Thompson, Alan Smith. 1979. "Mobile, Alabama, 1850–1861: Economic, Political, Physical, and Population Characteristics." Ph.D. diss., University of Alabama.

United States Congress. House Committee on Ways and Means. 1947. *Trade Agreements Program.* 80th Cong., 1st sess.

———. 1961. *Tariff Treatment of Shrimp Imports.* 87th Cong., 1st sess. H. Res. 6168.

United States Congress. House Subcommittee on Fisheries and Wildlife Conservation of the Committee on Merchant Marine and Fisheries.1960. *Fish and Wildlife Legislation*. 86th Cong., 1st sess. H. Res. 2777.

United States Congress. Senate Subcommittee on Merchant Marine and Fisheries of the Committee on Interstate and Foreign Commerce. 1956. *Fisheries Legislation*. 84th Cong., 1st sess. S. Res. 2379.

van Dresser, Cleland. 1950. "Pink Gold Strike in the Gulf." *Popular Mechanics Magazine* 94, no. 1 (July): 124–26, 230, 232.

Walker, Alyce Billings, ed. 1975. *Alabama: A Guide to the Deep South*. New rev. ed. New York: Hastings House.

Wallace, Richard K., and William Hosking. 1986. *Shrimp in Alabama*. Mobile, Ala.: Mississippi-Alabama Sea Grant Consortium, MASGP-86–012.

Warner, Betsy. 1982. *The Biology of the American Oyster*. Marine Education Center Leaflet No. 12. Biloxi, Miss.

White, David M. 1977. "Social Organization and the Sea: A Gulf Coast Shrimp Fishery." Ph.D. diss., Southern Methodist University.

———. 1989a. "Sea Turtles and Resistance to TEDs Among Shrimp Fishermen of the U.S. Gulf Coast." *Maritime Anthropological Studies* 2, no. 1: 69–79.

———. 1989b. "Knocking 'em Dead: The Formation and Dispersal of Work Fleets Among Alabama Shrimp Boats." In *Marine Resource Utilization*, edited by E. Paul Durrenberger, Lee Maril, and J. Thomas, 25–40. Mobile, Ala.: Mississippi-Alabama Sea Grant Consortium, MASG-88–039.

White, Howard A. 1970. *The Freedmen's Bureau in Louisiana*. Baton Rouge: Louisiana State University Press.

Works Progress Administration. 1939. "Interesting Transcriptions from the City Documents of the City of Mobile for 1823–1844." Manuscript at the Mobile Public Library Special Collection, Mobile, Ala.

Index

A Note on the Author

E. PAUL DURRENBERGER is professor of anthropology at the University of Iowa. He is the author of *Chayanov, Peasants, and Economic Anthropology*; the coauthor, with Nicola Tannenbaum, of *Analytical Perspectives on Shan Agriculture and Village Economics*; and the coeditor, with Gísli Pálsson, of *The Anthropology of Iceland*. He has published over eighty articles on a number of topics, including fishing.